Sexual Naturalization

ASIAN AMERICA

A series edited by Gordon H. Chang

The increasing size and diversity of the Asian American population, its growing significance in American society and culture, and the expanded appreciation, both popular and scholarly, of the importance of Asian Americans in the country's present and past—all these developments have converged to stimulate wide interest in scholarly work on topics related to the Asian American experience. The general recognition of the pivotal role that race and ethnicity have played in American life, and in relations between the United States and other countries, has also fostered this heightened attention.

Although Asian Americans were a subject of serious inquiry in the late nineteenth and early twentieth centuries, they were subsequently ignored by the mainstream scholarly community for several decades. In recent years, however, this neglect has ended, with an increasing number of writers examining a good many aspects of Asian American life and culture. Moreover, many students of American society are recognizing that the study of issues related to Asian America speak to, and may be essential for, many current discussions on the part of the informed public and various scholarly communities.

The Stanford series on Asian America seeks to address these interests. The series includes works from the humanities and social sciences, including history, anthropology, political science, American studies, law, literary criticism, sociology, and interdisciplinary and policy studies.

Sexual Naturalization

ASIAN AMERICANS AND
MISCEGENATION

Susan Koshy

STANFORD UNIVERSITY PRESS
STANFORD, CALIFORNIA
2004

Stanford University Press
Stanford, California
© 2004 by the Board of Trustees of the Leland Stanford Junior
University. All rights reserved.

Printed in the United States of America on acid-free, archival-quality
paper.

Library of Congress Cataloging-in-Publication Data
Koshy, Susan.
Sexual naturalization : Asian Americans and miscegenation / Susan
Koshy.
        p.   cm.
    Includes bibliographical references and index.
    ISBN 0-8047-4728-8 (cloth : alk. paper)—ISBN 0-8047-4729-6 (pbk. :
alk. paper)
        1. American fiction—History and criticism.   2. Miscegenation
in literature.   3. American fiction—Asian American authors—History
and criticism.   4. Politics and literature—United States.   5. Asian
Americans in literature.   6. Sex and law—United States.   7. Race
relations in literature.   8. Imperialism in literature.   9. Asians in
literature.   I. Title.
    PS374.M53K67 2004
    813.009'3552—dc22   2004018764

Typeset by BookMatters in 11/14 Adobe Garamond

Original Printing 2005

Last figure below indicates year of this printing:
13   12   11   10   09   08   07   06   05   04

For my parents

Contents

Acknowledgments

This book marks the end of a long journey. I am grateful to the many people who have helped me along the way in various capacities. I am especially grateful to the many journal editors I have worked with over the years, whose enthusiastic support and excellent advice have given me the intellectual space to explore new ideas and develop the tenacity and rigor that make research work exhilarating: Lauren Berlant, Paul Bové, Toby Miller, Bruce Robbins, Ellen Rooney, Khachig Tölöyan, and Mike Vazquez. I am also grateful for the support and friendship of many colleagues whose generosity and intellectual stimulation have energized me and kept me moving through the long labor of writing: David Anderson, Dennis Baron, Ali Behdad, Dale Billingsley, Maurizia Boscagli, Mary Patricia Brady, Martin Camargo, Karen Chandler, King Kok Cheung, Enda Duffy, Purnima Mankekar, Teshome Gabriel, Alan Golding, Suzette Henke, Vinay Lal, Neil Lazarus, Françoise Lionnet, Bill Maxwell, Bob Miller, Kathleen McHugh, Harryette Mullen, Tejaswani Niranjana, Franklin Odo, Kent Ono, Vincent Pecora, Catherine Prendergast, Jane Rhodes, Cedric Robinson, Rosanne Rocher, Nayan Shah, Jenny Sharpe, Shu-mei Shih, Siobhan Somerville, Paul Spickard, and Rajini Srikanth. Parama Roy's integrity, humor, and brilliant scholarship have been an inspiration to me. Rob Wilson's smarts, creativity and wit have made him an invaluable colleague and ally. I also want to thank R. Radhakrishnan, whose generosity and intellectual curiosity make him a valued colleague and fellow traveler. For exciting conversations, keen support, and his original takes on nearly every subject, I want to thank Henry Yu. For their terrific films and great conversations, my gratitude to Gurinder Chadha and Nisha Ganatra. Without my students, who put all my intellectual work into perspective, my work would not have been half as pleasurable or, for that matter, half as protracted: Priya Ananthakrishnan, Lynn Anyayahan, Emily Davis, Amy Jordan, Jennifer Li, Jocelyn Moore, Shazia Rehman, Mehnaz Sahibzada, Jaideep Singh, and Beena Varughese.

Gordon Chang has offered early and kind encouragement as well as his own superb scholarship, for which I offer my deepest gratitude. Muriel Bell of Stanford University Press has been infinitely patient, and I deeply appreciate her efforts in seeing this project to its completion. Carmen Borbón-Wu has kept me sane through this process and been a valuable resource. I am deeply appreciative of Judith Hibbard's expertise and extraordinary enthusiasm and Matt Stevens's superb and meticulous copyediting.

The work on this book has been supported by grants from the Institute for Social, Behavioral, and Economic Research and the Interdisciplinary Humanities Center at the University of California, Santa Barbara. A version of Chapter 2 appeared as an article in *differences: A Journal of Feminist Cultural Studies.*

Finally, I turn to the people to whom my debts are greatest. My parents, to whom this book is dedicated, have supported my work, although it has taken me so far afield from what they might have imagined. From my father's idealism, integrity, and love of knowledge I have learned not to settle for easy answers or to be enamored of difficult solutions. From my mother, I have learned that daily tasks unfold in steady rhythms. My siblings, whose periodic chants of "You must be done by now" and "It's just a book" have provided regular reminders that we all live in different time zones. Tanya, Sunjay, and Vinay were a part of my life while I was writing this book, and their presence has shaped this work in more ways than they could understand. I have no way of thanking the one person who has done more for me and asked less than anyone else. Without Vinod, this book would not be what it is. My thanks to him for being my truest companion, my most pitiless critic, and my most ardent interlocutor. True north, in all my journeys.

Sexual Naturalization

Introduction

Miscegenation discourse offers a rich field of study for understanding the constructedness of categories of race, gender, and nationality; the effects of their imbrication; and the force they gained by being grounded in the pre-eminent modern Western language of nature: the language of sexuality. *Sexual Naturalization* highlights the artificiality of the concept of miscegenation that policed sexual contacts across racial boundaries for over three hundred years. As I argue throughout this book, antimiscegenation laws turned sex acts into race acts and engendered new meanings for both. Antimiscegenation statutes not only demarcated and entrenched racial boundaries, they defined white bourgeois sexual mores as normative. By proscribing interracial sex, these laws defined it as deviant and dangerous and positioned the sexuality of racialized others in opposition to white middle-class sexual practices and family values.

In the case of Asian Americans, antimiscegenation laws reaffirmed their status as perpetual foreigners, as racial and sexual aliens. Not only were sexual relationships between the predominantly male Asian immigrants and white women outlawed, but, for a period, American women who married noncitizen Asian men were denaturalized.[1] While antimiscegenation laws also prohibited marriage between whites and other racial groups like blacks and native Americans, it was only marriage to Asian male aliens that carried the singular penalty of stripping white women of their citizenship. Furthermore, popular discourse identified Asian women as prostitutes and the "bachelor" communities of Asian immigrants as aberrant and pathological sexual formations. Thus, from the late 1800s to the mid-twentieth century, miscegenation laws worked in conjunction with immigration and naturalization laws to impede the reproduction of Asian immigrant communities, position Asians as racial aliens and sexual deviants, and secure the future of the United States as a white nation.

Most strikingly, immigration and miscegenation laws converged in a "biopolitics of the population" by providing critical regulatory mechanisms to the U.S. state to discipline the individual and aggregate social body of Asian Americans. As Foucault indicates, technologies of sex that centered on controlling the size and fitness of the population became "the anchorage points for the different varieties of racism of the nineteenth and twentieth century."[2] I argue that the interrelationship among the nation-state, technologies of sex, and the politics of race was amplified in the context of an immigrant country like the United States, where the influx of immigrants, capitalist expansion, and rapid urbanization provided a vast uncharted territory for the exercise of "biopower." Biopower refers to the political technology that "brought life and its mechanisms into the realm of explicit calculations and made knowledge/power an agent of transformation of human life."[3]

The presence of large numbers of new immigrants, often concentrated in urban centers, triggered fears of deviant and lawless sexuality, the proliferation of vice and prostitution, and the contamination of American genetic stock. In response to these changes, movements for social hygiene, sexual control, and racial purity gained ground, legitimating and intensifying the intrusion of the state into intimate relations. Thus, the expansion of antimiscegenation laws coincided with the creation of new laws to counter prostitution and deter vice and the implementation of eugenic measures to enforce the sterilization of criminals and the feebleminded; many of these laws targeted immigrants and the threats associated with their presence.[4] In addition, techniques of biopower, implemented through immigration restrictions on the entry of Asian women and laws against miscegenation, furthered the ends of capital by creating a highly productive and low-cost labor force. Biopower was also exercised through state efforts to preserve the American racial stock by cutting off immigration from Asia and Southern and Eastern Europe: the Chinese Exclusion Act of 1882, the Asiatic Barred Zone Law of 1917, the National Origins Act of 1924, and the Tydings-McDuffie Act of 1934 excluded Chinese; Asian Indians; Japanese and Southern and Eastern Europeans; and Filipinos, respectively.[5] Hence, in the United States, unlike in countries in Europe, immigration and miscegenation laws formed some of the primary sites for defining the internal and external frontiers of nationhood.

However, it is important to keep in mind the Foucauldian truism that (bio)power is productive and not merely repressive. The existence of antimiscegenation laws curtailed but did not end interracial relationships between whites and Asians. White-Asian couples intent on marrying often traveled to states that did not have such laws; some cohabited when they could not marry; one couple even devised the ingenious ruse of getting married on board a ship at sea to circumvent these laws.[6] Antimiscegenation laws also generated a large clientele among some Asian groups, such as Filipinos, for commercial sites of interracial intimacy like taxi-dance halls. In taxi-dance halls, customers were charged a dime for each dance with the mainly white or Mexican dancers, and it was not uncommon for Filipino or Chinese workers to run through a season's earnings in a few nights.[7] Finally, in the extraterritorial spaces outside the nation-state, interracial sex between white men and Asian women flourished in Asian treaty ports and U.S. colonial territories.

Antimiscegenation Laws: Making Race, Sex, Gender, and Nation

This study is located in the history of antimiscegenation regulation to show how the sexualization of Asians is inextricably linked to gender and racial regimes and to illuminate differences in the racialization of the diverse Asian American groups. I trace connections between white-Asian and other forms of white-nonwhite miscegenation to demonstrate that the unique features of Asian American racialization were shaped by and helped reformulate white and nonwhite racial meanings.

Although antimiscegenation statutes were enacted first in the South and endured the longest there, they acquired their most elaborate structure in the West, where Asian Americans were added to the numbers of prohibited groups.[8] Laws that originally banned sexual relationships between blacks and whites were eventually extended to prohibit marriages between whites and "Indians" (native Americans), "Mongolians" (a category that included Chinese, Japanese, and Koreans), "Hindus/Asiatic Indians" (the official terms for South Asians), and "Malays" (Filipinos). Over a period of time, thirty-eight states adopted antimiscegenation laws: all these states banned black-white intimacy, but fourteen states prohibited white-Asian intermarriage, and seven banned white-native American intermarriage. Finally, the California Supreme Court declared antimiscegenation laws unconstitutional in *Perez v. Sharp* (1948), and the U.S. Supreme Court overturned antimiscegenation laws in the landmark *Loving v. Virginia* (1967) decision.[9] Scholars have noted that antimiscegenation laws were implemented more strictly to discourage sexual ties between white women and nonwhite men, whereas white men have had free sexual access to nonwhite women through looser interpretations of the laws and the inability of women of color to testify against whites in court. Thus, a pattern emerges in which groups that were thought to be likely to have relationships with white women—like the largely male Asian immigrant groups (Asian Indians, Filipinos, Chinese, Japanese, and Koreans)—were subject to stringent enforcement.[10]

Prohibitions on miscegenation in the United States first emerged to demarcate rigid boundaries between slave and free, and black and white, at the end of the seventeenth century. The earliest U.S. antimiscegenation law, enacted in Maryland in 1661, did not prohibit marriages between blacks and whites, but it enslaved white women who married black men; the offspring of these unions were also enslaved. A year later, Virginia passed its own antimiscegenation law. These early laws blocked black access to white economic and property privileges through intermarriage. In the upper South, antimiscegenation statutes were reinforced by the adoption of the one-drop rule that barred mixed-race offspring of white-black unions from inheriting the privileges of whiteness.[11] In the lower South, sanctions against miscegenation were more loosely applied when the relationship comprised sexual contact between a white man and a black woman, thus allowing white men extensive sexual privileges. But sex between black men and white women was severely punished. The double standards encoded in these sexual norms enabled the emergence of forms of concubinage in this region, from the "fancy trade" in light-skinned women in Charleston and New Orleans to quadroon balls where freeborn mulatto women entered into financed sexual relations with white men, known as *placage*. Under *placage*, white men supported black women and their children for periods varying from a few years to a lifetime.[12]

After the Civil War, Southern Democrats coined the term *miscegenation* to denigrate the black quest for political equality, deploying a sexual metaphor to connote a political threat and thereby engendering widespread racial hysteria over union. The specter of miscegenation between black men and white women was used by vigilantes to terrorize blacks and justify lynchings of black men. Simultaneously, the rape of black women was also used as a mode of domination to undermine the black quest for social and political equality.[13]

By contrast, white-native American miscegenation represented a "conspicuous anomaly" in the U.S. racial landscape.[14] In the early period of white settlement, intermarriages between white men and native American women were accepted and even encouraged because they afforded white men access to land and trading rights.[15] The limited numbers of white women at that time and the role of native American women as cultural mediators in an alien environment enhanced the value of such relationships. Furthermore, the mixed-race offspring of such marriages were, in certain instances, able to claim a white identity. Indeed, the Virginia antimiscegenation law contained what was called the "Pocahontas exception," whereby persons with one-sixteenth or less native American blood were classified as whites.[16] Similarly, Louisiana also reclassified native Americans as whites. But by the late nineteenth century, white–native American unions drew increasing censure as opposition to other forms of miscegenation increased and several states, including Nevada, Oregon, North Carolina, and Arizona, banned these relationships.[17] During this period, in the frontier regions of the West, occupied by military garrisons and largely male mining communities, rape and prostitution defined the terms of interracial sexual contact between white men and native American women. The rape of native American women was justified as the victor's prerogative when white Americans conquered western territories. In addition, the political weakness of native American tribes in the West and the inability of native American women to testify against white men in court rendered them especially vulnerable to exploitation.[18]

White–Mexican sexual relationships followed patterns similar to white–native American sexual ties in that intermarriages were socially accepted and considered advantageous in the early stages of white settlement but became less so as Anglo power was consolidated through conquest and annexation. White-Latino intermarriage was never officially prohibited by law because treaty provisions granted conquered Spanish and Mexican citizens full American citizenship and a status equal to whites; nevertheless, the hybrid racial identities of Mexican people and their social subordination often led to prejudice against these unions.[19] However, the divergence between their white legal identities and their hybrid genealogies facilitated the intermarriage of people of Mexican ancestry with whites and nonwhites. Since people of Mexican origin were white by law, they were barred from marrying Asians or blacks but, in practice, county clerks often granted marriage licenses to such couples based on similar skin coloration between the partners.[20] For instance, Filipino and Asian Indian men frequently married women of Mexican origin; social tolerance of these marriages among Anglos clearly signaled that, notwithstanding their official whiteness, people of Mexican origin were socially nonwhite.[21]

Intermarriage between Anglo settlers and Mexican women had been encouraged by the newly independent Mexican government in the early 1800s; in fact, the government allowed intermarriage to be used as an avenue to naturalization and exempted foreigners married to Mexicans from trade restrictions. However, once the United States annexed Mexican territories, the incentive for Americans to marry Mexican women declined.[22] The postconquest period also led to shifts in acculturation in Anglo-Mexican intermarriages. Instead of Anglos and their mixed-race offspring being acculturated as Mexican, the post-conquest marriages resulted in Anglicization of Mexican spouses and offspring. Moreover, as people of Mexican ancestry became the minorities in these regions, Anglos drew on stereotypes that labeled them as racially and sexually inferior and "drew a distinction between 'good' (Spanish and assimilable) and 'bad' (Mexican and unassimilable) women, with the latter usually depicted as prostitutes."[23]

In general, the patterns of white–native American and white-Mexican miscegenation differed significantly from that of white-black miscegenation. The first two cases enabled some degree of social assimilation and provided mixed-race offspring restricted access to the privileges of whiteness. However, most white-black sex took place outside marriage and, thus, was denied the legal protections and privileges of matrimony.[24] These interracial sexual ties were defined by the status of blacks as the property of white men and placed black women in a position where they had little power over their own sexuality.

Unlike other forms of miscegenation regulation, antimiscegenation laws directed at Asian Americans were shaped by a need to police the sexuality of a primarily male immigrant labor force; the laws worked to impede their incorporation into America through marriage or through the creation of a subsequent generation of American-born citizens. The first legislation aimed at Asian Americans targeted Chinese immigrants who began arriving in the United States by the mid-nineteenth century. Public hostility toward the Chinese prompted an 1881 amendment to the California Civil Code that prohibited issuing marriage licenses to authorize the union of whites with "Mongolians." The California legislature passed an act criminalizing white-Chinese intermarriage in 1901 and then reenacted it in 1905 in response to popular anxieties about incoming Japanese immigrants. Several other states followed suit in prohibiting intermarriage between whites and "Mongolians." Specific provisions banning marriages with "Hindus" and "Malays" had to be added to prevent intermarriage with Asian Indians and Filipinos, who entered the country soon after restrictions were placed on the entry of Chinese and Japanese laborers.[25]

The punitive effects of antimiscegenation laws intensified with the passage of the Expatriation Act in 1907, which divested white women of their citizenship if they married foreigners. When women's groups protested against the principle that a woman's citizenship was derivative of her husband's, Congress passed the Cable Act in 1922. The Cable Act struck down the principle of derivative citizenship, except in cases where the women had married "aliens ineligible to citizenship," which is how Asians were classified. Hence, white women who crossed the color line to marry were selectively denationalized.[26] By the same principle, American-born women of Asian ancestry were stripped of their U.S. citizenship if they married foreign-born Asian men. Since a significant number of second-generation Asian women married immigrant men from their own communities, this law had a strong impact on Asian American communities. Another consequence of the Cable Act was that by eliminating the principle of derivative citizenship, it also made it harder for Chinese Americans to bring in their Chinese wives. The U.S. Supreme Court interpreted the Cable Act as barring Chinese women from joining their husbands since a woman's nationality was now deemed to be independent of her husband's.[27]

In the case of Chinese, Asian Indian, and Filipino workers, immigration laws restricting intraracial family formation and miscegenation statutes prohibiting interracial family formation created a condition of enforced bachelorhood.[28] White-Asian miscegenation statutes were unusually repressive because unlike all the other nonwhite groups, which had the option of forming same-race sexual relationships, the skewed gender ratios in Asian immigrant communities severely limited marital options. Moreover, the prevalence of prostitution in Asian ethnic enclaves and the same-sex living arrangements that characterized them were taken as proof of Oriental sexual deviance and unfitness for citizenship. What is ironic is that while the system of slavery provided incentives for black men and women to reproduce, the capitalist regime of the late nineteenth century benefited from the sexual subordination of Asian workers by passing on the costs of their social and sexual reproduction to their households in their homelands and profiting from their dependence on commercialized intimacies.[29]

The Japanese were the only Asian immigrant group who were able to build a significant proportion of same-race family units. This was in large part because the Japanese government used its political power to pressure the U.S. government to keep the immigration of Japanese women open for a relatively long period of time. Thus, by 1920, 46 percent of the Japanese in Hawai'i and 34.5 percent of the Japanese on the mainland were women. In comparison, until 1906, Chinese women never constituted more than 5 percent of the population, while Korean women represented only 20 percent of the adult Korean population in the United States.[30] More skewed were the gender ratios among the Filipino and Asian Indian communities: By 1930, only 3.8 percent of the adult Filipino population was female, and by 1914, only 0.24 percent of the Asian Indian population was female.[31] Notwithstanding the emergence of Japanese immigrants as a family-based community and the very low numbers who married white women (by some estimates there were only fifty such couples along the entire West Coast), anxieties about miscegenation were intense. Japanese family formation was purported to be an imperialist strategy to conquer the United States through reproductive power and weaken American racial stock. Other stereotypes focused on the hidden, lascivious designs of Japanese men on American girls, particularly in spaces of contact like schoolrooms.[32]

To a greater extent than Chinese and Japanese immigrants, Asian Indians and Filipinos worked actively to circumvent the laws by marrying white women and, when opposition to such marriages mounted, marrying women from the liminal racial groups, like Mexicans and native Americans. The ambiguous racial and political status of Asian Indians and Filipinos enabled these strategies. According to some anthropologists of the time, Asian Indians belonged to the Aryan/Caucasian racial group. Their ambiguous racial identity as darker-skinned Aryans allowed some Asian Indians to marry white women while the courts attempted to resolve the matter of their racial status. From the early 1900s until 1923, the courts offered contradictory rulings on the racial identity of Asian Indians. In 1923, in *United States v. Bhagat Singh Thind*, the Supreme Court ruled that while Asian Indians might be Caucasian by scientific precepts, they were nonwhite in the "common understanding," and that popular opinion should serve as the determining criterion of their racial identity.[33] Once they became nonwhite by law, some Asian Indian men began marrying Mexican women, and soon these Mexican-Hindu marriages became the dominant pattern of intermarriage in the Asian Indian community. These couples and their children were sufficiently numerous in the San Joaquin and Imperial Valleys to constitute a distinctive community.[34]

Filipino immigrants, like Asian Indians, faced an acute shortage of women of their own group and sought to marry and date across racial lines. The Filipino resistance to the control of their sexuality derived partly from the fact that they were the only Asian immigrants who were U.S. colonial subjects; hence, they were classified as American nationals rather than as aliens or citizens. This special status made them more willing to challenge their treatment in the United States. Antimiscegenation laws were also the first piece of legislation to target Filipinos directly; community leaders used the laws to mobilize the community. Nevertheless, Filipinos persisted in courting and dating white women in the face of opposition, and these relationships quickly became a flashpoint of conflict and triggered race riots. Filipinos challenged their inclusion in antimiscegenation statutes by arguing that they were not "Mongolians" and hence were exempt from intermarriage prohibitions. They took their fight to the courts and, by 1931, there were four cases pending in the Los Angeles Superior Court on the legality of white-Filipino marriages. Eventually, however, the California legislature adopted a law including "members of the Malay race" in its antimiscegenation laws. Faced with the legal defeat, Filipinos then circumvented the law by traveling out of state to marry white women. Others married Mexican, Japanese, Chinese, and native American women. Indeed, intermarriage among Filipinos was fairly extensive, and by 1946, more than half of the immigrants' children were biracial.[35]

Histories of miscegenation focus largely on the effect of restrictions on white-nonwhite sexual ties; however, an equally important effect of the antimiscegenation laws was that they fostered interracial sexual relationships among the marginalized groups. Since men far outnumbered women among all the Asian immigrant groups, many Asian men—Asian Indians and Filipinos, in particular—married or developed sexual relationships with Mexican, black, and native American women. As described earlier, marriages between Asian Indian men and Mexican women and between Filipino men and Mexican women were numerous. While a few Asian men married black women on the West Coast, the low position of blacks in the racial hierarchy and their smaller numbers on the West Coast seemed to have limited the number of these intermarriages. In the Mississippi Delta, however, liaisons between Chinese men and black women were established from the time Chinese men first arrived in the region in 1870 until the early decades of the twentieth century. Chinese men worked initially as sharecroppers and then established a niche for themselves running grocery stores in black neighborhoods. A significant number of these men married or cohabited with black women. But the pattern of black-Chinese relationships in Mississippi dissolved after the 1940s, when the changed immigration laws permitted the entry of the Chinese wives and kin of the Chinese men. In addition, the pressures exerted by the local white communities against black-Chinese relationships led to the eventual dissolution of black-Chinese family ties.[36]

While most accounts of white-Asian miscegenation focus on sexual relationships within the territorial boundaries of the nation-state, I highlight the critical importance of extraterritorial spaces to the management and production of white-Asian intimacies. This study argues that these extraterritorial spaces have been consistently absent from the historiography of miscegenation; it links their absence to the state-bound cartographies of American history and the invisibility of American imperialism.

I trace the genealogy of the white man—Asian woman dyad to the materialities of these colonial and neocolonial locations and point to their repressed links to national identity. The history of Asian women's exclusion from the U.S. nation-state turned repeatedly on the potential threat signified by their sexuality. During the early period of immigration, Asian women's bodies symbolized the power of the ethnic community to reproduce itself within the United States, and, hence, several immigration and naturalization laws targeted Asian women for exclusion. In fact, in the Chinese case, the exclusion of women preceded that of men. Prior to the Chinese Exclusion Act of 1882, the Page Law of 1875 restricted Chinese and other "Mongolian" prostitutes from entering the United States. Although prostitution was wide-spread in California and women of different nationalities participated in sex work, Chinese women were identified as a singular moral and public health danger: They were identified as carriers of unusually virulent strains of vene-real disease and as corrupters of young white boys. Subsequently, laws passed in 1903, 1907, and 1917 expanded the bases for barring Chinese women sus-pected of prostitution from entry into the country and for deporting alleged Chinese prostitutes already in the country.[37] The representation of Asian women's sexuality as different from white women's sexuality not only cor-roborated the thesis of Oriental degeneracy, it justified the segregation of Asians and whites.

But while Chinese women's sexual immorality provided the grounds for their exclusion from the nation, this imagined Oriental licentiousness heightened the allure of the extranational locales with which Asian women came to be identified—island paradises in the Pacific, treaty ports, and colo-nial possessions. Two interlocking issues emerge from the extra-territorial formations of the white man–Asian woman dyad: On the one hand, sexual contacts between white men and Asian women overseas emerged largely in the context of the sexual license and power afforded white men in treaty ports, military bases, or as occupying forces in Asia. On the other hand, U.S. immigration law made marriage the precondition for the continuation of these relationships in the United States, since long-term entry into the United States was restricted to the wives and children of U.S. citizens. Marriage was a prerequisite for immigration and assimilation. Thus, immi-gration law served as a mechanism of selective incorporation of interracial sexual relationships. Immigration law played a vital role in the normalization of white-Asian interracial intimacy. This is evident in two pieces of legisla-tion enacted in the pre-1965 period: the War Brides Act of 1945, which enabled U.S. servicemen to bring their foreign brides into the United States; and the Immigration Act of 1946, which permitted Asian spouses of U.S. cit-izens to bypass restrictive quotas on Asian immigrants and enter as "non-quota immigrants." Approximately 80 percent of the forty-five thousand Japanese immigrants who entered in the 1950s did so as wives of U.S. ser-vicemen; between 1950 and 1964, almost 40 percent of the fifteen thousand Korean immigrants came as G.I. wives; and nearly all the sixteen thousand Filipinas who entered the United States in the postwar years entered as the wives of servicemen.[38] Thus, from the postwar period until 1965, when Asian immigration was strictly limited, a selective avenue of immigration opened up for Asian women to enter as the wives of U.S. servicemen.

What has been treated as a footnote in the history of Asian immigration to the United States—the arrival of several thousand Asian women as the wives of U.S. servicemen—assumes a new significance when situated within the history of U.S. interracial heterosexual intimacies. This brief history of gendered migration played a significant role in reconstructing images of Asian femininity from sexually licentious to domesticatedly feminine; the recontextualization of white-Asian intimacy within marriage also increased the sexual capital of Asian American women.

The dual associations of Asian American women as hypersexualized and as marriageably feminine have their genealogy in these political and legal histories of contact and migration prior to 1965. These dual associations have continued to define and shape Asian American gender identities in the post-1965 period. The transformation of former military rest and recreation centers in Asian countries into popular sex tourist destinations after the 1970s and the emergence of a burgeoning mail-order bride industry between the United States and Asia have entrenched the eroticism and femininity associated with Asian American women.[39]

Interracial Intimacies and Genealogies of the Nation

Sexual Naturalization places racialized heterosexuality at the center of analytical attention and, in doing so, argues that heterosexuality is not a transparent or monolithic category. Various forms of heterosexual relations have been differently privileged in society because they are embedded in power relations and racial meanings. As I show, dominant norms of conjugal heterosexuality have been integral to securing the full personhood of subjects, ensuring access to property, according citizenship, and enforcing social hierarchies. But these norms have frequently been constructed in opposition to the sexuality of racialized others. Thus, examining the intersections of race and sex in the field of heterosexuality offers us new openings for understanding how normative meanings of family, gender, and nation have emerged at different historical conjunctures.

The subject of miscegenation opens up new directions in the study of race, representation, and nationhood and calls for a reevaluation of existing critical views of Asian American racialization. *Sexual Naturalization* sets out to accomplish three critical tasks: It remaps the history of U.S. sexuality by uncovering its extraterritorial formations; it questions existing critical paradigms about the gendering of Asian American racial identities; and finally, it theorizes racialized female sexual agency through the formulation of what I term *sexual capital*.

First, I contend that white-Asian miscegenation differs from the other forms of miscegenation in the United States because it was produced within two different frames: the territorial and the extraterritorial. Most historical accounts of white-Asian miscegenation rehearse the impact of miscegenation laws on the emergence of Asian communities in the United States; this territorialization of miscegenation leaves out the fact that white-Asian interracial intimacies flourished overseas during the time they were outlawed within the United States. More important, the territorial and extraterritorial contexts correspond roughly to gendered formations of race; the genealogy of the white man–Asian woman dyad emerged largely from extraterritorial intimacies, while the genealogy of the Asian man–white woman dyad was produced primarily through domestic sexual prohibitions. Furthermore, the extraterritorial represents the space identified with the forms of sexuality that had to be excluded from the moral order of the nation. I pursue the connections between these two sites because these links allow us to identify the affective ties and intimate arrangements excluded from and constitutive of U.S. nationhood and domesticity.

I also focus on the extraterritorial and territorial locations of white-Asian miscegenation discourse to render visible the embeddedness of Asian immigrants in transnational family networks, sexual arrangements, and affective ties: "Bachelor" Asian males were often married and had wives and children in their homelands.[40] Some subsequently married and had children in the United States and maintained two households over a lifetime; some slowly gave up one family and acquired another; some had one family, developed another, and then reunited with the first. The variations are numerous, and normative models of family, gender, and nation are unable to capture the historical variations in, and dynamic quality of, these arrangements and ties. In addition, the "sojourner" status attributed to Asian workers defined them primarily in terms of the families and lives they left behind, thus foreclosing their identification as settlers. By a strange tautology, their sojourner status became the effect of miscegenation laws and the justification for them. It was also the product of a labor regime that profited from their "bachelorhood" by transferring the costs of their social reproduction to their families overseas. My concern is with the extraterritorial and territorial dimensions of miscegenation because they render visible the terms of Asian American subjection and resistance.

Second, my analysis shows that effeminacy offers a reductive formulation for capturing the gender and sexual variations that have refracted the racial meanings of various Asian American masculinities over time.[41] Discourses of sexuality that determined the racialization of Asian Indians and Filipinos suggest that a threatening virility rather than effeminacy defined their alienness.

One of the striking features of representations of white-Filipino miscegenation—the seeming attractiveness of Filipino men to white women—conjured up the dangerous possibility that these relationships might reflect white women's desire and agency. It is useful to keep in mind that while Japanese and Chinese immigrant men had also been perceived as threats to white womanhood, the nature of that sexual threat was usually conveyed through images of coerced sexual relations with white women (raping, kidnapping, or bribing or drugging them into submission). This scenario of coerced sexual relations left intact the bourgeois ideal of the white woman's passionless domesticity. But the Filipino male raised the specter of consensual white-Asian miscegenation.

I argue that the allure of the Filipino male in public discourse on white-Filipino miscegenation, while seeming to make a point about Filipino sexuality, revealed instead a deep unease about the permeability of racial boundaries and the difficulty of policing women's sexuality during the economic and social crisis of the Depression. In other words, the Filipino male's sexual appeal was derived from his primitive origins, but the dangers of this savage sensuality were also refracted through the destabilization of class, race, and gender boundaries of the Depression era. In Chapter 3, I analyze Carlos Bulosan's *America Is in the Heart* (1946) as a strenuous attempt to deconstruct the popular attribution of deviant sexuality to Filipino Americans. My reading of Bulosan's text stresses that the construction of deviant heterosexuality in popular discourse had a colonial etymology. I argue that the text must be read against the archive of colonial representations of native/migrant Filipino sexuality. The colonial archive is defined by the *hypercorpo-*

reality of the native/migrant subject, by which I mean the reduction of Filipino subjectivity to primordial sensations, appetites, and propensities, and the corresponding equation of Filipino culture with a primitive level of social and cultural development.

Third, *Sexual Naturalization* argues that the study of miscegenation allows us to rethink the complex history and meanings of Asian American women's sexual agency. I coin the term *sexual capital* to capture the shifting value encoded in images of Asian American femininity within the United States over the course of the last century. By sexual capital, I refer to the aggregate of attributes that index desirability within the field of romantic or marital relationships in a given culture and thereby influence the life-chances and opportunities of an individual. Like Pierre Bourdieu's terms social and cultural capital, sexual capital involves certain nonmarket processes that have economic effects.[42] Sexual capital, like social and cultural capital, is linked but not reducible to economic capital. I introduce the term *sexual capital* to highlight the impact of gender and sexuality on mobility and to identify a particular set of constraints within which individuals function as agents.[43]

In this book, I compare John Luther Long's "Madame Butterfly" (1898) to Bharati Mukherjee's *Jasmine* (1989), written almost a century later, in order to trace a particular trajectory in which the Asian American woman moves from being a sexual commodity to becoming the possessor of sexual capital. I track the shift in the meanings of Asian American femininity over this period to show how this transformation underlies the construction of what I call the *sexual model minority*.[44]

Long's heroine, Cho-Cho-San, is a sexual commodity, a geisha who enters into a temporary marriage with an American sailor, Benjamin Franklin Pinkerton, who later abandons her and marries a white American woman, Adelaide. Long's story highlights Pinkerton's cavalier disregard for Cho-Cho-San, who, in his mind, exists outside the parameters of possible marriage or Americanization. Mukherjee's Jasmine, by contrast, figures the sexual capital of the Asian American woman in the 1980s. Jasmine is represented as an Asian love goddess who enters the United States with fake papers and then moves through a series of romantic relationships with middle-class white men, whom she loves and leaves as she desires. In the time span separating these two texts, the relative value of the Asian American woman's sexuality in comparison to the white woman's sexuality shifts: While Cho-Cho-San is seen as an inappropriate marriage partner for Pinkerton and is easily displaced by

Adelaide, Jasmine is seen as more desirable and more marriageable than the white women she displaces in her several relationships with white men.

Separating these two texts is a long and complex history that changes the meanings of the white man–Asian woman dyad. The Immigration Act of 1965, which reopened large-scale immigration from Asia after a nearly fifty-year hiatus, coincided with major social and political changes within the United States, and both factors contributed toward the rearticulation of the meanings of Asian American femininity. The breakdown of overt racial barriers through civil rights struggles, the positioning of Asian Americans as model minorities, and the valorization of multiculturalism created a more varied terrain within which racial, sexual, and class difference were refigured. In addition, the sexual revolution transformed sexual mores and encouraged greater sexual freedom, and the women's movement exposed the constraints of marriage on female aspirations, opened up the public sphere to women's participation, and severed the connection between domesticity and passionless femininity.

Within this transformed social landscape, Asian American femininity accrued sexual capital. When white American men were assailed by growing demands for equality made by white American women, the Asian American woman came to stand in for the more traditional model of family-centered femininity challenged by feminists.[45] Furthermore, I argue that through her association with the model minority, the Asian American woman was also differentiated from the black woman, who was linked to matriarchal, emasculating, and socially dysfunctional forms of femininity. The charged meanings of black femininity and family life were articulated in Daniel Patrick Moynihan's controversial study *The Negro Family: The Case for National Action,* in which he decried the "tangle of pathology" emblematized by black female-headed households, out-of-wedlock births, welfare dependency, and poverty.[46]

Thus, by a long and circuitous route we arrive at a postmodern American moment when Asian American women's sexuality, earlier defined as extra-territorial because the sexual license it represented had to be excluded from the moral order of the nation and marriage, is by the late twentieth century domesticated to mediate a crisis for white bourgeois sexuality. As a result, a sexualized gendered sign of racial difference (the Asian American woman) came to buttress and revive a besieged ideal of the *American* family. Moreover, since contemporary ideals of companionate marriage celebrate sexual vitality and eroticism *within* marriage, the Asian American woman, once a figure for sexual freedom *outside* marriage, has now become emblematic of the perfect match between family-centrism and sex appeal. Thus, the very racial difference that marks Cho-Cho-San as traditional represents, by the end of the following century, a desirable feminine attribute that can counter feminist challenges to white masculinity and traditional family structures. I categorize the structural position and function of this image of the Asian American woman as that of a *sexual model minority*. As a sexual model minority, the Asian American woman cannot entirely displace the white woman, whose appeal is reinforced by racial privilege and the power of embodying the norm, but she does, nevertheless, represent a powerfully seductive form of femininity that can function as a mode of crisis management in the cultural contest over different meanings of America. This is not to imply either that the objectification of Asian American women has ended or that they are no longer subject to racism, but it does suggest that the meanings of race and sexuality have been recast.

The Cultural Work of the Interracial Romance

Sexual Naturalization focuses on an area neglected in Foucault's theorizations of biopower, namely the role of literary and filmic texts in educating desire and directing it toward its appropriate objects. This book examines the "cultural work" of the white-Asian interracial romance in the United States over the last century.[47] I argue that narratives of white-Asian miscegenation dramatically transformed the landscape of desire in the United States, inventing new objects and relations of desire that established a powerful hold over U.S. culture, a capture of imaginative space that was out of all proportion to the demographic strength of the Asian presence in the United States. This redefinition of desire displaced and recast existing scripts of manliness, femininity, eroticism, and marriage by bringing forward new scenarios of sexual exchange and supplanting or transforming old ones.

The primary embodiments of white miscegenous desire prior to the arrival of Asians were the barbaric but noble Indian savage; the heroic, self-sacrificing Indian princess; the promiscuous squaw; the black rapist; the hypersexual black woman; and the erotically volatile mulatto woman. But the white-Asian interracial romance rewrote the existing cultural scripts. The emergence of the myth of the erotic Asian woman coincided with the waning significance of the other two cultural stereotypes of nonwhite feminine sensuality. The erotic force of the myth of Asian femininity was bolstered by the declining significance of the native American woman as a figure of desire in the popular imagination at this time. Concurrently, historical changes led to the slow fading of the sensually charged figure of the mulatto woman from the national consciousness. Joel Williamson writes that with emancipation, as racial mixing between whites and blacks almost ceased, intermarriages between blacks and mulattoes increased, leading to the erosion of the boundary between the two groups. The last census count of mulattoes was undertaken in 1920 and registered the declining significance of that racial category. The growing prominence of the Asian woman as an eroticized figure was reinforced by these demographic and categorical changes. Narratives of white-Asian miscegenation singled out for erotic attention the figure of the Asian woman, investing this figure with the traits of *exotic* eroticism that had until then been primarily associated with the mulatto woman.[48] The exoticism of the mulatto had stemmed from representations of her body as the fruit and sign of forbidden desire: Her racial mixture represented the transgression that had produced it and to which it invited continuous reenactment. By contrast, the exoticism of the Asian woman was associated with her identification with extraterritorial sexual license. Although the source of their exoticism was different, one was the heir to the other. One could argue, however, that the beginning of the twenty-first century has seen a reemergence of mixed-race identity as a sign of beauty and desirability in popular culture. In its latest incarnation, multiracial beauty serves as a seductive symbol of America's hybrid racial future, by figuring hybridity as a sign of beauty rather than of unmanageable conflict or violence.

A striking feature of stories of white-Asian miscegenation is their remarkable popularity at a time when the extent of white-Asian sexual contacts was rather limited and restricted to specific locations. The lack of correspondence between fiction and sociological reality has drawn comment from scholars, but its significance has not been probed further. However, I argue that this very discrepancy between fiction and sociology is the key to unlocking the cultural power of these scripts. These narratives are important precisely because they invented and therefore preceded the racialized sexual cultures that in subsequent decades attained greater sociological solidity. Myths of white-Asian desire were productive of, rather than reflective of, the sociological reality of white-Asian miscegenation, helping shift the meanings of Asian American masculinity and femininity over the decades. The productivity of these stories derives from their ability to act as an "incitement to desire" through "the dissemination and implantation of polymorphous sexualities."[49] As Henry Yu notes in his excellent essay on white-Asian miscegenation, the fascination of whites and Asians with the subject of racial mixing was created and fed by dime novels, pulp magazines, and pornography.[50] In addition, narratives of interracial desire were also popular in a range of other cultural sites, including film, short fiction published in elite magazines, plays, and opera. Collectively, these narratives created new modes of desirability and new criteria of worth that competed with and refigured dominant cultural norms.

Thus far, narratives of white-Asian miscegenation have received little scholarly scrutiny because of their axiomatic status as productions of white fantasy. Critics have pointed to their Orientalist tropes and stereotypical representations of Asians in explaining their popularity with a white mainstream public. However, this study uses the popularity and fascination exerted by narratives of miscegenation to argue for their importance, not their irrelevance. It places the cultural work of these texts at the center of analytic attention and demonstrates the instability of their identifications, which have been viewed reductively as either fixed or simply false. This book foregrounds the complexity of the negotiations performed by texts within this tradition.

The cultural power of these narratives was rooted in their choice of subject and its treatment. Their popular appeal derived from their exploration of a theme that has exercised a powerful fascination over people both during the time when antimiscegenation laws were in place and long after they were revoked. The imaginative energy of these texts is keenly attuned to the need to influence perceptions, win hearts, and transform the way in which the public thinks, believes, and even dreams. Accordingly, they propose imaginative resolutions of social contradictions and offer ways to make sense of the social world. But they perform this cultural work precisely by seeming not to perform it at all. Indeed, interracial romances provide a site where crucial political questions of the time came to be contested so persuasively because the domain of the romance represented a space removed from the material and political interests that contaminated the "real" world; this purported isolation of the romantic from the real was mobilized to legitimate its imaginative resolutions, endowing them with the force of "universal" ideals.

The power of the narrative of miscegenation lay in its ability to tap into and symbolically resolve questions about the racialized constitution of American national identity. If the interracial romance has enjoyed such a long life in the culture, it is primarily because the issues it raises about American-Asian encounters and the place of Asians in America—questions of race, gender, and class—continue to be relevant despite the repeal of exclusion and antimiscegenation laws. The interracial romance offered a flexible and multivalent narrative construct that was adapted by writers and filmmakers to articulate diverse, contradictory agendas. Early in the century, whites used it to reinforce or interrogate dominant perceptions of the assimilability of Asians, and later it was appropriated by Asian Americans to naturalize their claim to America even as they sought to redefine, subvert, or expand the meanings of Americanness in the name of socialist, international, or multicultural projects.

Narratives of miscegenous love transformed the political conflicts between Asians and Americans in the United States and Asia into romantic plots about the possibility of love between individuals of different races. This process of romantic reinscription translated systemic political conflicts of racism, exclusion, and imperialism into personal choices of love objects based on subjective truths and universal ideals. In the process of consuming these texts, readers/viewers were reconstituted from political subjects to sentimental subjects even as the enlistment of their sympathies was directed to the eminently political task of determining who belonged within the community on the basis of his or her ability to inspire and reciprocate lasting desire. Fundamentally, these narratives marshaled an emotional logic to test the political logic of social boundaries. But while tragic stories about the impossibility of love between the races often enlarged the sympathies of readers, they also engendered a pragmatic apprehension in an audience that acknowledged the necessity of racial divisions. Thus, both the ideal world of alternative social realities represented by miscegenous love and the art in which it was enshrined could serve as symbols for the ineluctable separation of art and reality. This is the impasse between art and worldliness on which D. W. Griffith's *Broken Blossoms* (1919) comes to rest.

Narratives of interracial desire came to be so influential because of their ability to address social questions precisely by seeming not to. They transformed political questions of difference that were the basis of social hierarchy by rendering them in the simulacrum of a "universal" language of the human heart. The story of miscegenous desire does its ideological work in two ways: first, by exploring the possibility of love across racial divisions despite the existence of social norms or laws that stigmatize such relations; and second, by representing the forms that such transgressive desires assume. In exploring the possibility of reciprocal interracial desire, these stories delineate the "anthropological minimum," or lowest common denominator, that is the precondition for romantic love. Such a threshold highlights the implicit preconditions that govern access to the domain of a putatively universal experience. Uday Mehta argues that the contradiction between liberalism's professions of inclusion and its historical practice of exclusion derived from certain cultural and psychological propensities that were seen as impeding the attainment of the anthropological minimum: "The universalistic reach of liberalism derives from the capacities that it identifies with human nature and from the presumption, which it encourages, that these capacities are sufficient and not merely necessary for an individual's political inclusion. . . . However, what is concealed behind the endorsement of these universal capacities are the specific cultural and psychological conditions woven in as preconditions for the actualization of these capacities."[51] In the case of the romance, the anthropological minimum is postulated through qualities of mind and heart that enable romantic union. My readings of the various texts in this study demonstrate that the sentimental incorporation enacted in the romance reframes political exclusions in the language of an affective, psychological, and cultural deficit.

Furthermore, romance offered a formula for naturalizing the narrative of nationhood in a land of immigrants where nationhood, lacking the weighty genealogical tropes of "tradition," language, or cultural antiquity, was in constant need of legitimating discourses that could transform the political abstraction of the nation into a deeply felt affective state. The language of sexual desire, permeated as it is in the Western context with the idea of consent, autonomy, and freedom, offered a powerful vehicle for examining, in the seemingly transpolitical space and language of the human heart, the possibility of forging binding ties that could provide the foundation of a common future. As Doris Sommer observes, "Romances are themselves synecdoches of the marriage between Eros and Polis."[52] As such, the romance offered an ideal narrative formula for exploring and constructing the emotional foundation of national membership at a time when the basis of such membership was deeply in question. Who of the many new arrivals in the country could become an American? On what basis would these determinations be made? Who could be assimilated to its ideals and who could not? The analysis of the interracial romance reveals the cultural construction of the racialized domestic genealogies that enabled a nation of immigrants to imagine itself as family.

I offer detailed readings of four narratives that reflect the changing structure of the romance over the last century.

In Part One, "Sexual Orients and the American National Imaginary," I examine two influential and popular narratives of white-Asian miscegenation produced by white Americans: John Luther Long's "Madame Butterfly" deals with the white man–Asian woman dyad, and D. W. Griffith's film *Broken Blossoms* represents the Asian man–white woman dyad. This pairing of texts is repeated in Part Two, "Engendering the Hybrid Nation," where I examine the representation of miscegenation through the different dyads in the texts of two Asian American writers, Carlos Bulosan and Bharati Mukherjee. The organization of the texts in this study is historical in order to track the shifts in racial and sexual ideologies encoded in these texts. This analysis reveals that gender and racial hierarchies were inscribed into cultural texts of white-Asian miscegenation in that the white man–Asian woman dyad came to assume quite different valences compared to the Asian man–white woman dyad. Literary and filmic representations played an important role in elaborating and enunciating the differences in these two variants of the white-Asian heterosexual romance. The white man–Asian woman dyad has historically been more serviceable to signifying the assimilability of Asian Americans than the Asian man–white woman dyad, which typically emplotted the cultural impossibility and sexual danger of incorporating Asians into the nation. Over the course of the twentieth century, the Asian man–white woman dyad has become the recessive narrative, while the white man–Asian woman dyad has become the dominant narrative for representing the Asian-American encounter.

Chapter 1 examines John Luther Long's "Madame Butterfly" as a narrative of extraterritorial desire in which the plot of interracial desire enables a critique of the political contradictions of informal empire. Long stages the claims of the Japanese geisha on the American sailor who marries and then abandons her as the site of a casual forgetting; in doing so, he emphasizes the gap between what happens outside national spaces and what is acknowledged within them. I argue that Long's choice of a Japanese woman as the heroine of the interracial love story is revealing because Japan occupied a unique status among Asian nations in relation to the United States—as both an imperial competitor in the Pacific and a country with a seemingly unique capacity for Western-style modernization. As a modernizing Asian nation with imperial ambitions, Japan challenged Western categories that opposed West and non-West and modern and traditional. Long's story reveals an ambivalence toward Japanese modernity, which he envisions as a form of mimic modernity, a sign of partial presence. His ambivalence toward the modern Japanese subject (represented through the heroine Cho-Cho-San and her aggressive suitor Yamadori) is partly resolved by gendering the forms of Japanese modernity and rendering these, in turn, as appropriate (feminine) and inappropriate (masculine). The redemptive potential of the reformed Japanese female subject is signified by her fitness for emigration to America and her potential for naturalization as an American citizen.

Chapter 2 shows that D. W. Griffith's film about the unrequited love of a Chinese shopkeeper for a poor English girl allegorizes the cultural impossibility of cross-racial desire even as its tribute to the spirituality and gentleness of the Chinese hero becomes a vehicle for criticizing the brutality and destructiveness of certain aspects of Western civilization. The chapter examines the way in which Griffith's critique of the West is displaced onto British decadence while tacitly suggesting the redemptive potential for Anglo-Saxon hegemony embodied in American innocence. The Asian man–white woman dyad is deployed by Griffith to signal the impossibility of assimilating Asians into the Western nation and the necessity for cultural separation. The aborted interracial romance naturalizes these racial and national divisions while calling for international peace and reconciliation in the aftermath of World War I.

Chapter 3 analyzes the way in which Carlos Bulosan rewrites the colonial family romance of U.S.-Philippines "special relations" encoded in the status of Filipinos as colonial "wards" and American "nationals." But although Bulosan repudiates the myth of benevolent white paternity contained in the colonial family romance, he retains the figure of redemptive white womanhood central to this fiction and uses it to ground an alternative conception of America envisioned as a universal fraternity. Bulosan's writings highlight the contradictions in American democracy by representing its oppression and injustice as masculine and its enlightenment and uplift as feminine. Within this framework, the Filipino American subject's platonic desire for white women comes to figure the migrant's love for the highest ideals of America. The Filipino American's desire for America is thus naturalized through the symbolic structure of the heterosexual romance even as the sexual purity of this love challenges popular attributions of deviant heterosexuality to Filipino Americans. In order to read the complexity of the political dimensions of Bulosan's work, it is crucial to situate it against the archive of colonial representations of native/migrant Filipino sexuality that it seeks to deconstruct and rewrite.

While Bulosan offers a powerful account of the outlawing of Filipino sexual and affective life within colonial regimes, his efforts to salvage the humanity of the Filipino subject depend on inscribing it within normalizing narratives of heterosexual love and family order. Bulosan's reliance on the "metacultural intelligibility" of the heterosexual romance in reinforcing his claim to America undermines the radical force of his decolonizing project because it leads him to ground his socialist vision of racial and class equality on a narrative of gender difference and sexual exclusion.[53]

Chapter 4 situates Bharati Mukherjee's *Jasmine* within a historical moment marked by popular apprehensions of a crisis in American identity attributed to the changes caused by the new immigration and the ethnic separatism identified with multiculturalism. Mukherjee's *Jasmine* transforms multiculturalism from a signifier of crisis to a mode of crisis management through a story of the new immigrant's willing embrace of America. I argue that this transformation is effected by deploying the figure of the sexual model minority. A closer examination of the novel reveals the repressions that are revealed in the seemingly random and agent-less violence that destroys or wounds all of Jasmine's lovers. The author's inability to attribute the agency of violence to a heroine who is nevertheless inexplicably associated with it reveals the disavowals through which Jasmine is produced as a celebratory story in which miscegenous love serves as a trope of willing assimilation. The narrative of miscegenation is important in Mukherjee's writing because it enables her to explore the sexual model minority role as a mode of female power in *Jasmine*.

Sexual Naturalization offers a major shift in discussions of miscegenation by focusing on the portrayal of interracial love in stories by whites *and* Asian

Americans. The popularity of early narratives of miscegenation produced by whites created a set of tropes and narrative formulas that assumed so much power in shaping the "common sense" about race, sex, and love that their deconstruction, revision, and appropriation became integral to the emergence of Asian American cultural production. By focusing exclusively on white representations of miscegenation, critics have overlooked the fact that representations of miscegenation have been part of an extended cross-racial contestation of ideas about race, sex, and nationhood over the last century.

This book does not attempt to provide an exhaustive survey of narratives of white-Asian miscegenation. Rather, I have attempted to bring to critical attention the key texts that deal with miscegenation, to reveal the links between signifying practices and power relations at a particular historical moment, and to trace the changing structure of the interracial romance. The emphasis on situating works in a historical and political context is better served by a close analysis of particular texts than an extensive coverage of the range of such texts. It is difficult to provide nuanced contextualization in an overview of the interracial romance because the relations between the United States and various Asian countries have undergone major realignments over the course of the last century. There are also important differences in the relationships between the different Asian groups and the United States, making it difficult to provide generalizations about Asianness pertaining to all the relevant groups.

The analysis of narratives of miscegenation not only opens up a new archive for understanding the constitution of American imperial nationality but it significantly revises established critical views of race, gender, and class formation. Race, class, gender, nationality, and sexuality are articulated categories that emerge in historical relation to one other. It is impossible to determine a priori the historical relationship between these social categories. While some of the narratives I examine repress a particular social category or use it as the equivalent of another, my purpose has been to tease out these ideological switches and substitutions in order to reveal the dynamic and interdependent relationship between these social categories. In an astute observation, Kobena Mercer warns against the practice of invoking race, class, and gender in a way that "flatten[s] out the complex and indeterminate relations by which subjectivity is constituted in the overdetermined spaces *between* relations of race, gender, ethnicity, and sexuality."[54]

PART ONE

Sexual Orients and the
American National Imaginary

ONE

Mimic Modernity: "Madame Butterfly" and the Erotics of Informal Empire

> Orientalism is better grasped as a set of constraints upon and limitations of thought than it is simply as a positive doctrine.
>
> —Edward W. Said, *Orientalism*

John Luther Long's short story "Madame Butterfly" (1898) was the first American incarnation of a white-Asian interracial romance that originated with Frenchman Pierre Loti's popular travelogue, *Madame Chrysanthemum* (1887). Long's story was subsequently adapted for stage by David Belasco (1900), revised repeatedly in early productions of Giacomo Puccini's opera *Madam Butterfly* (1904–6), and then revived in novels and pop musicals such as *The World of Suzie Wong* (1957) and *Miss Saigon* (1989).[1] Indeed, such was its ubiquity as a cultural script that David Henry Hwang felt compelled to write a "deconstructivist Madame Butterfly" to counter the Orientalist myths he felt it perpetuated.[2] Thus, over the course of a century, the Butterfly story emerged as a potent and fiercely contested cultural referent, once praised lavishly for its sympathetic rendering of its Japanese heroine but later satirized by writers like Hwang as an imperialist fantasy of the hyperfeminine Asian woman.

In the evolution of the Madame Butterfly narrative, Long's tale gradually faded from public consciousness while the Puccini version emerged as *the* Madame Butterfly story, erasing the memory of all its French and American predecessors.

But before Long's story achieved international popularity through Puccini's opera, it was subjected to repeated revisions by Belasco and Puccini. The frequency and nature of these changes point to the unsettling critique of U.S. racial nationalism and imperialism contained in the original story, which subsequent revisions sought incessantly to ameliorate. The opera's 1904 premiere at La Scala in Milan (in which the libretto followed Long's story very closely) turned out to be a spectacular fiasco. The disastrous reception prompted numerous alterations over the next two years, several times for Italian audiences starting with the Brescia performance in 1904 and then again for French audiences in the Paris premiere of 1906. The triumphant success of the revised Paris version sealed its status as the definitive script of *Madam Butterfly*.[3]

The powerful critique of U.S. imperialism distinguished John Luther Long's "Madame Butterfly" from earlier and later versions of the story. Long Americanized the French version of the interracial romance by recasting it through discourses of American Orientalism. These discourses, in turn, circumscribed the scope of his political critique. While scholars have suggested that Long's "Madame Butterfly" was an adaptation of Pierre Loti's *Madame Chrysanthemum*, Long attributed his inspiration to a true story about a Japanese geisha told to him by his sister Jane Correl, the wife of a missionary in Japan.[4] It appears likely that both sources contributed to the final shape of Long's "Madame Butterfly," but the discursive framework of Correl's account allowed Long to *Americanize* the story of a treaty-port liaison. Not only does Long substitute an American sailor—pointedly named Benjamin Franklin Pinkerton—for the Frenchman in Loti's autobiographical account, but he uses the story of the abandoned Japanese geisha and her child to explore how race, sex, gender, and class constitute the American national imaginary both in the domestic context of debates about immigration and in the geopolitical context of debates about American imperialism.

Appearing at the height of the Japonisme vogue in Europe, and feeding on the insatiable Western curiosity about Japan by offering the immediacy of a first-person account of the newly opened Oriental country, Loti's *Madame Chrysanthemum* gained an enormous following. Loti's travelogue provided a detailed account of an ostensibly exotic theme—his temporary marriage to a young Japanese woman. Temporary marriages like Loti's, between foreign men and Japanese women, were quite common in Japanese treaty ports at that time; the sexual arrangement was governed by Japanese customary law, whereby the man was expected to provide the woman with a house and payment in exchange for sexual services and housekeeping, and the marriage was considered to be dissolved when the man abandoned the woman. According to customary practice, the children of such unions belonged to the father, if he wished to claim them.

Madame Chrysanthemum was published when Loti had already established his reputation as a celebrated author of fiction and nonfiction in exotic settings, many of which focused on his relationships with Asian women. These accounts combined close descriptions of the locale with sensual descriptions of his sexual adventures. However, *Madame Chrysanthemum*—named after the Japanese geisha he marries while in Japan—is a conspicuously unromantic and unexotic account and represents a marked departure from his other romances.[5] In *Madame Chrysanthemum*, the absence of romance and the lack of exoticism are inscribed within the writer's hostile encounter with Japanese modernity, which he reads as a sign of the parodic, the artificial, and the ugly. Loti, like many other Western writers before and after him, showed a strong preference for an idealized and premodern Japan rather than the Westernizing Japan.[6] In Loti, the pointed antipathy toward Japanese modernity is expressed through his emphasis on the physical unattractiveness of the Japanese woman, her imperviousness to his presence, and the tedium of their sexual arrangement. Their relationship seldom escapes the frame of the coldly economic, and even the rare moments of sentiment or sexual interest depicted in the story are rapidly deflated. For instance, at the conclusion, in a rare mood of regret and sentimentality, the narrator bids farewell to Chrysanthemum and casts a nostalgic, lingering glance at her still-prostrate form framed in a ceremonial bow in the doorway. A few moments later, however, when he hurries back to retrieve a forgotten item, he discovers Chrysanthemum in the bedroom, wholly absorbed in biting and testing the gold coins he had left her as payment. The chastened Frenchman gathers his bag and bids a second farewell to his former wife, noting wryly the outwardly submissive appearance of the decorously prostrate young woman.

Despite Long's denial of literary indebtedness to Loti's book, critics point to certain structural resemblances in arguing for their intertextuality. They note the appearance in both texts of a sailor buddy who recommends the geisha as a recreation to the main character and references to certain common dates.[7]

But while there are similarities of plot between the two stories, Long's story reinscribes the Frenchman's narrative within the framework of American Orientalism. He rewrites Loti's sardonic port-of-call liaison between two distant partners as a tragic story about the unrequited love of a Japanese geisha. Long's story centers on a Japanese woman, called Cho-Cho-San or Butterfly in his tale, who enters into a temporary marriage with a callous American sailor, Benjamin Franklin Pinkerton. He urges her to convert to Christianity and to Americanize and promises to return after a brief period to take her to the United States. She waits for his return and gives birth to a blonde, blue-eyed baby in his absence. During this time, a wealthy Japanese man, Yamadori, proposes to her, but she rejects him, believing herself bound to Pinkerton in an "American marriage." After a few years, Pinkerton returns accompanied by Adelaide, the white American woman he married after leaving Japan. Pinkerton dispatches Adelaide to inspect and claim the child. Satisfied that the child looks white, Adelaide arranges to take him back with her to the United States. Cho-Cho-San learns of Pinkerton's remarriage and attempts suicide. After she plunges the knife into her breast, she changes her mind and decides to live for her child instead. When Adelaide arrives to pick up the child the following day, she finds the house empty.

Long replaces the opaque peripheral character of the geisha, the object of Loti's denigration, with the courageous Cho-Cho-San, driven by poverty and family obligations into selling herself into marriage with a barbarian, only to discover herself helplessly in love with him. The emphasis in Long's story is on Cho-Cho-San's victimization by Japanese customary law and the privileges extended through it to Americans in Japan, consequent upon the "opening" of Japan. By setting the action in a treaty port and centering it on a geisha's tragic predicament, Long highlights the double jeopardy of Japanese femininity caught between Japanese patriarchy and American racism. From Loti to Long, the geisha goes from being the unknowable object to the suffering subject in the asymmetries of power produced by Japanese entry into modernity. Long's narrative is attentive to the powerlessness of the Japanese woman in these shifting geopolitical alignments and explores tentatively the prospects for her empowerment.

Long's story of white-Asian miscegenation offers a "cognitive and libidinal map of U.S. geopolitics" because it reveals the strains in ideologies of American democracy created by American expansion in Asia and Asian immigration to the United States.[8] As I demonstrated in the introduction, the white man–Asian woman dyad emerged from a history of interracial intimacy in which the Asian woman was identified with forms of extraterritorial desire that are excluded from the moral order of marriage and nation-hood. Long's story invokes this repressed history of illicit interracial intimacy but does so to insist upon the links between the nation and its extraterrito-rial spaces. "Madame Butterfly" emphasizes the need to recognize the mutu-ally constitutive nature of these two spaces. Long also highlights the inextri-cable connections between American expansionism and Asian immigration to the United States by showing that Cho-Cho-San's desire to emigrate is the *effect* of Pinkerton's presence in her country.[9] Thus, he transforms the story of an overseas sexual adventure into a critique against nativism at home and imperialism abroad. In this respect, his story differs markedly from Loti's love story, which centers on a financed sexual arrangement that literally and figuratively begins and ends in Japan.

Long allegorizes the contradictions of informal empire through the moral crisis it creates within the bourgeois domestic order. Eva Saks observes that the outlawing of miscegenation created a crisis in representation because it had the effect of inverting traditional moral categories: "While punishing interracial fornication more severely than intraracial fornication, it punished interracial marriage most severely."[10] In the case of relationships between white men and Asian women overseas, this moral hypocrisy was reproduced through a territorial logic—what happened over there could be condoned and forgotten because it lay outside the moral and legal order that operated within the U.S. nation. It is precisely this moral contradiction contained within the thesis of extraterritoriality that John Luther Long critiques in "Madame Butterfly." Long's story suggests that the sexual license associated with the extraterritorial location of the Asian woman can be domesticated and normalized through marriage and assimilation.

By using the treaty port as a setting for his story of miscegenous love, Long revealed the production of American imperial nationality along the sea routes that bound the informal overseas empire to the continental United States. Like D. W. Griffith's later film, *Broken Blossoms* (1919), Long's story uses the Asian treaty port as a setting for renegotiating the meanings of American masculinity and nationhood in the shift from territorial nation-hood to informal empire.[11] The theme of informal empire is integral to late-nineteenth- and early-twentieth-century American literature but has until recently received little critical attention.[12] In his account of the "privileged settings" of American fiction, Philip Fisher lists the wilderness, the home-stead, and the city as the principal spaces where the meanings of American culture are explored. He explains that "privileged settings" are not necessarily the spaces where the key events take place, but, "instead, they are the ideal and simplified vanishing points toward which lines of sight and projects of every kind converge. . . . [F]or America, these settings have had an unusual force, because of the need for vanishing points and guiding patterns during the rapid construction of the culture."[13] Fisher's list of settings, while illuminating, restricts the meanings of Americanness to its continental boundaries and thus fails to recognize the formative influence of overseas empire in producing American national culture and ideology. The invisibility of extraterritorial locations such as the treaty port as a "privileged setting" can be seen as symptomatic of the exceptionality of imperialism and the erasure of Asia in accounts of the construction of American culture.

Asia formed a critical discursive site for framing the debates about imperialism and immigration in the United States at the turn of the twentieth century when Long was writing his fiction.[14] The passage of the Chinese Exclusion Act in 1882 marked the first time in the history of the United States that racial identity was used as a basis for excluding immigrants and denying them naturalization. After the act's passage, the anti-Oriental movement, which had its base among the white working class on the West Coast, directed its efforts to excluding Japanese immigrants who had begun entering the country in larger numbers to replace the excluded Chinese workers. Racial anxiety around the Japanese presence harnessed earlier Yellow Peril discourses mobilized against the Chinese, highlighting Asiatic unassimilability, depravity, and heathen practices; it also tapped into proimperialist discourses endorsing American expansionism in Asia and depicting Japanese imperialism in the region as menacing and dangerous. The term *informal empire,* which gained currency at this time, designated the newness of American imperialism and articulated the strategic advantage of neocolonialism as a uniquely American mode of power destined to supersede old-world European colonialism.[15] Thus, the growing Japanese population within the U.S. and Japanese imperial ambitions in Asia were seen by exclusionists as threatening Anglo-Saxon national identity and world dominance. Long's "Madame Butterfly," which appeared at this time, positioned itself against the jingoistic rhetoric of its time and sought to counter racism and imperialism through its depiction of the assimilability and desirability of the Japanese woman and its alternative vision of a U.S.-Japanese union.

In his interracial romance, Long criticizes the informality of American empire by depicting the asymmetry of American-Japanese relations; nevertheless, he leaves suggestively open the question of whether some other form of international collaboration—specifically of Japanese aesthetic culture with American political institutions—might not promise a utopian romance of rejuvenation for both countries. In this respect, Long's critique does not in the end escape the binary of tradition-modernity that underlies Orientalist discourse, although it does offer a trenchant critique of unregulated imperialism. Long's "Madame Butterfly" suggests that American institutions of law and marriage may liberate Japanese women from the tyranny of Japanese customary law, while Japanese premodern aestheticism and simplicity may counterbalance the negative influences of American modernity. In this manner, Long seeks to resolve the contradictions in American democracy by envisioning a symbolic marriage of the United States and Japan.

Despite its rejection of imperialism and racism, Long's critique was constrained by his reliance on discourses that were themselves embedded in American expansionism. Although the sentimental narrative of interracial romance enabled a critique of racial and sexual exclusions, it did not provide a discursive framework for apprehending Japanese modernity as "coeval" with U.S. modernity.[16] Rather, the gender hierarchy of the white man–Asian woman dyad reinforced the secondary positioning of Japan in relation to the United States. Yet, if Long's story does not provide an alternative vision of Japanese modernity, its conclusion does offer a metacommentary on the limitations of Orientalist tropes in representing the Japanese woman's resistance. In a striking narrative twist, Long stages the disappearance of his heroine from the story at the moment of her feminist emergence, signifying that her resistance serves as a vanishing point for textual representation. Cho-Cho-San and her baby literally vanish without a trace at the end of the story.

Missionary, Political, and Aesthetic Discourses in Long's "Madame Butterfly"

Long himself had never traveled to Japan and apprehended it entirely through the imagination of others. His dependence on missionary, aesthetic, and political discourses that are themselves linked to American expansionism produces an ambivalence toward Japanese modernity, which is represented as a form of *mimic modernity,* a sign of partial presence. Speaking of mimicry as

a strategy of colonial discourse, Homi K. Bhabha explains: "Colonial mimicry is the desire for a reformed, recognizable Other, as *a subject of a difference
that is almost the same, but not quite*. Which is to say, that the discourse of
mimicry is constructed around an *ambivalence*; in order to be effective, mimicry must continually produce its slippage, its excess, its difference."[17]

Feminist critics have called attention to Homi Bhabha's failure to address
the way in which gender identities inflect strategies of mimicry.[18] My analysis of Long's story seeks to foreground the gendering of mimicry and to link
it to a growing American global role in relation to which Japan emerged as
imperial competitor and as a not-quite-modern nation. Within Long's story,
the ambivalence toward the modern Japanese subject (represented through
the heroine Cho-Cho-San and her aggressive suitor Yamadori) is partly resolved by gendering the forms of Japanese modernity and rendering them,
in turn, as appropriate (feminine) and inappropriate (masculine). The redemptive potential of the reformed Japanese female subject is signified by
her fitness for emigration to America and her potential for naturalization as
an American citizen; the pathos of the Butterfly story lies in her being denied
these opportunities by the American sailor who abandons her. By contrast,
the mimic man in the story, Yamadori, is portrayed as sinister, manipulative,
and crass, appropriating American learning and language for his own
exploitative ends. The split in the representation of Japanese otherness is inscribed as the possibility of naturalizing appropriate forms of mimicry (the
female subject) and excluding inappropriate forms of mimicry from the field
of desire (the male subject).

The American imperative to Westernize Japan was caught between the
desire for Japanese markets and the fear that Japanese modernization could
result in the emergence of a strong Asian nation with its own imperial
designs. Summarizing the shifting currents in American representations of
Japan in the late nineteenth century, Akira Iriye comments, "To the traditional axiom of predominance in the western hemisphere, the Spanish-
American War added the theme of American expansion in the Pacific and
East Asia. Japanese activities in these regions, both actual and imagined,
could not easily be reconciled with such perceptions."[19] The effects of this
deep-seated American ambivalence toward Japanese modernity are reflected
in Long's story through the double vision of mimicry.

Long's sister, Jane Correl, lived as the wife of a missionary for many
years in Japan. In a short essay published in *Japan Magazine*, Jane Correl

recounted the story of a Japanese tea-girl, Cho-San, and her baby, who were abandoned by an American sailor and waited in vain for his return.[20] According to Correl, Cho-San lived near her house in Japan, and Correl had narrated the story to her brother on one of her visits to Philadelphia. Inspired by her tale, he wrote the story in a few days and asked her to review it for any details "not true to life."[21] Long had read widely about Japan and often discussed the details of his stories with his sister because of her first-hand knowledge about the country. Yet Long's attribution has been ignored by all other scholars or has been noted only in passing, possibly because it has been viewed primarily as a tactic used by the author to deflect criticisms of his unacknowledged borrowings from Loti's *Madame Chrysanthemum*.

Long's attribution of his story to his sister might be read as an indebtedness to the discursive production of Japan in missionary discourse, which offered one of the primary circuits for the dissemination of representations of Japan. Situating "Madame Butterfly" in this discursive context clarifies an important and overlooked aspect of its representation of the U.S.-Japanese relationship at the turn of the century. A recurring theme of missionary discourse in Hawai'i, the Philippines, and Japan featured the difficulty of evangelizing and educating natives when segments of the American expatriate community in these locations disgraced the very ideals the missionaries sought to identify as quintessentially American and Christian. Speaking of the double consciousness of Americanness embraced by Protestant missionaries in the Philippines, Kenton J. Clymer observes: "They helped reconcile Filipinos to their new fate and were allies of the government in what both perceived as a 'civilizing' mission. At the same time, they viewed themselves as the conscience of the American experiment and did not hesitate to judge other Americans harshly for not living up to what they believed was the best in the American tradition."[22] Missionaries were often ambivalent and frequently critical about the conduct of their fellow countrymen because they felt it jeopardized their own work and the legitimacy of the civilizing mission. The proliferation of vices and un-Christian behavior among the other expatriates was often explained in terms of class differences within the expatriate community—the infidelity, racial condescension, and immorality of sailors, gamblers, and businessmen were censured by the missionaries, while the teachers and higher-ranking civilian administrators were viewed favorably by the missionaries. Speaking for many others involved in mission work, Charles F. Rath commented grimly, "As I look and see the flag of my country floating in the breeze which is the emblem of a Christian government, and then look around me and see the men sent over here to represent us, I feel ashamed."[23]

In Hawai'i and Japan, combating sexual promiscuity and prostitution became a focal point of missionary work.[24] The role of the Western male in the promotion and perpetuation of these vices turned him into one of the primary antagonists in missionary efforts at reform. Patricia Grimshaw explains that missionary wives in Hawai'i focused their outrage at unhallowed sexual relations between their fellow countrymen and the natives: "It was the conjunction of the Western male's sexual predacity and the Hawaiian's easiness about sexuality which most affronted missionaries' sense of propriety."[25] In the civilizational schema that rationalized efforts to evangelize and modernize the natives, the foundational assumption of the degradation of native life and of the urgent need for the humanizing intervention of the missionaries was undercut by the activities and propensities of fellow Americans whose behavior fell well below the standards upheld to the natives as qualitatively superior to their own ways. Within missionary discourse, then, the sexual predacity of white men served not as a vehicle for anti-imperialist critique but as a marker of class differences within the expatriate groups and the sign of a major internal threat to the success of the civilizing mission.

Within this context, the marked contrast between Pinkerton and the cultivated Consul Sharpless becomes meaningful as a contrast between a worthy and an unworthy representative of American values in Japan rather than a wholesale condemnation of the American presence in Japan. In missionary discourse, this critique of the sexual morality of sailors and other expatriates was consonant with the strong support of America's modernizing and Christianizing influence in the Pacific. In missionary discourse, this difference between good and bad Americans was not expressed as concern about the effects of expansionism on natives but about the undermining of the moral claims of the civilizing mission and of the difficulty of regulating the behavior of segments of the expatriate community. Long deploys this structural contrast to point to the difficulty of maintaining American ideals far from home.

While Pinkerton plays the pivotal role in "Madame Butterfly" as the primary agent of Butterfly's tragedy, the significance of Consul Sharpless has been overlooked in critical discussions of the text. He is presented in many ways as the lover Pinkerton should have been. Sharpless's role as the recipient of Butterfly's confessions, as the intermediary between the couple, and as the interlocutor who is constantly prompted by Butterfly to ascribe motives to Pinkerton and confirm her doting interpretation of his character, positions him as a reluctant representative of Pinkerton, an unhappy surrogate, and a foil to the callous sailor. In particular, the first meeting between Butterfly and Sharpless is structured around the contrast between Sharpless and the absent Pinkerton. The difference between the two men, both serving as representatives of America in different capacities, is heightened by Butterfly's reminiscences and rehearsal of her courtship with Pinkerton. The sympathetic consul is cast in the role of auditor; during a series of impromptu re-enactments he is a stand-in for her lover. The consul's receptivity to her charm and beauty, his pity for her situation, and his musings about Pinkerton's character are expressed in the sentiment that he would undoubtedly have behaved differently if he had been in Pinkerton's place:

> Well, Pinkerton *might* have meant to return to her. Any other man probably
> would. . . . There was a saying in the navy that if any one could forget a
> played game or a spent bottle more quickly than Pinkerton, he had not
> yet been born. . . . For himself, he was quite sure—had he been Pinkerton,
> of course—that it would have survived something greater. And finally his
> own views prevailed with him as if they were Pinkerton's, and he believed
> that he would be delighted to return and resume his charming life with her
> on Higashi Hill. (Long, "Madame Butterfly" [hereafter, "MB"], 62–63)

In the course of their meetings, Sharpless and Butterfly develop a running joke between them that the consul is the "mos' bes' nize man in all the whole worl,' " with the exception of Pinkerton, a qualification Butterfly always makes apologetically in the course of her elaborate, formal courtesies toward the consul. Pinkerton charges the consul with the task of paying money to Butterfly for her maintenance and with the unpleasant duty of informing her that he is now remarried ("MB," 61). Through all these proceedings, the pointed contrast between Pinkerton and his agent and spokesperson underscores the gap between the representative and the represented. Since both of them also serve in Japan as the representatives of their government, they symbolize a fissure in the American presence in Japan—a division between those who uphold the ideals of their country and possess a genuine respect and affection for Japan and those who tarnish these same ideals and treat the Japanese as dispensable playthings with a backward culture.

What are the fissures of this internally differentiated idea of America? Long seems to suggest that the Butterfly story is produced within a masculine naval culture that, in the context of American domination in the Pacific, has acquired the privileges of extraterritorial promiscuity that can operate unchecked by Japanese customary law and American legal sanctions. This not only creates a crisis in how and what America comes to signify in the course of trans-Pacific expansionism but also creates fissures between different sectors of its overseas establishment. Hence, however loath he may be to do so, the consul has to mediate between the American sailor and the Japanese geisha. Despite the fact that his values pit him against his compatriot, he maintains a public reticence about Pinkerton's behavior, thus reducing his own role to that of a helpless spectator to the unfolding tragedy. American ideals can, therefore, provide a cover for the international sexual adventurism of Pinkerton and his like, even as the necessity to attest to their existence binds functionaries like Sharpless to a posture of noninterference in extranational space. When Sharpless sees how devastated Butterfly is when she discovers that Pinkerton has remarried, he curses him under his breath, "Pinkerton, and all such as he" ("MB," 82). Even as the story opens, the narrative is framed by the story of the Pink Geisha, recounted in an elegiac mode by Pinkerton's sailor friend Sayre and offering in encapsulated form a story that circulates within the naval crowd and seems to be endlessly reenacted within these circles: "He went back; couldn't find her" ("MB," 2).

Sharpless's positioning as the conscience of his callous compatriot and his role as a moral touchstone of American ideals is quite different from the sailor-buddy relationship that frames Loti's tale. Long's contrast between the sailor and the consul has its roots in the discursive framework of Long's acknowledged source, his sister's story of Cho-San. The structural contrast between the narrator's best friend, Yves, and "Loti" in *Madame Chrysanthemum* turns on their ability to establish a relationship with the geisha as an index of their resourcefulness in adapting to their new surroundings. In Loti's travelogue, Yves does develop a close relationship with Chrysanthemum, and the narrator spies the two in long, companionable conversations. Seen for the first time as the possible object of another man's desire, the hitherto unattractive Chrysanthemum acquires a new allure for the narrator, only to revert to her status as a nondescript convenience when the narrator discovers that her relationship with Yves is purely platonic. That the narrator and Yves are Frenchmen is of less significance than that they are sailors, although both factors establish the basis for their camaraderie. Unlike Long, Loti is not concerned with his characters' ability to uphold their country's national ideals.

Although Long contrasts the attitudes of the two sailors, Sayre and Pinkerton, to establish that Pinkerton is more callous than other sailors, his central contrast is between Pinkerton and the consul. Both characters are seen not only as representatives of their *country* but also as representatives of their *class*. The story raises the question of whether the democratic ideals embraced by an American like Sharpless can accommodate the dishonorable actions of Pinkerton.

Other aspects of the sailor's portrayal can also be contextualized within the discursive production of missionaries in Japan, which displayed clear differences from the writings of their counterparts in other parts of Asia. The widespread Western perception of Japanese modernity and of Japan's anomalous status among Asian nations affected the attitudes of missionaries toward the natives. Japan was early identified as a major field of evangelical endeavor but was quickly superseded by other Asian mission destinations that conformed more closely to the conventional notion of degraded, backward, and heathen nations: Japan was simply too modern to attract many missionaries.[26] However, the missionaries who did work there developed more progressive and egalitarian attitudes toward the natives than their counterparts in other parts of Asia and were known, in particular, for advocating racial equality. Many missionaries protested discriminatory legislation against Japanese immigrants in the United States and supported open immigration from Japan and Japanese naturalization in the United States.[27] In addition, since Japanese missionary work included immersion in the language and culture, it was not uncommon for missionaries to acquire "a pronounced belief that Japanese culture had its own unique advantages and values."[28] Furthermore, since Japanese laws banned proselytizing until 1873, a major focus of mission work in Japan was in social improvement, especially in the area of women's education and in the eradication of the extensive system of licensed prostitution that flourished in treaty ports.[29] Thus, when examined within the context of the missionary enterprise in Japan—its formulation of social problems and their causes, the primacy of women's liberation from native patriarchal custom, and the corrupting influence of foreign sailors in the treaty ports—the Butterfly story as a prototype of treaty-port liaisons comes to acquire new and more complex meanings. The racial arrogance of Pinkerton, his refusal to treat his marriage to the Japanese woman as a binding one, his unwillingness to allow her to emigrate to the United States, his contempt for Cho-Cho-San's culture, and his sexual opportunism reveal a composite figure whose attributes can be traced back to the double-pronged missionary critique of U.S.-Japanese relations in the United States (immigration) and in Asia (customary sexual arrangements that contravene Christian ideas of marriage).

This view is reinforced by the emphasis given in Long's tale, as compared to Loti's, to the cruelty of Japanese customary law, which is as much the cause of Cho-Cho-San's distress as the sexual adventurism of the American sailor that it sanctions. The overhaul of the Japanese legal system represented a major area of Western intervention in the Japanese social structure and provided an important focus of missionaries' reform work as well.[30] The story's emphasis on the law as the medium for the exploitation of Cho-Cho-San by Pinkerton and Yamadori is unambiguous, as is its pitiful elaboration of the circumstances that force Cho-Cho-San to enter into the marriage with a "barbarian." Cho-Cho-San explains that she became a geisha after her father killed himself and the family fell into poverty ("MB," 55). Therefore, the double-pronged critique of Western license and oppressive native custom (that was improved through Western reform) suggests that the story is both a critique of aspects of the Western presence *and* an endorsement of its improving influence that draws on the double-consciousness of missionary writing about Japan.

The critique of the American presence in Japan in Long's story is also foregrounded by the gender politics that underscores the interracial romance. Nowhere is the influence of Westernization more powerfully evoked than in the transformation of the central character from a demure Japanese geisha to a feisty and spirited New Woman who taunts Yamadori about his abuse of the Japanese custom of temporary marriages and his treatment of women as dispensable objects. In fact, the Yamadori character and the elaborate look-at meeting arranged by the go-between, in which the prospective suitor views the young woman he wants to marry while she serves him tea, introduce a feminist theme that has no equivalent in Loti's story. This scene stands out because it reveals a paradoxical defiance in Cho-Cho-San, showing her as naively and blindly devoted to Pinkerton but trenchantly critical, assertive, and confidently ironic toward the Japanese man who approaches her with an offer of remarriage. As a result, she emerges as a curious graft of a full-fledged New Woman and an exotic and childishly petulant geisha. How are we to understand this hybrid creation, which runs against the grain of popular stereotypes of geishas? She is composed of the strains of the sentimental child-heroine, the delicate Oriental woman of popular literature, and the New Woman who embodied the transformations of the nineteenth-century women's movement.[31] What are the implications of superimposing the representation of the New Woman on the figure of the geisha as a gendered figuration of Japanese modernity?

The valorization of the feminine subject of Japanese modernity and the critique of her masculine counterpart point to an underlying ambivalence toward the subject of Japanese modernity in Long's fiction as well as in American representations of Japan at that time. In the 1890s, American representations of Japan were somewhat inchoate and were shaped by conflicting images of the Japanese that emanated from aesthetic, missionary, and political discourses. Aesthetic discourses celebrated Japanese art and culture in the register of simplicity, delicacy, and craftsmanship; missionary discourses affirmed certain aspects of Japanese culture and pointed to the need for Western intervention and improvement in others; and political discourses acknowledged growing Japanese power and constituted this progressively as threat or competition. The ambivalence toward Japanese modernity produced by discrepant representations of the Japanese in aesthetic, missionary, and political discourses is resolved in Long's fiction by the splitting of Japanese modernity into an arrogant, tyrannical masculine subject and a pliable, charming, and idealistic feminine subject.

The gendering of Japanese modernity corresponds to a culture/politics dichotomy within which "the color and poetry that is Japan" is associated with the feminine subject and the political and economic power of Japan is associated with the masculine subject. This bifurcation was based on the contradictory representation of Japan in American aesthetics and politics as object of desire and object of threat. On the one hand, Japanese arts were at the center of an Oriental vogue in late Victorian America, while, on the other hand, Japanese political power came to be viewed as an imminent threat in political discourses that highlighted the emergence of a modern, militarized, imperial Japan and constituted Japanese immigrants in America as an invading horde.[32]

The identification of Japanese culture with the feminine and its association with simplicity and naturalness had their antecedents in the development of the discourse of aesthetic Orientalism in the United States. For instance, Neil Harris explains that during the Centennial Exhibition in Philadelphia in 1876, where the Japanese exhibit offered one of the earliest exposures of Japanese culture to many Americans, "despite occasional recognition of Japanese efforts at modernization, most attention was lavished on Japanese art and craftwork."[33] Evidence of Japanese modernization and Westernization at the exhibit was greeted with an ambivalence that had its roots in the uncertainty of Americans about the consequences of modernization in their own lives (labor unrest, massive immigration, urbanization) and their capacity to withstand its destabilizing effects; in this context, the nostalgic affirmation of crafts and the passing era of artisanship was all the more intense. As T. J. Jackson Lears points out, this form of antimodernism, which created an idealized space for the valorization of the Orient and the warrior and craftsmanship ideals identified with it, "was not simply escapism; it was ambivalent, often coexisting with enthusiasm for material progress."[34] The American privileging of the natural in Japanese art was an effort to assert and preserve those modes of feeling and value most threatened by industrialization in America. As Mari Yoshihara observes, "Being part of the discourse which defined and contained Asia as the West's 'Other,' the discussion of Asian art always associated Asia with premodern simplicity, naturalness, tradition."[35] At the early stages, those who embraced Japanesque design were the upper classes in New England, among whose number were some of the most prominent Japanologists, who were instrumental in introducing Japanese culture to Americans. But the growing commodification of Japanese art and the popularizing influence of Japanese exhibits at world's fairs led to the circulation of Japanese arts in a middle-class consumer market, from where they entered the middle-class household as decorative objects framed as an Oriental accent or motif in household furnishings and design. Thus, Yoshihara concludes, the circulation of Japanese art within American culture led to a gendering of Orientalism: "In the period when Asia emerged as both object of desire and as a threat, Americans carefully managed both desire and threat by domesticating and containing Asia within the feminized space of the household."[36]

The beauty associated with the arts and crafts in Japan are embodied in Cho-Cho-San's delicacy, purity, simplicity, and grace, while the worldliness of Yamadori's legal knowledge, aggression, self-possession, and manipulativeness signify a less congenial vision of Japan. Ironically, Pinkerton is criticized in Long's story for treating Cho-Cho-San as "jus' a picture off of a fan," and yet his own fiction depends on the identification of the Japanese woman with the attributes of Japanese art ("MB," 20).

Yamadori's character in Long's text is a composite figure that draws together those aspects of Japanese modernity that most troubled the classificatory schemas with which the West apprehended the meanings and value of Asian civilizations. The exceptional status of Japan among Asian nations was based on its rapid modernization and the deft skill with which the Japanese absorbed foreign knowledge without surrendering either their sovereignty or their own imperial ambitions, creating a classificatory problem for Westerners habituated to thinking of Asian nations as either primitive (Hawai'i, Philippines) or decrepit (China, India). Carl Dawson explains that in an era fascinated with the idea of civilization, Japan raised puzzling questions since it defied categorization as either primitive or civilized: "Japan was worthy of respect on the one hand and typically Oriental—or inconsequential—on the other. As for the Japanese, in early Meiji years, they had moved aggressively to destroy Oriental affiliations and sought international recognition by wholesale Westernization."[37] Historians have traced the ambivalence toward the Japanese to the inability of Western nations to exercise much control over Japanese development, to which, nevertheless, they were invited to contribute (and for which they were well compensated): "But the Japanese were uncommon in their determination and their success in keeping the foreign experts away from the levers of power, from the making of policy. The foreigners were 'on tap, not on top.'"[38] After the Sino-Japanese War (1894–95), in particular, military, political, and economic competition between the United States and Japan began to intensify and was given additional impetus by the Spanish-American War and the Russo-Japanese War.

Yamadori is depicted as a Westernized figure, but the effects of Westernization are distinctly parodic and self-aggrandizing; he is the mimic man with a long genealogy in colonial discourse, a figure of flawed colonial emulation. The authorial commentary on Yamadori's attire when he arrives for the look-at meeting is disparaging and presents his Westernization as crass mimicry: "Yamadori suggested somewhat the ready-made clothier—inevitable evidence of his transformation; otherwise he was the average modern Japanese, with high-gibbeted trousers, high collar, high hat, and eyeglass" ("MB," 39). His Westernization acquires an uglier aspect, however, in an exchange between Cho-Cho-San and the marriage broker Goro, when Cho-Cho-San connects his frequent Japanese divorces to his American travel. When Cho-Cho-San asks the go-between how often Yamadori has been married, she learns that he has already been married twice. She then asks pointedly whether both his divorces took place after his visits to the United States and is told that she is correct. She then mockingly asks the go-between whether Yamadori keeps marrying for fun, whenever he feels like it ("MB," 37).[39]

In Long's critique, the freedom, mobility, and contact with the West that has become available to the modern Japanese man has only intensified patriarchal oppression, creating a need for the emancipation of Japanese women that can be achieved through their Westernization. Long emphasizes that Yamadori, a man "bred to the law," deploys his legal knowledge to entrench his patriarchal power ("MB," 33). Moreover, he does not hesitate to use his authority as a traveled man to produce a conveniently distorted account of the West to scare Cho-Cho-San into accepting his proposal. He paints a grim and exaggerated picture of the fate awaiting her and her child if she emigrates to the United States. Cho-Cho-San refuses to believe him, clinging instead to the equally fictitious version of life in the United States fed to her by Pinkerton. The masculine subject of Japanese modernity is depicted as a figure who commands power in his own surroundings and is capable of appropriating and deploying his new knowledge ruthlessly for his own ends.

By contrast, the mode of Westernization represented by Cho-Cho-San's emergence constructs a narrative that was not only at the center of missionary discourse in Japan but posits the improving influence of the American presence in Japan. Cho-Cho-San's comic triumph over Yamadori during the look-at meeting derives from her fluency with the Japanese feminine roles she performs to entice him and then tosses aside to assert the independence she has acquired from her American marriage. When Cho-Cho-San points bitterly to the predicament of women in temporary marriages and proudly holds up her own child for Goro to see as testimony of a more enduring ideal of marriage, Goro's aversion is expressed as horror at the consequences of women's Americanization: "He hoped there were not going to be any more such women in Japan as the result of foreign marriages" ("MB," 33). By tracing Butterfly's transformation from a demure geisha to a New Woman, Long's story indicates that the emancipation of Japanese women from oppressive native custom represents a site of constructive Westernization.

The script of the native woman's salvation through the agency of her

Westernization was central to missionary discourse on Japan. Its discursive centrality stemmed from a number of interrelated factors, including the feminization of the mission workforce at the turn of the century, the rearticulation of feminism within the evangelical movement, and the widely held conviction of the special status accorded to women within Christianity. The growth of the foreign mission movement coincided with the closing of the frontier and the burgeoning national interest in an overseas empire and drew large numbers of women recruits, thereby facilitating an interpenetration of women's emancipation with humanitarian expansionism. By 1890, 60 percent of the mission force comprised single or married women, just as they were also the numerical majority of the foreign-missions public.[40] Women within the movement were motivated by deeply held convictions of the elevated status of Western women in contrast to their heathen sisters and of their special role in ministering to and uplifting members of their own sex: "Evangelicals nurtured the deep-seated conviction that Christianity sustained a high status for women; the place of women in pagan societies was portrayed, by contrast, as desperately degraded. Such pitiful members of the female sex urgently needed the benefits of Christianity, drudges as they were for their lords and masters, slaves as they were to male sensuality."[41] Mission work, therefore, allowed for participation in American expansionism in terms of a specifically female calling that focused on the redemption of heathen women, to whom male missionaries did not have access.

In Japan, the two most important arenas of missionary activity were woman-centered: education and the abolition of prostitution. But as historians of the foreign mission movement note, the interest of missionaries in women's elevation was tactical and was closely linked to establishing the oppressiveness of native patriarchal constraint as a way of winning souls and legitimizing evangelical work. Thus, the degradation of native women, often exaggerated and dramatized in missionary propaganda, formed a dominant trope of missionary discourse that constructed as its narrative corollary the cruel or tyrannical native man from whose sensuality and power the women were to be freed.[42]

The introduction of the subplot of Yamadori and Cho-Cho-San is an important interpolation to the broad outlines of the Loti story. What bearing, then, does the inclusion of the Yamadori proposal and Cho-Cho-San's response to it have on the romance between Cho-Cho-San and Pinkerton?

Moreover, given the discursive framework of missionary accounts of Japanese women's condition and Long's own attribution of the story to his sister, how is this theme rearticulated within Long's narrative?

While the encounter between Yamadori and Cho-Cho-San adheres to the framework of Westernization as the means for the native woman's salvation common to missionary discourse, the conclusion of the story provides a crucial narrative swerve that questions the adequacy of Orientalist representations of Japanese women's oppression. It shifts the focus from the local context of the Japanese woman's oppression, which conforms to missionary discursive constructs, to the wider frame of Cho-Cho-San's defiance of Pinkerton's and Adelaide's claim on the child, legitimized by Japanese customary practice. Through this shift, Long makes visible the complex inter-articulation of the emancipated white woman's complicity, the white man's sexual predacity, and the Japanese man's modernization in framing the subjection and emergence of the Japanese woman. But while Long does lay out the conditions of her subjection, he has no means of envisioning the trajectory of her emergence, except through the awkward allegory staged in the look-at meeting when Cho-Cho-San sheds her role as a demure geisha and steps forward as a prototype of the New Woman. However, at the conclusion of the story, in a symbolic enactment of the exhaustion of the trope of mimicry in representing the geisha's resistance, Long stages her disappearance from the text, her defiance serving as it were as a vanishing point for textual representation: "When Mrs. Pinkerton called next day at the little house on Higashi Hill, it was quite empty" ("MB," 86). In her last metamorphosis, Butterfly passes out of the line of vision and outside the field of desire inscribed by Orientalist discourse.

If one of the effects of prohibitions against miscegenation was to turn sex acts into race acts, miscegenation narratives offered a powerful vehicle for reconstructing sexual norms by telling stories about whether love across racial lines was possible or desirable. "Madame Butterfly" exposes white domesticity and nationhood as a fiction by showing that it is built by erasing the memory of extraterritorial intimacies. Long's depiction of Pinkerton's wife, Adelaide, is clearly unsympathetic and shows her as condescending toward Cho-Cho-San and unquestioning about enforcing Pinkerton's claim on the child if it looks white. Adelaide inspects the child first during a brief visit to the house before deciding to take him. The complicity of the white wife in maintaining the fiction of white domesticity offers a sharp critique of the racial exclusions through which the meanings of family and nation are produced. It also suggests that a focus on racial boundaries in defining sexual propriety has obscured the corruption of modern sexual norms. Moreover, the hypocrisy and racism of the white couple is contrasted to the purist, if naive, faith of the Japanese geisha in the ideal of "American marriage." Rather than representing a threat to American family values, Long shows that the Japanese woman's Occidental desire serves as a repository for the domestic ideals of American marriage. The strategy of locating the purest American ideals in the desires of Asian immigrants who seek to be a part of the United States reappears in Carlos Bulosan's *America Is in the Heart* (1946).

D. W. Griffith's film of white-Asian miscegenation again uses the unrequited love of an Asian for a white to offer a critique of the breakdown of sexual norms in modernity. But where the white man–Asian woman dyad enables an argument for Asian assimilation and naturalization, the threat to white paternity represented by the coupling of the Asian man with the white woman generates an implicit argument for racial segregation through a narrative of the cultural impossibility of cross-racial desire.

In addition, the narrative of the Japanese woman's desire for an "American marriage" also functions as a sign of her rebellion against ethnic/native patriarchal constraint in Long's story. This structural feature of the story of white-Asian miscegenation became an integral element of the white man–Asian woman romance in many of its later forms. As we will see, Mukherjee's *Jasmine* (1989), written nearly a century later, explores the idea of sexual agency in miscegenation as a means of representing Asian American feminist agency and exploring modes of female power. In this chapter, I have examined the colonial etymology of formulations of the Asian woman's liberation through Westernization, showing how Long's narrative acknowledges the discursive limits of Orientalist discourses in representing the Asian woman as a feminist subject. Mukherjee's heroine, by contrast, asserts sexual agency through self-Orientalizing strategies in her several relationships with white men. But compared to Long's story, the later novel is less heedful of the paradoxes of power contained in the allure of exotic woman.

TWO

Eugenic Romances of American Nationhood

A "hieroglyphist prejudice" had produced the same effect of interested blindness. Far from proceeding . . . from ethnocentric scorn, the occultation takes the form of an hyperbolical admiration. We have not finished demonstrating the necessity of this pattern. Our century is not free from it; each time that ethnocentrism is precipitately and ostentatiously reversed, some effort silently hides behind all the spectacular effects to consolidate an inside and to draw from it some domestic benefit.

—Jacques Derrida, *Of Grammatology*

Appearing two decades after John Luther Long's "Madame Butterfly," D. W. Griffith's *Broken Blossoms* (1919), a spectacularly popular film dealing with white-Asian miscegenation, seems, like Long's story, to present a sympathetic view of interracial romance at a time of widespread anti-Oriental hostility in the United States.[1] However, the historical moment of Griffith's work, his choice of medium, and the racial ideologies associated with his oeuvre differed significantly from Long's. By centering their plots respectively on female and male Asian subjects, these stories configure miscegenation as the racial imaginary of a new political future in quite different terms. Despite the surface similarities in the liberal sympathies of the two interracial romances, their underlying racial and sexual politics differ markedly.

Broken Blossoms was released soon after the end of World War I. This historical event shook Griffith's confident faith in the legitimacy of Anglo-Saxon domination that he had so fervently idealized in his notorious box-office success, *The Birth of a Nation* (1915).[2] Critics have noted that his film about World War I, *Hearts of the World* (1918), failed because he sought to capture the vast upheavals of the war in a chivalric idiom and melodramatic schema of good versus evil reminiscent of *Birth*. *Hearts of the World* demonized the Germans and idealized the French and Americans, recapitulating many of the white-black structural oppositions of *Birth*.[3] The film was made with the encouragement and assistance of the British government, which solicited Griffith to use his cinematic skills to make a film that would persuade the Americans to join the war. Although *Hearts of the World* was a commercial success and received favorable reviews, Lillian Gish, who worked very closely with Griffith on the film, writes that "I don't believe that Mr. Griffith ever forgave himself for making *Hearts of the World.* 'War is the villain,' he repeated, 'not any particular people.'"[4] *Hearts of the World* is widely acknowledged as a turning point in Griffith's career, and the films that he made after that, including *Broken Blossoms*, have been described as signaling a withdrawal into pastoralism and tradition and marking "a flight from modernity, on screen and off."[5]

Broken Blossoms, set in the East London slums against the backdrop of World War I, is the story of the tragic love of a Chinese shopkeeper for a young English girl, Lucy. Lucy is the illegitimate daughter of Battling Burrows, a brutish drunkard and a boxer who beats and abuses her. One day Burrows attacks her in a fit of rage and she escapes from her home and finds refuge with a Chinese shopkeeper, who is referred to as the Yellow Man in the film. The Yellow Man has long been silently in love with Lucy and offers her sanctuary when the battered and terrified girl falls unconscious in his shop. One of Burrows's friends spies Lucy in the Yellow Man's bedchamber and informs her father, who drags her home and beats her to death. The Yellow Man arrives too late to save Lucy but kills Burrows to avenge her death. Grief-stricken, he carries Lucy's body home; after laying her down and praying, he kills himself.

Broken Blossoms does not comment directly on the events of the war; instead, by telling an intimate, pictorially haunting love story that ends in the death of all the principals, it portrays a world where innocence and beauty are brutally crushed by violence and degeneracy. The violence and degeneracy that drive the action are symptomatic of a larger social crisis symbolized by the war, but its effects are dramatized within the intimate sphere of a family drama. The deaths of the main characters are infinitesimal when set against the forty thousand English battlefield casualties that are mentioned at the end of the film by the policemen who arrive too late to bring justice or avert death.

The triangulated relationship between Lucy, Burrows, and the Yellow Man allegorizes the crisis signified by a war that Griffith depicts as emanating from a degeneracy at the heart of Western civilization. Eastern civilization, in the figure of the Yellow Man, offers a counterpoint to Western brutality but is depicted as too weak and effete to supersede it; thus, in this Griffith film, there are no heroes. Instead, the heroic qualities of physical strength and spiritual strength have been split and embodied in the two antagonists, thereby emblematizing an impasse in conceiving the future.

Birth's brave new world of Anglo-Saxon supremacy represented by the Ku Klux Klan—to whom Griffith assigns paternity for the birth of the American nation—seems far removed from the dark, brutal, and degenerate world of the East London slums during World War I. *Broken Blossoms* represents an alternate legacy of the Anglo-Saxons, who are identified in an intertitle as "the barbarous Anglo-Saxons, sons of turmoil and strife." The short space of four years that separated the two films was filled with a long war that appears to have forced Griffith to reassess the ideal of white supremacy he had earlier celebrated. Richard Schickel, Griffith's biographer, describes the effect of the war on the filmmaker as transformative: "In short, Griffith had arrived at the very event that would undo the cultural consensus that had formed his sensibility and informed all his work."[6]

Griffith's indictment of Western civilization in *Broken Blossoms* is specifically a condemnation of British imperial domination that leaves open the possibility that a younger, historically innocent heir (America) of the Anglo-Saxon legacy may yet appear to succeed the British. This possibility is only an embryonic one in the film, the merest hint of possibilities in the configuration of American nationalism and masculinity; it is defined less through an elaboration of its specific characteristics than through juxtaposition with representations of English and Chinese manhood defined through the extremes of excess or lack of virility. Thus, *Broken Blossoms* is not a revocation of the thesis of Anglo-Saxon supremacy upheld in *Birth* but a complex rearticulation of it at a different historical conjuncture. The mode of that rearticulation emphasizes American national identity as innocent of the will to power associated with the brutality and sadism of the English. Furthermore, the formulation of Americanness is inchoate and remains tangential to the main narrative so that it appears to function outside the clash between the Old World civilizations of Britain and China—the American sailors make only a brief appearance in the opening sequence of the film. Finally, the American presence in the Chinese treaty port is shown as transient and casual. In all these aspects, American manhood serves as a metonym for a Western presence associated with informality, manifested as a noncoercive extraterritorial presence and possessing an innocent vitality missing in other forms of manliness in the film.

This representation of American manhood complements discourses that emerged in the early decades of the twentieth century to postulate a new global role for Americans through the exercise of a uniquely American mode of power. The American decision to join the Allies in World War I intensified public debate about the need for American succession to the helm of world leadership. The announcement of the American decision to join the war came when the British government and aristocracy were feting Griffith in London and hoping to persuade the famous American filmmaker to make a war film that would convince Americans to fight alongside the Allies. The British public showered its gratitude on Griffith, who enthusiastically embraced the American decision in his many public appearances in England.[7] Indeed, as Karl Brown notes, the late American involvement in the war seemed like an enactment of one of Griffith's signature filmic devices, the ride to the rescue.[8]

At the war's end, the United States emerged as the dominant industrial power, and President Woodrow Wilson took a leading role in laying the groundwork for a reconstructed international order. Wilson's plans for an enduring peace settlement and a new global order were articulated in the famous "Fourteen Points" speech before the victorious Allies in 1918. He also played a pivotal role in founding the League of Nations, which was envisioned as an international body that would mediate disputes between nations and thus prevent the outbreak of another major war. The Wilsonian rhetoric of disarmament, anticolonialism, and international reconciliation did not eventually result in the United States joining the League of Nations, but it did project a geopolitical role for the United States that positioned it outside of the old European imperial regimes with the unique capacity to forge a new international order.

The message of an American-led international order promulgated in Wilsonian rhetoric resonated with the efforts of filmmakers like Griffith, who sought to legitimize the new medium of cinema by couching its power and appeal in a universalism that could promote international brotherhood and equality: "Are we not making the world safe for democracy, American Democracy, through motion pictures?"[9] According to Griffith, cinema not only made possible the globalization of American democracy, it also created a "universal language" that could transcend all linguistic and cultural divisions: "We've found a universal language—a power that can make men brothers and end war forever."[10] Miriam Hansen explains that this myth of film's universal language was the major trope dominating public, aesthetic, and critical discourse on cinema at the time of its formation.[11] The rhetoric of American dominion expressed through cultural persuasion rather than political conquest received its early articulation among proponents of cinema as a new democratic art form. Griffith, like many other prominent spokespersons in the film industry, recognized the potential of American film to wield an unprecedented influence on a global scale. In using his film *Broken Blossoms* to offer a critique of Old World regimes and modes of power, Griffith instantiates the exercise of this power both through the film's medium and its message. One might argue that Griffith recognized at an early stage the role of film as a primary vehicle for what Joseph Nye in *The Paradox of American Power* (2002) has, nearly a century later, identified as the "soft power" of American empire.[12] Nye offers a useful elaboration of the operations of this form of power: "Soft power lies in the ability to attract and persuade rather than coerce. It means that others want what the United States wants, and there is less need to use carrots and sticks. Hard power, the ability to coerce, grows out of a country's military and economic might. Soft power arises from the attractiveness of a country's culture, political ideals, and policies."[13] Griffith's awareness of the power of film to convert the world to American political ideals and cultural values displays a remarkably prescient grasp of the power of the new American medium and its future influence.

Griffith's vision of the political power of cinema is confirmed by the unease with which the British began to view the increasing influence of American movies. The "soft power" or hegemonic force associated with American cinema came to assume unsettling implications when viewed from the other side of the Atlantic. By as early as the 1920s, many British commentators had begun to identify American movies as a serious threat to their imperial dominance. The Prince of Wales sounded the alarm in a speech before the British National Film League in 1923. Commenting on the speech, the London *Morning Post* declared, "The film is to America what the flag was once to Britain. By its means, Uncle Sam may hope some day, if he be not checked in time, to Americanize the world."[14] This theme was echoed again in Lord Newton's speech before the House of Lords two years later:

"The Americans realized almost instantaneously that the cinema was a heaven-sent method of advertising themselves, their country, their methods, their wares, their ideas and even their language, and they had seized on it as a method of persuading the whole world that America was really the only country that counted."[15]

The anxieties of the British about the growing global influence of the Americans were linked to apprehensions about their own imperial decline. Historians like Paul Kennedy have dated the waning of British imperial ascendancy to World War I, while Corelli Barnett notes that by the 1920s, "the British empire was one of the most outstanding examples of strategic overextension in history."[16] Despite some differences among historians in pinpointing the year that marks the decline of British imperial power, there seems to be wide agreement that American global power came to be exercised overtly during World War II. In an important recent book on the differences between British and American empire, Patrick Karl O'Brien and Armand Klesse date the period of hegemony of the two world powers as Britain, 1846–1914, and the United States, 1941–2001.[17] In his seminal study, Charles Kindleberger contends that after 1918 Britain was too weak to play the role of an effective hegemon, while the United States was too hemmed in by protectionism and isolationism to undertake the role until World War II. Kindleberger describes the intervening period between the two empires as a "hegemonic interregnum."[18]

The cultural work of Griffith's *Broken Blossoms* is illuminated by locating it within the context of the "hegemonic interregnum" between British and American empire. The film's production during this period accounts for its thesis of the degeneration of Anglo-Saxon domination in its British avatar; this context also clarifies the indeterminacy that attends the articulation of future possibilities for international reconciliation; and, finally, it suggests why the representation of the American role in the vision of an alternative world order is so nebulous, appearing more as a trace in the brief opening sequence with the American sailors and in the ideology of the medium through which Griffith's story is projected than as an antagonist in the drama.

Thus, a film set in East London and based on the short story "The Chink and the Child" (1917) by British writer Thomas Burke offered a medium for an American filmmaker to take up the question of Western modernity in a trans-Atlantic context foregrounded by post–World War I debates about

America's succession to world dominance and the prospects for a new international order.[19] Griffith condemns the destructive course that Western civilization has taken while incorporating a narrative proviso (the opening sequence with the American sailors) that seems to place Americans outside his general indictment of Western modernity.

The corpus of Griffith criticism is extensive, and the research of feminist and ethnic studies scholars, in particular, have offered rich analyses of the representation of race and sexuality in his work. Critics have largely overlooked the national identities that inflect these forms of difference and have assumed a common Anglo-American culture as the source of representations of miscegenation in Griffith and Burke. This analysis departs from previous work in examining the way in which geopolitical shifts in the second decade of the twentieth century strained the notion of a common Anglo-Saxon identity binding the United States to Britain, precipitating an American anticolonial critique in the interests of positing a new globalism. Such a maneuver is consonant with what James Thomson, Peter W. Stanley, and John Curtis Perry characterize as the "anticolonial imperialism" that defined American informal empire at the turn of the century.[20] Discourses of American primacy in the early decades of the twentieth century articulated themselves against and in relation to already existing world powers. The U.S. definition of its benevolent relationship to the Orient/China was a critical part of its claim to representing a new form of global hegemony.

The "hyperbolical admiration" for the Oriental as the repository of pacifist, spiritual, and aesthetic ideals is staged within an opposition to British brutality and violence that in ceding moral virtue to the Oriental nevertheless denies him virility and full personhood. The Yellow Man is unable to protect or save Lucy, the young white virgin who embodies—as in so many Griffith films—the truest and deepest ideals of Western civilization. Thus, as Derrida's comments on the "hieroglyphist prejudice" in Western culture suggest, the move in which ethnocentrism is "precipitately and ostentatiously reversed" hides an effort to "consolidate an inside and draw from it some domestic benefit." The representation of American masculinity as the third term in a triadic structure that opposes British and Chinese masculinity allows Griffith to retain his idealization of Anglo-Saxon American nationhood while framing the larger crisis represented by the war in terms of the culpability of Old World regimes.

The Trope of Degeneration and the Poetics of Social Crisis

> Crucially, degeneration in the second half of the nineteenth century served not only to characterize other races (for instance in the view that other races had degenerated from the ideal physique of the white races), but also to pose a vision of internal dangers and crises within Europe. Crime, suicide, alcoholism and prostitution were understood as "social pathologies" endangering the European races, constituting a degenerative process within them.
>
> —Daniel Pick, *Faces of Degeneration*

The setting of Griffith's *Broken Blossoms* is the East London district of Limehouse, which was popularly known as the haunt of prostitutes, alcoholics, half-castes, Jews, Orientals, and opium addicts—what Gareth Stedman Jones has referred to as "outcast London."[21] Its topography offers a compelling visual setting for the trope of degeneration that organizes the meanings of racial, gender, class, and national difference in the film. The lexicon of degeneration, which emerged in the late nineteenth and early twentieth century in discourses of race science, heredity, eugenics, and evolution, offered a "poetics of social crisis" that transcribed the contradictions of imperial modernity into the language of natural science.[22]

The word *degeneration* was used by Benedict Augustin Morel in 1857 as a medical term to describe the process by which human beings were destroyed by moral and physical contaminants like disease, opium, alcohol, prostitution, moral flaws, and nervous disorders. The term gave a biological foundation to biblical ideas of the Fall of Man from an Adamic ideal and sought to account for human susceptibility to external influences ranging from alcohol to climate. The idea was picked up by anthropometrists, eugenicists, lawyers, and many in the English intelligentsia by the 1880s, appearing in the writings of Havelock Ellis and Francis Galton and spreading from Europe to the United States, where it was taken up by race scientists and eugenicists such as Francis Walker and Charles Davenport.[23]

Foucault's work helps locate these intellectual developments within the context of the growth of "biopower" and the discursive formations that proliferated within it. The trope of degeneration gained its formidable power to organize a "poetics of social crisis" because of its implantation within the larger apparatus of biopower, or the collective institutional forces aimed at "the calculated management of life."[24] Biopower was manifested in the active intervention of the state into the management of the life-processes of the individual and social body through the apparatus of medicine, demography, and statistics; these efforts focused on separating out the abnormal and the pathological from the healthy social body. As the "statisation of the biological"progressed, biopower achieved an extensive and deep reach and penetration of social life.[25] Foucault notes that it was only when racism became linked to biopower in the nineteenth century that racism assumed its most virulent form. He specifies that by the late nineteenth century, technologies of sex were mobilized around issues of race primarily through "the series composed of perversion-heredity-degenerescence."[26]

One of the most compelling insights in Foucault's study of sexuality is that the regime of sexuality is best understood within the context of the rise of liberalism that undermined descent-based social hierarchies associated with the aristocracy and sought new ways of naturalizing the inequities in the social order.[27] However, an important qualification to this Foucauldian formulation is that while the rise of liberalism undercut descent-based hierarchies among dominant white groups, it mobilized discourses of race to consolidate descent-based identities among nonwhite groups. That said, Foucault's larger point about the concurrent rise of liberalism and state-directed racisms is an invaluable one. This insight is linked to his larger argument that discourses of race are characterized by "polyvalent mobilities" that can be yoked to progressive and conservative projects. Indeed, the trope of degeneration became widespread and was so deeply implanted precisely because it brought together a range of concerns and therefore could be appropriated by a promiscuous range of political projects. For instance, in Griffith's film, the identification of the working-class Englishman and the Chinese man as subject to degeneration points to the need for a regeneration of Western civilization through some other agency. While the film insists on the nobility of the Yellow Man, by depicting his degeneration in the West it makes a biological argument for his exclusion from the Western nation. Thus *Broken Blossoms* accommodates a separatist argument within its liberal politics.

The power of the trope of degeneration at the turn of the century lay in its acknowledgement of the existence of a social crisis and its interpretation of this crisis in terms that addressed liberal and conservative anxieties about modernity. Critics such as Gareth Stedman Jones and Daniel Pick suggest that the rhetoric of degeneration emerged in Britain amid widespread con-

cerns about the widening electoral constituency after 1857, the rise of organized socialism, and the increase in demonstrations and riots after the 1880s.[28]
The lexicon of degeneration sought to define the crisis "by articulating in
biological terms what was felt to be the widening political contradiction between national prosperity and empire on the one hand, and persistent urban
poverty, criminal sub-culture and social pathology on the other."[29] Like allied
discourses of race science and eugenics, it addressed a welter of politico-
economic concerns about industrialization, the growth of slums and urban
sprawl, and large-scale migration from the rural areas and abroad.[30] These
anxieties climaxed in Britain during the setbacks of the Anglo-Boer War and
the reports of the poor physiques of the recruits and resulted in the passage
of the Alien Immigration Act of 1905, which targeted Jews, prostitutes, anar-
chists, criminals, and the destitute for expulsion. At the heart of the English
production of the discourse of degeneration was "the convergence of a sup-
posed crisis of the city as a viable system, with deep conservative and liberal
fears of socialism, democracy and 'mass society.'"[31]

By contrast, in the United States the discourse of degeneration combined
with the theories of race science and eugenics to focus with particular intensity on immigration restriction. Eugenicists focused in particular on immigration from Asia and from Eastern and Southern Europe, arguing that the
mixture with these inferior races was weakening the superior Anglo-Saxon
national stock. In a letter to a fellow exclusionist, leading eugenicist Charles
Davenport wrote, "The idea of a 'melting-pot' belongs to a pre-Mendelian
age," adding, "Now we recognize that characters are inherited as units and
do not readily break up."[32] In 1891, Francis Walker, the superintendent of the
1870 and 1880 census, fuelled racial anxieties by hypothesizing that the lower
birthrates of native-born Americans as compared to immigrants was a sign
of the imminent racial decline of Anglo-Saxons in the United States. This
thesis was reiterated in President Theodore Roosevelt's famous declaration to
the National Congress of Mothers on March 13, 1905, that Anglo-Saxons
were committing "race suicide" if they did not propagate the race. In his
manifesto *The Passing of the Great Race* (1916), which proved to be enor-
mously influential, Madison Grant argued against "mongrelization," stating
that the result of the mixing of races was the dominance of the "inferior"
racial strains. Through the efforts of biometrists, eugenicists, and other race
scientists, the necessity of artificial or state selection to replace Darwinian
natural selection began to be propounded.[33] What Foucault calls the "stati-

sation of the biological" was articulated in the United States as negative eugenics rather than primarily as positive eugenics as in Britain; the former emphasized preventing the propagation of the unfit, while the latter promoted the breeding of the fit.

Thus, the British and American deployments of degeneration and allied race science theories took two distinct trajectories, the former organized around a grammar of class and the latter around a grammar of race. Daniel Kevles identifies the fundamental difference between British and American eugenics thus: "While British eugenicists talked of the threat of the immigrants from Ireland and the Continent, they fretted a good deal more about the threat to the national fiber arising from the differential birthrate and the consequent weakening of their imperial competitive abilities in relation to France and Germany. British eugenics was marked by a hostility decidedly more of class than of race."[34]

In the United States, the period of the growing influence of scientific racism coincided with the massive influx of immigrants and the attendant perception of social crisis; hence, the "perversion-heredity-degenerescence" series was deployed to rearticulate the meanings of American national identity in the context of the new immigration. This strain of American racial nationalism combined with anti-Catholic and antiradical forms of nativism, leading to the passage of the 1921 and 1924 Immigration Acts. By severely restricting immigration from Southern and Eastern Europe and closing off all immigration from Asia, except the Philippines, these created the first major large-scale hiatus in immigration to the United States. The 1924 Immigration Act was signed by President Calvin Coolidge, who as vice president had declared, "America must be kept American. Biological laws show . . . that Nordics deteriorate when mixed with other races."[35]

During the period that Griffith was making his film, the trope of degeneration figured prominently in contestations of the racial meanings of American nationhood with respect to its domestic identity and its external geopolitical role. Griffith used the trope of degeneration to resolve the question of the Yellow Man's place in the Western nation, but his use of this trope to determine the domestic boundaries of the Western nation is beset by a deep equivocation. In the domestic context, the trope of degeneration operates a *poetics of crisis* that works in tension with the *politics of equality* contained in the film's liberal message of racial reconciliation. This ambivalence bears out Foucault's observation that discourses of inclusion, humanitarianism, and equality in liberalism can coexist with exclusionary and discriminatory cultural logics.

In an insightful essay titled "Liberal Strategies of Exclusion," Uday Mehta examines liberalism's political claims of inclusion against its historical practices of exclusion. He uses the term *anthropological minimum* to refer to the lowest common denominator of human attributes and capacities on which liberalism grounds its claims to universalism.[36] He explains, however, that a contradiction emerged between liberalism's professions of inclusion and its historical practice of exclusion because certain cultural and psychological propensities were seen as impeding the attainment of this minimum: "The universalistic reach of liberalism derives from the capacities that it identifies with human nature and from the presumption, which it encourages, that these capacities are sufficient and not merely necessary for an individual's political inclusion. . . . However, what is concealed behind the endorsement of these universal capacities are the specific cultural and psychological conditions woven in as preconditions for the actualization of these capacities."[37] The tension between inclusion and exclusion develops because "behind the capacities ascribed to all human beings there exist a thicker set of social credentials that constitute the real bases of political inclusion."[38]

In *Broken Blossoms*, the trope of degeneration short-circuits the articulation of an "anthropological minimum" that is independent of place and culture. While the idea of degeneration was conventionally used in race science and evolutionary theory to identify regressive segments of the white race or to prove the atavism of nonwhite peoples, Griffith uses it to show the degeneration of the Yellow Man in the West. He depicts the fall of the Yellow Man from his tranquil, serene existence as a well-born Chinese man in his homeland to a blighted, opium-addicted wretch in the heart of Limehouse. All the moral poisons associated with degeneration—such as prostitution, alcohol, and opium—are endemic to the Limehouse world and sap his moral faculties and physical strength. However, although the film presents his degeneration in a sympathetic light by linking it to his migration and his decision to live in an alien environment, the corollary of the thesis of his degeneration in the West is a naturalization of his belonging in the East.[39] Which is to say that Griffith's deployment of the trope of degeneration postulates a naturalistic logic to national and cultural separatism and makes separatism the precondition for the fulfillment of the *human* attributes of the Yellow Man.

On a parallel level, the Yellow Man has many of the attributes of kindness, courage, and generosity that define the conventional romantic hero and yet he is unable to inspire desire or romantic interest in the young white heroine because his racial difference refracts these attributes so they are figured as a sign of his passivity and lack of virility.[40] Accordingly, the Yellow Man fails to achieve the "anthropological minimum" necessary for romantic union, although the film's intertitles idealize the possibility of interracial love. The trope of degeneration works here to set up naturalistic and psychological provisos to the articulation of a politics of equality, thereby creating a tension between the dynamics of the love story and the film's political message.

Griffith also mobilizes the trope of degeneration to define American identity in terms of an emergent global role that distinguishes it from Old World empires. He uses the trope of the degeneration of the Englishman to posit a global crisis that implicitly invokes the need for a new incarnation of Anglo-Saxon global leadership. English masculinity is represented in the figure of Battling Burrows, who is described in one of the intertitles as "a gorilla of the jungles of East London." The physically overdeveloped, brutish boxer is a vivid embodiment of the corrupting force of his environment—he drinks ferociously, spends his time with prostitutes, and vents his frustrations by tyrannizing and beating his illegitimate daughter, Lucy. But unlike the Yellow Man, Burrows is shown as a product of his environment rather than an alien figure within it and is, thus, deserving of condemnation.

Burrows's relationship to Lucy and the Yellow Man allegorizes the crisis of Western modernity that is figured spatially in the topography of the city and temporally through the war. The moral degeneration of the working-class Englishman represents the exhaustion of that branch of the Anglo-Saxon race that had assumed the leadership of the world. His presexual daughter symbolizes the precious heritage of Western civilization that awaits rescue and redemption; but although the Yellow Man is in love with her and attempts to save her, his racial characteristics render him too effete to perform the task and he fails. In representing English nationalism/Western civilization through the father-daughter relationship between Burrows and Lucy, Griffith drew on the conventional gendering of the dual temporality of nationalism. Anne McClintock elaborates on this doubling: "Women are represented as the atavistic and authentic body of national tradition (inert, backward-looking and natural), embodying nationalism's conservative principle of continuity. Men, by contrast, represent the progressive agent of national modernity (forward-thrusting, potent and historic) embodying nationalism's progressive, or revolutionary principle of discontinuity."[41] Thus, although Lucy lives with Burrows in Limehouse, she is immune to its corrupting influences, her virginity and spiritual purity signifying the primordial continuity of Western civilization, while her father symbolizes its historicity and potential for change. His association with the historicity of English national identity transforms the question about his nature and his propensity for degeneration into a larger question about the future of Anglo-Saxon dominion over the world. If the English father is a corrupt father who can no longer protect the child entrusted to his care, then what fate awaits the world?

The film does hint at the redemptive possibilities contained in American masculinity, but this possibility remains an embryonic one. It necessarily exists outside the frame of the main dramatic action to signal both its tangentiality to the central conflict between the Englishman and the Yellow Man and to confer an historical innocence on American manhood as compared to English manhood. Within the discursive parameters established by the trope of degeneration in the film, however, it is the youth and high spirits of the "skylarking American sailors" in the opening sequence, and their association with health and vitality, that contains the seeds of a reborn social order. But the film concludes with the death of all the principals and the prospects for hope are submerged in the closing mood of sadness and waste. The trope of degeneration, nevertheless, renders visible the complex negotiations through which the internal and external meanings of Americanness are produced during the "hegemonic interregnum" between British and U.S. global ascendancy.

The Afterbirth of a Nation: Broken Blossoms and Racial Reconstructions

In *Broken Blossoms*, Griffith reworked the representation of American nationhood and masculinity that he had elaborated in *Birth*. The representation of Americanness is abbreviated in *Broken Blossoms* and is developed implicitly by juxtaposition to alternative national figurations of masculinity rather than through direct dramatic development. *Birth* and *Broken Blossoms* both use a narrative of miscegenation to define the boundaries of white nationhood. In comparing the representation of white-black miscegenation and white-Asian miscegenation, I seek to emphasize the extent to which the racial meanings of Asiannesss have been worked out in relation to whiteness and blackness. While scholars have examined the mutually constitutive nature of white-black or white-Asian identities, less research has been done in examining the ways in which the identities of racialized minorities have been elaborated in relation to each other.[42] Since Asian American racial formation took place belatedly through its insertion into the already existing white-black binary, its meanings have emerged in relation to both terms of the binary and to the other racialized minority identities and needs to be read within the context of this multilayered process of racial formation.

At the time of its release in 1919, *Broken Blossoms* was widely praised for its poetic beauty, its aesthetic innovations, and its liberal message of racial tolerance. The *New York Times* dubbed *Broken Blossoms* "a masterpiece in moving pictures," praising its pictures as surpassing "anything hitherto seen on the screen in beauty and dramatic force."[43] Shot in only eighteen days, at a total cost of seventy thousand dollars, *Broken Blossoms* went on to earn seven hundred thousand dollars in profits, making less money than only two other Griffith films, *Birth* and *Way Down East* (1920). More important, the nearly universal approbation received by *Broken Blossoms* was seen as marking a sharp break from Griffith's other major filmic treatment of miscegenation, *Birth,* in which his racist representation of blacks provoked a storm of protests.

The riddle of *Broken Blossoms* is that it followed *Birth* quite quickly but seems, on the surface, so far removed from it. Had the director revoked his racist views? Or perhaps, as Lillian Gish maintained, he had always been "incapable of prejudice against any group" and had only finally made a film in 1919 that unambiguously reflected this liberalism.[44] The films were separated by a gap of four years, but although both films deal with miscegenation as the foundational metaphor of a new political future, Griffith's representation of miscegenation seems to have undergone a complete transformation over this period. *Birth* is based on Thomas Dixon's racist novel *The Clansman* (1905) and its stage adaptation. The film offers an epic "history" of Reconstruction through a tale of two families, the Stonemans (Northerners) and the Camerons (Southerners), whose burgeoning friendship is destroyed by the Civil War only to be redeemed after the triumphant march of the Ku Klux Klan restores order to a South threatened by black anarchy. The political drama is allegorized as a sexual drama and embodied in the threatened rapes of a Cameron and a Stoneman daughter by a black and a mulatto man, respectively. The Klan appears as a chivalric white brotherhood, an image of the reborn nation, riding to the rescue of white womanhood, a quasi-religious avenging force that castrates and kills the suspected black rapist and frees Elsie Stoneman from the clutches of the lecherous mulatto. As Michael Rogin elucidates, although white men were the primary agents of miscegenation in the South, Griffith's film erases the history of this desire and reinvents them as the saviors of a reunified nation.[45] In *Birth*, miscegenation can only be envisaged as rape and signifies anarchy and the imminent destruction of the nation.[46]

In *Broken Blossoms*, the miscegenous love of a Chinese shopkeeper for Lucy, a fifteen-year-old English girl, is enshrined as the purest of loves and vividly contrasted to the sadistic and incestuous desire of the white father for the girl. In a film in which the only other male lead, the father, is a melodramatic villain, the Chinese man, an idealistic dreamer, appears to be the hero of the story. Noting the conspicuous difference between Griffith's representation of blacks and other racial minorities like native Americans and Asians, some critics have sought explanations in his Southern roots. Richard Schickel traces Griffith's attitudes toward blacks to the "almost unconscious racism of his time and place" but highlights, by contrast, what he sees as his lack of prejudice toward other racial groups: "We can perhaps stipulate that Griffith's prejudice did not extend beyond blacks and that it was mostly quiescent when the possibility of sexual congress across racial lines was absent."[47] Other critics have treated *Broken Blossoms* independently of *Birth* and can, therefore, take its poetic treatment of the relationship between the Yellow Man and Lucy as testimony of Griffith's liberalism. In these readings, *Broken Blossoms* is seen as a plea for international reconciliation and understanding between the races, a message rendered more poignant in the wake of World War I.[48]

The view that Griffith's representation of the Yellow Man in *Broken Blossoms* is antiracist derives largely from a focus on what Griffith didn't do with the character (in relation to contemporary representations of Asians) rather than what he did do with it.[49] The period of the film's release was a time of virulent anti-Asian sentiment, and Asians came to be associated in the public discourse on immigration restriction, job competition, urban reform, and overseas expansionism with filth, degeneracy, immorality, and treachery. In the arena of cultural production, stereotypes of the "good" and the "bad" Asian proliferated in popular fiction, where the former were depicted as "brute hordes" or "sinister villains," and the latter as "loyal and lovable allies, sidekicks, and servants."[50] Similarly, Hollywood depictions of Asians drew on "Yellow Peril" discourses of the imminent danger to white civilization from Asians, whether that danger was constructed as sexual threat, imminent invasion, or moral corruption.[51] Films like *The Yellow Menace* (1916), *The Perils of Pauline* (1919), *Patria* (1919), *Crooked Streets* (1920), and the various Dr. Fu Manchu films draw on this framework. In early Hollywood cinema, miscegenation narratives offered the primary narrative construct for articulating and mediating the anxieties generated by the Asian presence: "Whether plotting from within or invading from outside the country, he [the Asian] represented a constant threat to American values—and, more specifically, to American womanhood."[52] A major Hollywood production with an Asian protagonist, Cecil B. DeMille's *The Cheat* (1915), depicts a Japanese villain who can usefully be seen as a prototype of Asian masculinity against which Griffith's divergence from Hollywood Oriental fictions may be measured. The Japanese protagonist of DeMille's film, Hishuru Tori, a wealthy, cultivated, and treacherous man, insinuates himself into the Long Island smart set and uses the opportunity to enter into a bargain with a glamorous and recklessly extravagant married woman to repay her debts in exchange for sexual favors. When she later attempts to extricate herself from the bargain by offering him repayment in cash instead, he brands her with a hot poker before trying to rape her. She shoots and wounds him before making her escape.

Griffith's idealistic Yellow Man, who sublimates his lust for the helpless Lucy into "the holiest of affections" and kills himself after avenging her death, seems far removed from DeMille's Tori and others because in Griffith's film the greatest danger to white womanhood is from the degenerate white man, not the Yellow Man. In addition, the film identifies the East with gentleness, idealism, and spirituality and the West with brutality and violence. Indeed, this reversal of conventional associations posed a problem for the director, who was apprehensive of the chances of success for a film that presented such an admiring view of the Asian man. Vance Kepley Jr. explains that Griffith marketed *Broken Blossoms* as an "art film" in a concerted effort to distance his work from sensational anti-Oriental discourses and Yellow Peril films that catered to a mass public. By charging an exorbitant three-dollar admission fee, Griffith hit upon a "cunningly brilliant distribution scheme" that would restrict the audience for the initial release to the cultural elite. Griffith intended that this select group of elite patrons would define the reception of the film, after which it would be released to the regular film-going public, consisting largely of working-class, immigrant, and women viewers. He thus used the category of the art film to convey a sense of the film's distinctiveness and superiority to the regular racist Hollywood fare and as a legitimizing form for conveying what he saw as its lofty message of racial reconciliation.[53] The assumptions underlying this marketing strategy derive from the identification of racism with a white working-class sensibility and are reproduced in the film's story, in which racist brutality is displaced onto the white working-class figure of Battling Burrows and safely transposed to the London East End.

Overall, earlier criticism of Griffith's work has tended to construct the relationship between *Birth* and *Broken Blossoms* as a rupture, either by treating the two films independently or by demarcating a boundary between Griffith's representation of blacks (seen as racist) and his representation of other minorities like Asians and native Americans (seen as benign). These readings assume that racism is manifested only in the production of negative images and that liberalism is incompatible with discriminatory effects. However, as I argued earlier following Derrida, the reversal of ethnocentrism sometimes produces a "hyperbolical admiration" that can mask its own exclusionary operations. Similarly, the Foucauldian genealogy that connects the convergence of technologies of sex around issues of race to the need for new legitimizations of social inequity in a liberal social order points to the imbrication of liberal ideals in shifting and dynamic forms of racial exclusion. With this in mind, we might more productively excavate the film's liberalism as the site for the construction of racial boundaries and social hierarchies rather than see it as transcending them.

One of the first critics to discern a nebulous evasiveness in Griffith's liberal idealism was Sergei Eisenstein, who astutely describes the subject of *Broken Blossoms* as "love of mankind 'in general.'"[54] However, Eisenstein develops this insight about Griffith's sentimental liberalism exclusively in relation to the representation of class difference in his films and leaves out the complicating intersections of race and gender. According to Eisenstein, the structure of the Griffith montage constructs class contrasts in a way that reflects the inability of the filmmaker to move beyond bourgeois pathos to a truly dialectical vision (the montage trope of Russian filmmakers) that can envision revolutionary alternatives to the conditions being critiqued. Eisenstein observes, "And, naturally, the montage concept of Griffith, as a primarily parallel montage, appears to be a copy of his dualistic picture of the world, running in two parallel lines of poor and rich towards some hypothetical 'reconciliation' where . . . the parallel lines would cross, that is, in infinity, just as inaccessible as that 'reconciliation.'"[55]

Extending this insight about the ideological limitations of Griffith's bourgeois sentimentalism to his treatment of miscegenation, one finds a similar parallelism and dualism in the representation of racial contrasts that operates ideologically as an argument for racial separatism. In *Birth,* the dualism that undergirds the segregationist argument is more overt because of the focus on American national identity in terms of white-black union. Griffith's investment in producing the meanings of a reborn American national identity as white supremacy forced a more violent and unambiguous dramatization of the need for racial segregation. Moreover, given the long history of the black presence in the United States and his choice of subject—the Civil War and Reconstruction—Griffith was forced to resolve the question of union in historical time in *Birth*, albeit through a deferral.

In the case of white-Asian union, however, a more hazy and benign reconciliation of the parallelism of racial difference became possible. A slew of legislation from the 1850s onward, sharply curtailing or denying Chinese and other Asians rights of entry, naturalization, land ownership, and interracial marriage, meant that the Asian was not only more tenuously located in American history but that his or her very identity had been defined as that of an alien by race. Furthermore, the political weakness of China in relation to the West at the turn of the century reinforced perceptions of the inability of Chinese to inhabit the conditions of Western modernity. Thus, the Chinese were discursively constructed as aliens in Western time (the native subject as backward) and Western space (the immigrant subject as unassimilable). This doubled "foreignness" of the Asian allowed for a resolution in an *inter*national rather than an *intra*national context (as in *Birth*) by a dramatization of the Yellow Man's alienation in the West and the tragic consequences of his decision to leave his home. In *Broken Blossoms,* cultural difference and degeneration provide the grounds for racial separatism, whereas in *Birth* political and sexual anarchy provide the justification for racial segregation. Moreover, unlike the historical centrality of the black presence in *Birth*, the historical tangentiality of the Chinese in the United States enabled a displacement of the resolution of Anglo-Asian miscegenous desire outside historical time to a sacred hereafter.[56] Thus, contrary to the view that *Broken Blossoms* offers a reversal of the prohibition against miscegenation dramatized in *Birth*, it aestheticizes the prohibition by inscribing cultural separatism as tragic necessity. Structurally and thematically, the film insists on the parallelism of racial difference and defers racial hybridity to an inaccessible infinity.

Moreover, while Griffith constructs the racial divide between the black man and the white woman through the rape fantasy in *Birth*, he creates the racial divide between the Oriental man and the white girl through the non-consummated interracial romance in *Broken Blossoms*.[57] By centering the story on a Chinese man instead of a black man as the potential agent of miscegenation, Griffith could invoke an interracial union that would fail, not because of the animality of the colored man, as in *Birth*, but despite the goodness of the colored man. Thus, we must turn to Griffith's use of the interracial romance to grasp the ideological continuities and shifts in his representation of miscegenation between the two films. In *Broken Blossoms*, romance operates a discourse of reciprocal desire and compatibility that in plotting the tragic impossibility of union across Anglo-Asian racial divisions naturalizes and entrenches them. Liberalism's most cherished axioms of choice, equality, and autonomy appear here as affective states and outcomes, which engage in "human" terms the exclusion of the Asian from union. The persuasive power of the story lies in its exaltation of romance for its transcendence of social and political interests, even as it uses romance as a vehicle for securing these very interests. Romance also invites the identification of the audience in the fictional resolution of social contradictions by postulating a common language of the human heart.

The Asian emerges, tragically but inescapably, as an improbable object of desire for the white woman, embodying all the qualities of tenderness, devotion, and faithfulness that qualify as heroic in the world of romance, yet unable to inspire reciprocal desire in the beloved. Thus, it is precisely in the arena of locating and elaborating an "anthropological minimum" for entry into romantic union that interracial romance does its ideological work. Sadly, the love between Lucy and the Yellow Man can never be realized, regardless of Burrows's violent opposition, because the Asian is an abject lover, impossible to conceive as her equal, and the presexual white girl seems incapable of desiring him. Thus, tellingly, the unidirectional flow of desire from the Asian man to the white girl reproduces the racial hierarchy that the film's exaltation of romance and its condemnation of racism seem to reject.

The crucial question here is to what or whom the narrative attributes the failure of the interracial romance. *Broken Blossoms* equivocates, foregrounding the untimeliness of the relationship, the white girl's youthfulness and lack of desire, and the abject nature of the Yellow Man. Prior to Burrows's violent efforts to separate Lucy from the Yellow Man, the prospect of romance between the two runs into an impasse because of Lucy's lack of desire for the Yellow Man. It is crucial to keep in mind that Battling Burrows's violent reaction to the relationship is based upon a misunderstanding of its nature. As the terrified Lucy screams to her father, "It ain't wot you think!" But, while the earlier section of the film diffuses agency for the nonconsummation of interracial romance, the climax channels it into the figure of the melodramatic villain and, thus, offers an emotional resolution for the narrative deadlock. In addition, by plainly identifying Burrows as the villain, through opposition, Griffith's own position emerges as ostensibly liberal and antiracist, thereby obscuring the affinities between his own racial unease and its pathological form represented by Burrows. The film thus displaces racism on to the figure of the white, working-class father, thereby obfuscating its own aestheticized injunction against miscegenation. In rejecting the vision of Lucy and the Yellow Man as lovers, Griffith takes recourse to a nebulous universalism that paradoxically exalts love between the races while demonstrating its impossibility.

The melodramatic climax distracts attention from the disabling of the interracial romance through the representation of the white woman as a presexual innocent and of the Yellow Man as an abject lover. These symbiotic representations of innocence and abjection allow Griffith to exercise absolute control over the representation of the Other in *Broken Blossoms,* and betray his profound unease with the possibilities of their relationship. It enables Griffith to symbolically take over the body of white womanhood and allows the filmmaker's racial and masculine anxieties about miscegenation to impersonate innocence and ventriloquize the absence of desire of the white woman for the Yellow Man. In the film version, Lucy is shown as inert in the struggle between the men to lay claim to her body. At the time of their first meeting, Lucy collapses unconscious in the Yellow Man's shop; she does not seek him out for succor. She receives his attentions without reciprocating them and seems bemused by and grateful for his kindness. After her father discovers her in the Yellow Man's room, she is dragged back home by him and beaten to death; later, the Yellow Man carries her lifeless body back to his room before his suicide. The nonconsummation of the relationship between the Yellow Man and Lucy is exalted as a manifestation of its purity; however, the necessary effect of such purity is sterility.

In the film, the Yellow Man makes his living selling curios in Limehouse. Not unlike the curios he sells, the Yellow Man is set apart from his environment, his value inscribed in terms of the culture from which he is removed; he exists in his present context only as a novelty, incapable of absorption within it. He can satisfy Lucy's longing for beauty through offering her beautiful objects, but he cannot inspire desire in her for himself. In a remarkable shot that captures this incomplete circuit of desire and possession, the Yellow Man gazes longingly through the shop window at Lucy, whose own gaze is fixed on the exquisite objects on display in the window case. In Griffith's interracial romance, desire is rerouted to Oriental objects rather than Oriental subjects.

In this instance, desire for the Orient/al is produced as a form of *extraterritorial desire*, a sign of the exotic that can be *acquired and consumed* (the fate of Cho-Cho-San in "Madame Butterfly") but is predicated on distance, on the foundational condition of belonging to another world, and hence must be *excluded from the space of the family and the nation*. Extraterritoriality is one of the key signifiers of American Orientalism because it maps the space of domination within the regime of informal empire as presence in a space that is not-quite-annexed and not-quite-autonomous, hence *extra*territorial. Extraterritoriality reflects the tension between ideas of nation and empire that is irresolvable because it cannot be absorbed entirely in either. It is just this tension of location that attaches to the presence of the Yellow Man in *Broken Blossoms*. While on the one hand, Griffith criticizes the bigotry of characters like Battling Burrows who cannot accept the Yellow Man's presence in London, on the other he places the Yellow Man in China through the depiction of his physical and moral degeneration in London. The use of the biological trope of degeneration to define the Yellow Man's belonging and displacement is reinforced by the use of the language of the "natural" affections or romantic love to establish the impossibility of white-Asian love.

The exaltation of a transcendent ideal of romance aestheticizes and obscures the film's injunction against miscegenation. The effectiveness of Griffith's technique is evident in the readiness with which viewers respond to the film as a tragically thwarted romance. Taking the film's imaginary resolution at face value, Sandy Flitterman-Lewis observes, "The couple is in fact united in *the most ethereal of marriages* beyond life. The implied resolution is a fantasy of union, in keeping with the peculiarly ephemeral quality of the film."[58] I would argue, however, that to accept such a reading is to overlook the very clear, though subtle, barriers to miscegenation that are conveyed through the characterization of the young girl and the Yellow Man and to disregard the antagonism between interracial intercourse and romance that is framed by an ideology of natural affections in the story. In essence, such a reading is symptomatic of the power of romantic conventions to shape viewers' desires and proof of the artfulness with which *Broken Blossoms* transmutes its opposition to miscegenation into an idealization of romance.

Miscegenation serves as a figure in both films for positing an alternative political order to white supremacy; in the earlier film, it is violently suppressed by chivalric white knights riding to the rescue of the nation; in the later film, there are no glorious white heroes, only a failed ride-to-the-rescue by the Yellow Man. As in *Birth*, the equation of whiteness and heroism remains unchanged, and without a white hero, it appears, we must relinquish the hope of redemption. Thus, *Broken Blossoms* can be read not as an apology for the racism of *Birth* but alongside *Birth* as productive of a distinctively American variety of racism that aestheticizes the injunction against miscegenation by offering interracial romance as a solution to racial difference while simultaneously demonstrating the impossibility of such romance.

More recently, feminist and ethnic studies scholars have begun to examine the connections between *Birth* and *Broken Blossoms* in an effort to unpack the ambiguities of the film's liberalism. Julia Lesage argues that *Broken Blossoms* is a "cinematic rejoinder to charges of racism" because it uses a story of interracial love to evade an exploration of racism, concentrating instead on class and gender politics under capitalism. She contends that the Yellow Man, portrayed as a doomed romantic hero, is a projection of the director and represents with his counterpart, Battling Burrows, the crippling forms of masculinity available under capitalism.[59] But Lesage's argument that the figure of the Yellow Man is evacuated of racial referentiality overlooks the force of associations that attached to this figure in popular culture, making it impossible for Griffith to use it merely as a projecting surface, as she suggests. Although the Yellow Man does have some attributes of the romantic hero, these attributes, in inhabiting the body of an Asian in a narrative of miscegenation, undergo a critical transformation, becoming effete, a sign of lack and failure, thus averting in the end the dramatic momentum toward interracial union.

Unlike Lesage, John Tchen argues that *Broken Blossoms* is "an elaboration of *[Birth's]* ideological thrust" because it is centrally about race, as well as gender and class. He suggests that *Broken Blossoms* examines the necessity of benevolent white paternalism not as heroic presence against the backdrop of national emergence, as in *Birth,* but as brutish failure against the backdrop of urban decay. The Oriental signifies the consolations to which an unprotected white daughter might turn if the white father fails to fulfill his duties and responsibilities, just as the black represented the defilement and violence to which the unprotected white daughter could fall prey, if not vigilantly guarded.[60] Like Tchen, Gina Marchetti highlights the pivotal importance of race in understanding the film's "contradictory mix of high-minded moralizing and lasciviousness, of racial stereotypes and pleas for tolerance, of aestheticism and exploitative violence."[61] Marchetti discerns in *Broken Blossoms* "a rape-lynching fantasy remarkably similar to the 'Bible Belt pornography' that drives *Birth*" and suggests that these two films "use the fantasy of rape and the possibility of lynching to reaffirm the boundaries of a white-defined, patriarchal, Anglo-American culture."[62] Tchen and Marchetti offer more complex readings of the continuities between *Birth* and *Broken Blossoms* because their interpretations take into account the representation of Asian masculinity in American popular culture and engage the force of the cultural prohibition against miscegenation in both films.

But although the similarities in the racial ideology of both films has begun to be examined in recent criticism, the focus has remained on the representation of *non*-whiteness and its function as the definitional other against which the meaning of white paternity is produced. Except for class differences between the aristocratic Southerner in *Birth* and his working-class counterpart in *Broken Blossoms*, critics have assumed that the whiteness of white paternity is not further specified in the films. As a result, in these interpretations, whiteness acquires a certain transparency and coherence that is encapsulated by references to "patriarchal Anglo-American culture" as the common subject of *Birth* and *Broken Blossoms*. That Griffith's *Broken Blossoms*, like

Burke's short story, is set in London is then readily explained by extending the analysis of American racial ideology to a British context by positing the existence of a common Anglo-American culture. For instance, Marchetti explains that "given the links between American and British relations with China, the fact that an English story about the Limehouse slums should strike a responsive chord with Griffith and the 1919 film audience should come as no surprise."[63] On the other hand, Tchen's analysis emphasizes the contrast between Griffith's representation of the Oriental and Burke's, but he forecloses the insights opened up by this idea by attributing the contrast to divergent Victorian responses to the theme of the city; here again, the critic reverts to the explanatory framework of a trans-Atlantic cultural commonality that connects Griffith and Burke.[64] But are the British Orientalism of Burke's story and the American Orientalism of Griffith's film an undifferentiated whole defined by a monolithic whiteness, or are there nationalist logics that complicate the articulations of race, gender, and class in the film and story?

Trans-Atlantic Mediations, Orientalism, and the National Logic of Racial Segregation and Global Expansion

> Discourses of sexuality do more than define the distinctions of the bourgeois self; in identifying marginal members of the body politic, they have mapped the moral parameters of European nations. These deeply sedimented discourses on sexual morality could redraw the "interior frontiers" of national communities, frontiers that were secured through—and sometimes in collision with—the boundaries of race.
>
> —Ann Laura Stoler, *Race and the Education of Desire*

By locating Griffith's revisions to Burke's short story within the discursive field of American and British Orientalism, I offer a reading of the film that situates its representation of American national identity—through a story of British working-class racism and degeneracy—in the uncertain geopolitical context of an emergent new international order at the end of World War I. The challenge to white paternity viewed on a national scale in *Birth* is projected on a global scale in *Broken Blossoms*. But the confident affirmation of American heroism in the figure of the Little Colonel is replaced by the bleak pessimism of the failure of Anglo-Saxon heroism in the figure of the degenerate Londoner Battling Burrows.

The film's obsessive gendering of all social difference marks a stark contrast to the British short story's strategy of racializing class. Accordingly, the short story presents the possibility of a romance between its Chinese protagonist and its poor white heroine as further evidence of lower-class degeneracy. By contrast, Griffith's film version genders race and class. Thus, the film furnishes the story's working-class white girl with a bourgeois sensibility, thereby transforming her into a heroine, while depicting her male counterparts as insufficiently or excessively masculine: the Yellow Man is stereotypically feminized, and the working-class father is depicted as a degenerate brute. While the white (American) middle-class man who could protect and win the love of the innocent English girl is a figure barely hinted at in the film, he is structurally necessary to it. Anglo-Saxon Britain is no longer adequate to preserve the Western woman. With this move, the film can be seen as displacing a British Orientalism in favor of an American one, even as its betrays a deep pessimism about the emergence of this or any other alternative.

Despite its setting in the East London slums, the film is discursively located in the United States through its national logic of racial segregation and global expansion. Griffith Americanized his British source in two main ways: by increasing the racial divide between the white girl and the Yellow Man and by projecting a benevolent image of American identity, in contradistinction from its British counterpart. The racial divide between the Yellow Man and Lucy is highlighted through a sentimental narrative of the impossibility of interracial romance that required Griffith to substantially rework Burke's depiction of the two characters as lovers. Griffith transformed Burke's Cheng Huan, who is portrayed as an exotic Londoner, into the unassimilable figure of the Yellow Man, who remains irrevocably Chinese in a world where racial crossings are doomed by their cultural logic. Furthermore, the shift to the figure of the Asian enabled Griffith to explore the meaning of American national identity in the context of global expansion, although he does so indirectly, by anatomizing the failure of British heroism rather than by asserting the prospects of American heroism, as he did in *Birth*.

Griffith's film increases the racial divide between the young white girl and the Yellow Man by transforming Lucy into an icon of white feminine sexual purity. Griffith had to significantly rework Burke's materials in order to arrive at his representation of presexual feminine innocence. The contrast between the two Lucys is readily apparent in elements of the film that were derived from Burke's story but conflict with changes made in Griffith's adaptation. For instance, the opening intertitle of *Broken Blossoms* reads: "It is a tale of temple bells, sounding at sunset before the image of the Buddha; *it is a tale of love and lovers; it is a tale of tears*" (emphasis mine). Griffith's wording derived from the opening paragraph of Burke's story: "It is a tale of love and lovers that they tell in the low-lit Causeway. . . . It is a tale for tears."[65] But whereas Burke's story accommodates a vision of Lucy and the Yellow Man as "lovers," Griffith's film does not. Was the reference to "love and lovers" an inadvertent error reflecting the rush with which the intertitles were put together, or does it reflect a view of miscegenation that Griffith grafted from Burke's tale and strained to incorporate but ultimately evaded through a series of deferrals and displacements? Does the view of Lucy and Cheng as lovers reflect a possibility that Griffith sought to incorporate at the level of suggestion but circumvent at the level of plot?

In "The Chink and the Child," Lucy is even younger, a mere twelve years, but Burke depicts their relationship as erotically charged and reciprocal. Burke's sensationalism deliberately plays up the violation of the taboos of miscegenation and pedophilia within the seamy world of his Limehouse lowlife characters. He describes in titillating detail the Yellow Man's growing fascination with Lucy as "he began to watch for her and for that strangely provocative something about the toss of the head and the hang of the little blue skirt as it coyly kissed her knee."[66] Unlike Griffith's fifteen-year-old Lucy, Burke's twelve-year-old eagerly receives and returns the Yellow Man's embraces:

> He took her hand and kissed it; repeated the kiss upon her cheek and lip and little bosom, twining his fingers in her hair. Docilely, and echoing the smile of his lemon lips in a way that thrilled him almost to laughter, she returned his kisses impetuously, gladly. . . .
>
> Oh, beautifully they loved. For two days he held her. Soft caresses from his yellow hands and long, devout kisses were all their demonstration.[67]

The crucial difference in the two versions is in Lucy's response. Burke, like Griffith, insists on the "holiness" of the Yellow Man's affections. Despite their rapturous passion for Lucy, Burke's and Griffith's Chinese man does not have sex with his adored object but confines his devotion to ardent kisses and tender care. Within Burke's story, purity can coexist with sensuality and mutual attachment in the relationship between the lovers. But Griffith's

Lucy is a presexual creature whose purity requires the absence of agency and sexual desire, qualities reinforced by Lillian Gish's acting and physical presence. Gish's frail folded shoulders, the downcast gaze and the timorous, huddled posture heighten the inversion of the character and her inability to register or regard the world on her own terms or initiate actions on her own behalf. Henrik Sartov's ethereal long-lens close-ups of Gish and Billy Bitzer's irising of the lens intensify the sense of Lucy's preternaturally fragile beauty and cloistered innocence; she emerges through their visual effects as an icon of immaculate white child-femininity.[68] As Richard Dyer's essay on Gish's persona emphasizes, Gish, more eloquently than any other female star of silent film, emblematized the equation of virtue, whiteness, and femininity, and Griffith drew on this aspect of her persona in many of his melodramas: "Her body and performance can seem to emanate the same qualities the light is molding. This is why all that white light took so breathtakingly, why she shines so compellingly in the dark."[69]

In the film, the sexual innocence of the white woman has as its counterpart the abjection of the Yellow Man, the two producing in conjunction a scenario of "conspicuous nonconsummation."[70] The representation of the Chinese male in popular culture was polyvalent, encompassing a range of attributes from effeminacy, servility, and decadence to lechery, treachery, and rapacity. For Griffith, the stereotype of Oriental subservience and passivity offered a mechanism for disabling the narrative of white-Asian miscegenation without recourse to an overtly negative representation.

Frank Chin and Jeffrey Paul Chan, who have analyzed representations of Asian American manhood in popular culture, write that "the white stereotype of the Asian is unique in that it is the only racial stereotype completely devoid of manhood."[71] Chin and Chan's argument that Asian American masculinity was seen as "completely devoid of manhood" turns on an opposition between the lack of masculinity associated with Asian Americans and the excess of masculinity associated with other images of nonwhite masculinity, such as those of black studs, Mexican machos, or Indian rapists. As I argued in the introduction, representations of Chinese masculinity in the early part of the twentieth century were complex and historically variable, ranging from associations of sexual deviance to effeminacy and passivity.

The flashpoint of controversy in Griffith's representation of white-black miscegenation was the association of blacks with sexual and political anarchy and his legitimation of white control even through terror and violence. On the other hand, in *Broken Blossoms,* the Yellow Man is shown as consumed by desire for the white girl, and in one dramatic shot he approaches Lucy, his face a menacing mask of lust, but then his higher nature prevails, and he is seen sublimating lust into worship as he kisses the sleeve of her robe. This moment in the film recapitulates the dual proposal scenes in *Birth,* in which Mae Marsh and Lillian Gish are shown similarly recoiling from a mulatto and a black suitor. But the later film significantly reconstructs the depiction of miscegenation as rape by drawing on the associations of the effeminacy and passivity of the Asian male. Griffith's representation of the Yellow Man is more ambivalent than Chin and Chan's formulations allow, although the film's metaphoric structure does use the Yellow Man's effeminacy to defuse the element of sexual danger and undercut the romantic and reproductive possibilities of his union with Lucy.[72]

Griffith's reliance on the feminization of the Yellow Man is evident in the significant revisions he makes to Burke's portrayal of Cheng. The Chinese man in the short story is a dissolute wanderer and frequenter of opium dens, whose passion for Lucy is a reflection of an inchoate poetic sensibility submerged by the exigencies of a shiftless existence:

> But a poet he was, tinged with the materialism of his race, and in his poor listening heart strange echoes would awake of which he himself was barely conscious. . . .
>
> He had come to London by devious ways. He had loafed on the Bund at Shanghai. The fateful intervention of a crimp had landed him on a boat . . . to Limehouse, where he remained for two reasons—because it cost him nothing to live there, and because he was too lazy to find a boat to take him back to Shanghai.[73]

None of these qualities make him effeminate, however. They simply cast him in the mold of lowlife characters who populated numerous late Victorian accounts of East London, the embodiments of a degeneration that existed as a persistent contradiction in the heart of metropolitan modernity. As Anne McClintock explains, in imperial England, "The rhetoric of race was used to invent distinctions between what we would now call *classes*."[74] She notes that Jews, prostitutes, and the working classes were distinguished from the normative, white, middle-class male in racial terms in such formulations as "white Negroes." These characterizations were anxious figures of the ever-present possibility of racial decline, the obverse of the narrative of evolution.[75]

Within this discursive domain, Burke's Chinatown is a metonym for East London, a powerful signifier of the *racial* degeneracy of the lower orders, reflected in and exacerbated by their promiscuous couplings. The brothel Cheng Huan visits is the scene of this promiscuity, its space defined by the collapse of boundary distinctions, contamination, and decay, all the signifiers of degeneracy. Its inmates provide a precise taxonomy of the degenerate races and their atavistic counterparts within the European race: "Low couches lay around the walls, and strange men decorated them: Chinese, Japs, Malays, Lascars, with one or two white girls. . . . On one of the lounges a scorbutic nigger sat with a Jewess from Shadwell. . . . The atmosphere churned. The dirt of years, tobacco of many growings, opium, betel nut, and moist flesh allied themselves in one grand assault against the nostrils."[76]

The absent referent in this scene is the regulative ideal that defines Burke's middle-class readership, whom Karl Brown refers to as "the whole English-*reading* world."[77] The inhabitants of Burke's Chinatown tales are part of a seamy, lurid, and amoral underworld that titillates and throws into relief the rectitude, sobriety, and order of a racially homogenous bourgeois society to which his literate public belongs.[78]

But while race provides a metaphor for class discriminations in the British Orientalism of Burke's story, gender provides a metaphor for race distinctions in the American Orientalism of Griffith's film. The Yellow Man's effeminacy is created in multiple registers of desire and power in the film: he is a dreamer, not a doer; he is a pacifist, not an aggressor; he nurtures Lucy, but cannot save her. The passivity of Lucy and the Yellow Man derives from melodramatic conventions, which typically feature passive protagonists, "sympathetic innocents who have done nothing to deserve their miseries."[79] But the active/passive dichotomy of melodrama draws on a male/female opposition, since women are associated with passivity in bourgeois society.[80] Griffith develops this moral dualism by superimposing the male/female dichotomy onto the opposition of West/East, with the spirituality of the East seen as the source of both its beauty and its weakness. Moreover, Richard Barthelmess's performance as the Yellow Man provides a highly stylized rendering of Chineseness with the slow movements, hunched body, and delicate gestures, which draw extensively on a repertoire of conventionally feminine bodily signs. Critics have noted, for instance, the striking similarity in posture between Lucy and the Yellow Man. Charles Affron observes: "Griffith's caricatural notions about Chinese posture perhaps have something to do with the hunched torso, but he uses it throughout the film when presenting Lillian Gish as well."[81] Barthelmess's performance was widely praised for its delicacy and this quality lauded as a mark of its authentic Chineseness.[82] The opposition between the Yellow Man and Battling Burrows, reinforced by the use of soft-focus shots for the former and harshly lit shots for the latter, dramatizes the gendering of their opposition.

In addition, Lucy's childlike unresponsiveness to the Yellow Man's passion initiates a transformation in his role from potential lover to surrogate mother, further highlighting the feminine associations of his characterization. In Burke's story, the lover's role encompasses a maternal element, but in Griffith's film, it is displaced by the maternal. In order to expand the maternal role, Griffith had to substantially modify Burke's story. He does this by incorporating into the script a touching souvenir Lucy hoards, a letter written by her mother, leaving her daughter a piece of silk and a strip of ribbon for her future wedding. The mother's vestigial role in Burke's story— a mere narrative device to establish Lucy's illegitimacy and emphasize her isolation and defenselessness in Burrows's household—is extended in the film. In the story, the mother represents an origin the daughter transcends through her purity and sweetness, even as the mother's fate signifies the desperation and powerlessness of women to be reiterated in the daughter's tragic end. The film mother is a fallen woman like her literary counterpart, but Griffith is careful to show her rehabilitation in her longings for an appropriately bourgeois closure for her daughter's future: a decent wedding. When the Yellow Man discovers Lucy in his shop, he lavishes on her gifts of silk and ribbons that recall her mother's gifts and hopes; but instead of becoming the wished-for lover, he becomes the surrogate mother. He feeds her, tends to the cuts on her battered body, brushes and dresses her hair, and watches over her as she sleeps. It seems that the ideal of maternal love, articulated as surrogate motherhood, offered a means for Griffith to cathect the radically transformative energies unleashed by a narrative of miscegenation.

The film's association of the Yellow Man with the lost mother also operates at another symbolic level through the representation of China as a lost paradise of wholeness, stability, and harmony that invokes the lost innocence of childhood. The film is suffused with nostalgia for this lost world of timeless serenity. The connection between Griffith's representations of native Americans and Asians, often pointed to by critics as similarly sympathetic, is striking in this respect. Gregory Jay's study of the representations of Indians in Griffith's Biograph Company films stresses that "what distinguishes Griffith's work in the Indian genre is the way his plots and narratives revolve around nostalgia for lost paradises: the antebellum South, the pastoral world of the Indians, the innocence of childhood, and the mother."[83] The Chinese world to which the film insists the Yellow Man belongs resembles these other worlds in representing a civilization and a culture rendered anachronistic with the emergence of Western modernity. In *Broken Blossoms*, the theme of cultural separatism is reiterated through the symbolic connections between the figure of the lost mother and the Chinese man, while simultaneously providing a rationale for the failure of interracial desire.

Griffith's decision to begin his film with a sequence depicting the Yellow Man's life in China enables him to dramatize his degeneration in the West. Contrasted to the rest of the film, which is set in the darkly lit, bleak, claustrophobic streets of Limehouse, the opening Chinese sequence is brightly lit. This sequence is pervaded by bustling activity in the street scenes and tranquility and harmony in the temple scenes. Many of the shots are medium or long shots that frame several characters, either friends, families, or religious groupings, all of whom appear to be *bound together* by the nature of their activities. The emphasis is on community and belonging. The shots evoke the stability of the culture through images of intergenerational continuity: the vignettes of the young women's visit to the old fortune teller, the exchange between the old man and the mother and her daughters, the priest's mentorship of the idealistic Yellow Man. This is in contrast to shots of the Yellow Man in Limehouse, his isolation highlighted by his pensive, unseeing gaze and the irising of the lens. In one of the few shots that use the irising in the Chinese sequence, he is shown finger and gaze pointed upward, preaching the Buddha's word to the unheeding American sailors. The irising of the lens marks it temporally as an archetypal moment and highlights the exalted nature of the speaker and his elevation above his squabbling auditors. But even here, his beatific posture affirms not his alienation from his surroundings but his belonging in it. Dudley Andrew insightfully analyzes the construction of the "spirituality" of the Chinese in these early sequences:

> The beauty and brightness of the Yellow Man presents itself from the very first within the sanctuary of an established order. The perfect symmetry of Griffith's découpage in the temple expresses clearly the Yellow Man's

strength and the source of that strength. In the heart of this scene is a close-up of prayer beads followed by an insert shot of a monk striking a gong and another of several monks before a dominating Buddha. The Yellow Man's teacher reads from a text as Griffith cuts back to his concluding long shots. Griffith thus doubles the mise-en-scène with an editing strategy that structures the Yellow Man permanently within this world of eternal values. His very motionlessness is testimony to the rightness of this world and of him, its worthy inheritor.[84]

The Chinese world of these sequences presents an example of the familiar colonial trope of "anachronistic space" in which "geographical difference across *space* is figured as historical difference across *time*."[85] Social Darwinist paradigms spatialized time by assigning the West to progress and modernity and consigning non-European cultures to an anterior time of premodernity to justify Western subjugation of the non-West and to legitimize its civilizing mission. In *Broken Blossoms*, Chinese culture is figured through images of generation and stability and yet is seen as inhabiting a zone of "tradition" that casts it as timeless and inherently antithetical to modernity. History enters the narrative as a racial presence in the form of the American sailors who create the narrative disturbance that will propel the story forward. Their quarrel crystallizes the Yellow Man's decision to leave on his mission to the West. Prior to the encounter with the sailors, the world the Yellow Man inhabits is an unchanging one, occupying not the chronological time of history but the cyclical time of generations. The static representational quality of this section is defined by the use of noncontinuous tableaux, each of which is autonomous, rather than being bound to the contiguous shots in sequential relation. What is important is that "they are marked *as* tableaux; that is, the dramatic power of the introduction is lodged in static representations rather than in any sequenced relationship of events."[86] The editing strategy, mise-en-scène, and composition of the shots stress the Yellow Man's belonging in this space and the tragic error of his choice to leave for the West.

In beginning his film with the Yellow Man's life in China, Griffith revised Burke's text. As discussed above, the opening intertitle of the film offers a threefold narrative frame for the story: "*It is a tale of temple bells, sounding at sunset before the image of the Buddha*; it is a tale of love and lovers; it is a tale of tears" (emphasis mine). Of these, only the first frame is of Griffith's own authorship and was not derived from Burke's story. The emphasis on the

Chinese section and its significance is reiterated through the use of the early shot of the priest striking the gong in a flashback in the Limehouse section when the Yellow Man visits a brothel (introduced by the intertitle, "In this scarlet house of sin, does he ever hear the temple bells?") and as a closing image in the film to signify everything the Yellow Man was and has subsequently lost. The narrative trajectory of the Yellow Man's journey to the West highlights his degeneration in the alien and inhospitable environment. The corollary of this narrative logic is the appropriateness of his place in China and the tragic consequences of cultural crossing, which are dramatized through the story of failed miscegenation.

The Yellow Man's visual transformation, recreated through costume, posture, and composition, is stark. He goes from being a splendidly robed, dignified, and eloquent man to a pathetic, silent, huddled figure in shabby black pajamas. His arrival in Limehouse is prefaced by the intertitle, "Now—Limehouse knows him only as a Chink storekeeper." Griffith reverses the colonial trope of the white man's degeneration in the dark parts of the world to show the Yellow Man's degeneration in the West, but this statement of the spiritual superiority of the Yellow Man is inextricable from the notion of his rootedness in the East. Thus, although the film explores the possibility of transcending racial differences through love, its outcome affirms the logic of racial separation.

Burke's story, by contrast, omits any reference to Cheng Huan's life in China and starts instead with his journey to Limehouse. The racialization of lower-class identity in Burke's story allows for the representation of Cheng Huan as belonging to Limehouse; thus, his origin in China paradoxically establishes his place in Limehouse. Burke's story is based on the alterity of East London to London, while Griffith's constructs the alterity of East to West. The short story allows Cheng to be portrayed as an exotic Londoner, whereas Griffith's Yellow Man remains immutably Chinese. For Burke, Cheng's journey to England does not constitute a "fall" of any kind since he has been from the start a shiftless, dissolute character. On the contrary, in this version, his love for Lucy signifies the awakening of a dormant poetic sensibility.

Moreover, Burke's literary reputation derived from his status as a chronicler of London life, a distinction he proclaimed in the titles of his nonfictional and autobiographical writings: *Nights in Town: A London Autobiography* (1915), *Out and about London* (1919), *The London Spy: A Book of Town*

Travels (1922), and *Son of London* (1946). His Chinatown stories, the most popular of all his work, only confirmed this reputation since his stories engaged a Victorian discourse that had pathologized the topography of East London. Note, for instance, how an early critic, Edwin Björkman, describes two of the defining traits of Burke's writing:

> The first of these is the soil from which he sprang; the London East End; the life of the slums; the sounds and sights and mysterious doings of the dock district, where "on the flood-tide, floats from Limehouse the bitter-sweet alluring smell of Asia." The second is the metropolis itself, in its vast and protean entirety, which every evening . . . "affords an event as full of passion and wonder as any Eastern occasion."[87]

Interestingly enough, Björkman evokes the distinctiveness of Burke's East London through metaphors of Asia. The topographical interpenetration of Asia and London in Burke's East London landscape mirrors the writer's construction of Lucy and Cheng as lovers. Griffith's narrative of averted miscegenation derives from a different topography of Chinatown.

The genealogy of Griffith's Chinatown can be traced to medical, demographic, and missionary discourses that developed in the late nineteenth century in the United States and were dedicated to enumerating and defining the norms of domesticity in public health reports, census forms, and domestic management manuals. In these discourses, Chinatown emerged as a signifier for deviant forms of domesticity, its spaces packed with overcrowded "bachelor" households, brothels, opium dens, and amorphous female-headed households. Thus, in the disciplinary apparatus of biopower in the United States, the topography of Chinatown came to be associated with infection, domestic chaos, and moral corruption, an urban site of what Nayan Shah calls "queer domesticity," the sum of those social ties and practices against which white domesticity and heteronormativity was produced and consolidated.[88] Griffith invokes these associations visually in his sensationalized depiction of the Chinatown opium den that the Yellow Man visits through a sequence of close-ups of white prostitutes and Oriental men, reclining in a drug-induced stupor, the women's bodies displayed in wanton abandon to the camera and their male companions. The atmosphere in the opium den is seamier and more insidious and debauched than the contrasting space of white sociality, the pub, in which Battling Burrows meets up with his buddies and jostles boisterously with white prostitutes. The perverse social relations identified with Chinatown are embodied in the miscegenous couplings associated with the opium den and symbolize the antithesis to the lost ideal of white heteronormativity that the film mourns but seems unable to resurrect.

The film's representation of this racially marked topography emerges from a discourse of American Orientalism in which Chinatown serves as a figure of the unassimilable and the alien. The interchangeability between signifiers of colored and white working-class identity that was possible within the British Orientalism of the nineteenth and early twentieth century was less conceivable in the United States, where the discourse of immigration, the discourse of whiteness, and the discourse of Manifest Destiny in the Pacific produced as their truth-effects the opposition between whiteness and Asianness. The debates leading to the Chinese Exclusion Act of 1882 and the legislation itself inaugurated the racialization of immigration discourse and transformed an open immigration policy into a racially selective one.[89] This legislation was the first in a series of immigration and naturalization laws that denied—first the Chinese, then subsequently other Asians—incorporation into the political body of the United States as citizens, marking them as aliens and outsiders by race. Similarly, as many scholars of whiteness have demonstrated, in the United States, the movement to exclude Asians was led by "not-yet-white" working-class groups, who in the process were able to shift the debate about American identity in their own favor, from a question of nativity to a question of race.[90] Rather than identify along class lines with other immigrants of color, these groups identified along racial lines, rejecting class consciousness in favor of race consciousness as whites. Finally, U.S. colonization of the Philippines and Hawai'i in 1898 reinforced the idea of Asians as a people civilizationally remote from Americans and unassimilable within Western modernity. The impermeability between white working-class and colored working-class identity is played out as the impossibility of interracial union in Griffith's setting.[91]

By contrast, in Britain, the population faced no comparable influx of nonwhite immigration or economic competition from nonwhites. The growing immigration, during the 1880s, of Eastern European Jews was checked by the 1905 Aliens Act, while immigration from the colonies was negligible. Rather, white middle-class hegemony in Britain was asserted through racializing the lower orders as part of the effort to discipline them. Thus, miscegenation in Burke's narrative is a metaphor for the fluidity of racial boundaries among the lower classes; Burke's Lucy is not the immaculate conception that Griffith's is.[92]

Why, then, did Griffith retain the Limehouse setting and why didn't he simply transpose the story to a Chinatown in the United States? I would suggest that the answer lies in his vision of the tangentiality of Americans to a global narrative of "Western" guilt and oppression. In other words, this was a story that could best be told by using English characters and an English setting. Griffith could use British imperialism as a metonym for Western aggression and offer a scathing critique of its arrogance and brutality, while eliding the vexed question of the specific nature and degree of U.S. participation in Western imperialism and racism. For a filmmaker whose previous engagement with miscegenation in the United States had unleashed a firestorm, the English setting allowed for the creation of a certain distance in dealing with the charged narrative of miscegenation. The international rather than the national context of *Broken Blossoms* (and its subject of world peace rather than national integration) offered a more amorphous space for articulating the relationship between race and sexuality through the loose construction of categories of "Western" and "Eastern" identity. But even within this broad framework, Griffith incorporated a short sequence that serves as a proviso to his generalized indictment of Western aggression; he introduces a sequence establishing American innocence, or at least limited culpability, in his metanarrative of Western guilt.

Griffith interposes a brief, early sequence involving American sailors in the Chinese port city, who squabble among themselves, knock each other down, then get up and walk off together amicably.[93] The sensitive Yellow Man, who is a witness to their quarrel, is appalled by their rough ways and attempts to intervene only to be pushed down in the melee. His attempt to preach the philosophy of nonviolence is a failure. This sequence is introduced by the intertitle "skylarking American sailors" and is suggestive of playfulness, excessive high spirits and instinctive rather than deliberate roughness. This is the only specific reference to Americans in the film, an episode that does not exist in Burke's story. Therefore, it represents an interpolation by Griffith that serves to establish the informality and casualness of the American presence in the Orient and its marked contrast with its European counterpart. The episode concludes with the following words: "Just a sociable free fight for the Jackies—but the sensitive Yellow Man shrinks in horror." Through the lightness of its tone, this comment suggests an element of cultural misperception underlying the episode. Dudley Andrew's interpretation of this sequence emphasizes the effectiveness of Griffith's technique here: "The sailors know no rule of life save rough and tumble fun, healthy unreflective instincts. The Yellow Man, on the other hand, is shown to be the product of a sophisticated culture and tradition."[94]

The contrast Andrew focuses on is the one between the Yellow Man and the Americans. But there is another more subtle implied contrast, between the American and British forms of Western aggression, which is as critical to Griffith's narrative: the contrast between the casual, instinctive roughness of the American sailors and the deliberate sadism and perversion of Burrows. Youth exonerates the aggression of the former, while sadism pathologizes the aggression of the latter (*Battling* Burrows). Here, as in *Birth*, though to a lesser degree, the shift to the U.S. national context involves Griffith in extenuation and legitimation. *Broken Blossoms*'s global filiation of "the barbarous Anglo-Saxons, sons of turmoil and strife," is a more easily indictable conception for the Southerner Griffith than *Birth*'s ideal of Anglo-Saxon identity celebrated in the mystical brotherhood of the Klan. The American presence in the port city is signified through the sailors who wear the uniform of their country, but what is highlighted is the casualness of that presence and its thoughtlessness. The contrast between Griffith's and John Luther Long's representations of the informality of the American presence in the Asian treaty port is also striking.

The analysis of Griffith's revisions to Burke's text reveals the complex trans-Atlantic mediations that complicate the politics of race, class, and gender in the film and highlights the post-coloniality of American national identity at a specific historical moment. The crisis in Western modernity signified by World War I prompts Griffith's critique of Western imperialism and racism, locating culpability for racism among lower-class whites and for imperialism with the formalized colonial domination of the British. The disinterestedness of the narrative is persuasively established by its message of liberal universalism and the seeming absence of the United States from the story, except in the brief appearance of the American sailors. The post-coloniality of American identity invokes a genealogy of kinship with Britain that disavows its tyranny, affirms cultural affinity, and asserts historical innocence, thereby anticipating the possibility of a passing on of the Anglo-Saxon legacy of world domination to a more benevolent heir. This is not to say that the film locates such transformative possibilities in American culture; on the contrary, the short sequence with the American sailors is too brief to do anything more than hint at such a prospect. Nevertheless, the Americans appear as the only characters whose presence in modernity is marked as neither anachronistic (China) nor degenerate (Britain). In other words, the structure of such national mediations is triangulated; the lack or excess associated with China and Britain respectively posits an alternative, some of the attributes of which resonate with the idea of Americanness in the film. What we then arrive at is the prospect of American global ascendancy by default rather than by design, a formulation that anticipates in compelling ways the manner in which American geopolitical domination will be represented in political discourse in the decades to come. In Griffith's film, this notion is still inchoate and it is overwhelmed by a dark pessimism about the state of the world.

PART TWO

Engendering the Hybrid Nation

THREE

Unincorporated Territories of Desire: Hypercorporeality and Miscegenation in Carlos Bulosan's Writings

> The dominant race of the country has a perfect right to exclude all other races from equal rights with its own people and to prescribe such rights as they may possess. . . . Our government is in control of a large body of people of the insular possessions, for whom it is acting as a sort of guardian and it has extended certain rights and privileges to them. . . . Here we see a large body of young men, ever-increasing, working amongst us, associating with our citizens, all of whom are under the guardianship and to some extent the tutelage of our national government, and for whom we feel the deepest interest, of course, naturally . . . the question ought to be determined whether or not they can come into this country and intermarry with our American girls or bring their Filipino girls here to intermarry with our American men, if that situation should arise.
>
> —Judge Carlos S. Hardy, *California v. Yatko*, No. 24795, Superior Court of Los Angeles County, May 11, 1925

Through the representation of sexual affinities and appropriate attachments, stories of white-Asian miscegenation produced by white writers and film-makers at the turn of the twentieth century helped create and secure the internal and external frontiers of the U.S. nation. In these stories, desire for Asians is defined as extraterritorial, existing outside and yet constitutive of the moral, cultural, and racial order of the nation. Depicted as a form of desire extraneous to the civilized morality of the nation, extraterritorial desire signifies sexual license and/or sexual freedom. Thus, Asian sexuality could be cast as a regenerative force as in John Luther Long's "Madame Butterfly" or as a degenerative or effete force as in D. W. Griffith's *Broken Blossoms*. In both aspects, however, representations of Asian sexuality are harnessed to a larger critique of Western modernity.

The popularity of these early interracial romances and the limited number of creative works by artists of Asian origin endowed these early stories with unusual power to define and shape the cultural "common sense" about race, nation, gender, and sexuality. However, as more Asian American writers began producing their own narratives by the middle of the twentieth century, the appropriation and reformulation of scripts of Asian American sexuality offered an important arena for challenging the naturalizing force of dominant ideologies of difference.

In the work of two Asian American writers, Carlos Bulosan and Bharati Mukherjee, representations of white-Asian intimacy provide a central narrative framework for exploring the terms of Asian American subjection and hybridizing the American national imaginary. The interracial romance enables Bulosan and Mukherjee to make a *generative* claim on Americanness in the absence of a *genealogical* claim to belonging. However, because of the historical alienation of the Asian American subject from the nation—stemming from their exclusion from political citizenship in the early stages of immigration and their exclusion from cultural citizenship in the later stages of immigration—the claim to belonging always also involves a reconceptualization of American national identity.[1] In Bulosan's work, "America" comes to signify a reborn democracy and a radical internationalism, and in Mukherjee's writings, it signifies an emerging multiracial collectivity defined not by political membership but by the individual capacity for desire and reinvention.

Carlos Bulosan's writings, influential and widely known in his time, have recently drawn scholarly attention because of the growing interest in theorizing the Philippine-U.S. colonial relationship and in examining Filipino American literature.[2] Carlos Bulosan's most well-known work, *America Is in the Heart,* was written in 1946, by which time he had established himself as an acclaimed writer nationally and internationally.[3] In a *Look* magazine poll, *America Is in the Heart* was voted one of the fifty most important books ever published. The book, classified variously as an autobiographical novel or a collective biography, sought, in Bulosan's words, "to give literate voice to the voiceless one hundred thousand Filipinos in the United States, Hawaii, and Alaska."[4]

America Is in the Heart is divided into four parts. In the first part, the narrator, Allos, or Carlos as he is later called, recounts his family story of dispossession in the Philippines and their futile struggles to recover their land.[5] His family's loss is symptomatic of the social upheavals and dislocations produced by U.S. colonialism, absentee landlordism, and peasant rebellions. Part II tells of his migration to the United States in the 1930s as part of a migration wave that transplanted approximately one hundred thousand Filipinos to the United States and Hawai'i. This section describes the racism and class exploitation faced by Filipinos in America. Part III delineates Carlos's political development through union activisim and involvement in Filipino civil rights struggles in the United States and includes an incident where Carlos is chased by a white mob during an anti-Filipino riot, is beaten, and has his testicles crushed. Carlos's growing socialist consciousness draws him to the Communist Party and he develops a sense of solidarity with international anti-fascist movements. Part IV details how Carlos's political concerns lead him to see himself as part of an international fraternity of writers and intellectuals passionately committed to social justice and peace.

Much of the scholarship on Bulosan has focused on his anticolonial critique, his socialist vision, and his internationalism.[6] More recently, however, feminist critics have identified the gender hierarchies that underlie his political vision of universal fraternity and, in doing so, have expanded established understandings of the "political" in Bulosan's work.[7] A few critics have also noted Bulosan's preoccupation with narratives of white-Asian desire and have read it as symptomatic of "erotic desire stemming from the colonial complex"[8] or as a manifestation of the feminization of "the singular desire called 'America.'"[9]

While scholars have acknowledged the unusual convergence of the political and the personal in Bulosan's work—especially in *America Is in the Heart*, which is subtitled *A Personal History*—the significance of sexuality to his revolutionary project has yet to be explored in a sustained way. My analysis locates Bulosan's representations of white-Filipino intimacy within the history of early Filipino immigration and political struggles to highlight the way in which his vision of politics dismantles the separation between the private and the public sphere on which the bourgeois order is grounded. Miscegenation appears as a defining theme in Bulosan's work because Filipino resistance to sexual and bodily control was a key site of political struggle during the first few decades of Filipino immigration and was articulated on two levels—as the struggle for labor rights and the struggle against sexual oppression. The link between both forms of resistance was the subjection of the Filipino worker within the labor regime of capitalism. As a group of predominantly male migrant workers performing "stoop labor," whose work required mobility and few family encumbrances, Filipino laborers were profitable to capitalists because the cost of their social reproduction was passed on to families overseas and the sexual needs of the workers generated profits for emerging forms of sexual commerce. As I point out in the introduction, while the system of slavery offered incentives for black men and women to reproduce, the labor regime of twentieth-century capitalism profited from the sexual deprivation of Asian American workers.

Critics of Bulosan have generally registered an unease with the representation of affect and sexuality in his writings, seeing this dimension of his work as either apolitical or as compromising his political vision. Bulosan's "sentimental humanism" has been interpreted as a sign of political weakness or as an index of his assimilationism. I argue, instead, that Bulosan's interest in affective states and sexual relationships stems from an understanding of how deeply intimate relations were penetrated by what Foucault calls the regime of biopower.[10] Bulosan's writings reveal that the politics of empire and the regime of capitalism were implemented in and through the intimate world of sexuality and affect and engender its master tropes of affinity and exclusion. Rather than being an accommodation with sentimentalism, *America Is in the Heart* is a passionate protest against the colonization of the lifeworld of the Filipino peasant and migrant worker. Hence, Bulosan's "sentimental humanism" is not a contradiction of but is continuous with his revolutionary politics.

Bulosan's conjunction of the "personal" with the "historical" in *America Is in the Heart* warrants reinvestigation as a political project. Bulosan's effort to decolonize the lifeworld of the Filipino loses its political edge if framed within the opposition between public and private spheres that has defined Western modernity and relegated intimacy, sexuality, and affection to the private sphere. The emphasis on intimacy and interiority in Bulosan needs to be understood as a passionate outcry against the raw exposure and relentless publicity to which Filipino sexuality was subjected within colonial regimes of biopower and the immigrant surveillance apparatus of public health, census enumeration, and law enforcement. Foucault explains that biopower is the defining mode of power in the bourgeois social order. It encompasses a range of regulatory controls over the life-processes of individual bodies and the social body and is directed at the "calculated management of life."[11] He explains that the effect of technologies of biopower was to "distribut[e] the living in the domain of value and utility."[12]

As *America Is in the Heart* graphically depicts, the bodies of Filipino natives and migrant workers were photographed, anatomized, exhibited, tortured, stripped, and thus subjected to the colonial gaze and the law. Bulosan also reveals how the body is the site of multiple subjections for the Filipino worker—through the exploitation of his labor, the dangerous exposure of his body to disease, starvation, and bodily injury, the policing of his sexuality, and the commodification of his leisure.[13] By harnessing the tropes of intimacy and familialism to chronicle political struggles for citizenship, independence, and international worker's rights, Bulosan dismantles the privatization of intimacy and sexuality that underscores the bourgeois order in which, "along with the sex it legitimates, intimacy has been privatized; the discourse contexts that narrate true personhood have been segregated from those that represent citizens, workers, or professionals."[14] Thus, Bulosan's revisionist project contains radical possibilities for re-reading the political through the personal because he attempted to transpose to an interior realm unmapped by colonial and racist discourses the worth of the native/(im)migrant subject and the source of his dignity and revolutionary agency.

The politicization of the personal had its source in the Filipino experience of migration and displacement under colonialism. Historians and legal scholars have pointed to two distinctive features of the Filipino experience in the United States that elucidate the conjunction between affective states and resistance in Bulosan's writing: first, they emphasize the degree to which racial antagonism toward Filipinos was transcribed in sexual terms, whether as sexual competition over white women or criticisms of the primitive sensuality and allure of Filipino males; and second, they point to the unusual intensity of the Filipino response to sexual prohibitions on cross-racial intimacies.[15] When faced with restrictions on their sexual and marital choices, Filipinos wrote petitions, held meetings, organized community forums, and fought court cases contesting their inclusion in antimiscegenation laws. As one legal scholar notes, "Their collective, confrontational approach to restrictions on sexual and marital freedom is unique in the annals of antimiscegenation law."[16]

Filipino American resistance to state control over their intimate lives was a political response to the penetration of their lives by biopower. Although labor activism is a well-documented site of Filipino political activity in the United States, Foucault's theorization of biopower clarifies how other forms of struggle against bodily exploitation constitute crucial modes of political resistance. The Filipino American experience and Bulosan's representations of it in his writings call for a revision of conventional models of politics and resistance. Bulosan's critique of antimiscegenation prohibitions is inextricably linked to his critique of the life-denying forces of capitalism and colonialism.

However, although Bulosan's work anatomizes the effects of biopower on Filipino Americans, his reliance on the heterosexual romance to naturalize his claim to America undercuts the radical potential of his revolutionary politics. The strategy of countering white national imaginings through a narrative of miscegenous heterosexuality is a contradictory one because it redefines racial boundaries by reinstalling heteronormativity; which is to say it offers a strategy of subversion through normalization. Although the claim to a "normal" sexuality may offer a strategy for countering dominant images of native or (im)migrant sexual otherness or deviancy, it carries the risk of engendering an inclusionary politics rather than a transformative one, of changing the demography of the hegemonic group rather than reconfiguring the coordinates of power.

Filipino Americans and "Biohistory"

> But a power whose task is to take charge of life needs continuous regulatory and corrective mechanisms. . . . Such a power has to qualify, measure, appraise, and hierarchize, rather than display itself in murderous splendor; it does not have to draw the line that separates the enemies of the sovereign from his obedient subjects; it effects distributions around the norm.
>
> —Michel Foucault, *The History of Sexuality,* vol. 1

Filipinos began arriving in the United States in significant numbers in the second decade of the twentieth century, when recruiters turned to the Philippines to fill labor needs after the passage of laws excluding laborers from China (1882), Japan (1907), and India (1917). By 1930, approximately thirty thousand Filipinos lived on the mainland, 93 percent of whom were male and the vast majority between the ages of sixteen and thirty years.[17] Racial hostility toward Filipinos was particularly virulent because the period of Filipino immigration coincided with the years of the Great Depression. Furthermore, anti-Asian exclusion forces that had successfully mobilized to exclude all other Asian-origin groups were highly organized by the time Filipinos began entering the country and could readily formulate opposition to the new arrivals by reworking earlier Yellow Peril and anti-Asian discourses.

But a crucial difference between Filipinos and earlier waves of Asian immigrants was that Filipinos were the only Asian-origin group who were U.S. colonial subjects and entered the United States under a special status that defined them as "wards" of the U.S. government.[18] They were classified as "noncitizen nationals," an ambiguous category that made them neither aliens nor citizens. Thus, although exclusion movements directed against Filipinos could invoke anti-Asian discourses, they also had to reformulate opposition to the Filipino presence in terms of the special relationship that defined U.S.-Philippine colonial ties. Thus, ironically, the law through which Filipinos were eventually excluded from the United States, the Tydings-McDuffie Act of 1934, established the Philippines as a commonwealth and provided independence after ten years. Prospective Philippine independence enabled the reclassification of Filipinos as aliens, thereby rendering them ineligible for entry into the United States. The distinctive and contradictory status of the Philippines as an "unincorporated territory" of the United States determined the terms of Filipino American subjection and differentiated Filipino American from other Asian American political subjectivities.[19]

The annexation of the Philippines (and other territories such as Hawai'i, Puerto Rico, and Guam) posed an enormous constitutional and philosophical problem for American nationalism and generated fierce debates over whether annexation necessarily conferred citizenship upon the inhabitants of these territories. The doctrine of "unincorporated territory" was developed in a series of 1901 Supreme Court rulings; as it developed, this doctrine allowed for differences in political status among the inhabitants of the various territories. While Hawai'ians were granted citizenship in 1900 and Puerto Ricans in 1917, Filipinos were designated "noncitizen nationals," which meant that they were subject to the jurisdiction of the United States but would not have the rights of citizens. The United States denied Filipinos the rights of U.S. citizenship while purportedly affirming their special status through their classification as "nationals," which, it was to be understood, distinguished them from all other noncitizens who were merely classified as "aliens."[20] Those opposing the extension of citizenship to Filipinos argued that the Philippines was the largest, remotest, most racially distant, and least developed of the territories and, thus, unsuitable for assimilation within the United States. The barbaric state of Filipinos provided an organizing grammar for establishing their racial and sexual difference.

Earlier waves of Asian immigration comprising Chinese, Japanese,

Koreans, and Asian Indians had also aroused racial antagonism centered on the threats posed as economic competitors, carriers of diseases, and sexually promiscuous and morally degraded groups. But anti-Filipino discourse was uniquely charged by its focus on Filipino sexual deviance and the threat it posed to a civilized order. Filipino intimate relations with white women emerged as one of the most volatile sites of racial conflict and tension.

At the time Filipino migrants arrived in the United States, antimiscegenation laws prohibiting marriages between whites and "Mongolians" already existed in several states. Tensions around white-Filipino intermarriage began to rise in California by the early 1920s, but the question of the legality of such unions was complicated by confusion over whether Filipinos were included under existing antimiscegenation laws banning unions between whites and "Mongolians." Although the courts offered conflicting judgments on whether "Malays" were Mongolians, the matter was finally resolved in 1933, when the California legislature amended the antimiscegenation law to include "Malays." When the governor signed the bill into law, it *retroactively* voided and made illegitimate all previous white-Filipino marriages.[21] Eventually eight other states specifically named "Malays" as one of the groups prohibited from marrying whites (Arizona, Georgia, Maryland, Nevada, South Dakota, Utah, Virginia, and Wyoming).[22]

The skewed gender ratios in Filipino communities and white hostility toward sexual relationships between Filipino men and white women forced many Filipino men to turn to commercialized forms of intimacy, whether in brothels or in taxi-dance halls. Taxi-dance halls provided one of the few social outlets for Filipinos, and here they could mingle with white and Mexican women.[23] However, the public spectacle of white-Filipino intimacies in taxi-dance halls soon turned them into flashpoints of racial violence and hatred. In congressional hearings on Filipino immigration, these venues were described as "a provocative cause of the intense feelings against the Filipinos on the part of Caucasians in many communities."[24] The Filipinos who flocked to the taxi-dance halls were generally seen as sexually exploiting and corrupting white women and were described by Justice of the Peace D. W. Rohrbach as "little brown men attired like 'Solomon in all his glory,' strutting like peacocks and endeavoring to attract the eyes of young American and Mexican girls."[25] The taxi-dance halls fuelled racial hostility that erupted into anti-Filipino riots in several parts of California in the late 1920s and early 1930s; the most well-known of these incidents was the Watsonville riots in which a mob of five hundred white men attacked Filipinos, shooting and killing one and clubbing and injuring numerous others.[26]

The frequency with which economic competition was articulated as sexual competition differentiates the racialization of Filipino from that of other Asian groups in the United States. Some critics have suggested that the higher level of sexual tension arose from the greater interest that Filipino men demonstrated in establishing relationships with white women, in comparison to Japanese, Chinese, Koreans, and Indians. Other critics counter that as "nationals" rather than aliens, Filipinos may have felt a greater entitlement to mingle freely with Americans as equals.[27] However, a crucial factor that has been overlooked in these discussions is that the economic hardships of the Depression, the weakening of constraints on women's mobility, and the growth of commercialized sexual activity increased the possibilities and opportunities for sexual ties across the color line. The eroticization of racial boundaries at these sites turned them into dangerous contact zones in the popular imagination and incensed white community members who turned to violence and legislation to police these racial and sexual boundaries.

Dominant accounts of relationships between Filipino men and white women fixated on the seeming attractiveness of Filipino men to white women, conjuring up the dangerous possibility that these relationships might reflect white women's desire and agency. While Japanese and Chinese immigrant men had also been perceived as threats to white womanhood, most often the nature of that sexual threat was conveyed through images of coerced sexual relations with white women (raping, kidnapping, or bribing or drugging them into sexual slavery). The scenario of coerced sexual relations left intact the bourgeois ideal of the white woman's passionless domesticity; the sexual danger could be addressed through the chivalric rhetoric of protecting white women from Asian men. But the Filipino male raised the specter of consensual white-Asian miscegenation. The attractiveness of Filipino men to certain white women was a recurrent theme in many accounts of white-Filipino liaisons, and the appeal of Filipino men was attributed to their primitive sensuality, the flamboyance of their "Latin" ways, and their willingness to spend money on their clothes and on women. Against the backdrop of the Depression, the stereotype of Filipinos as "flashy dressers" was a loaded one because it offered a dual metaphor of Filipino theft—their theft of the jobs and women of white working-class men, the one a prelude to the other. In an article in the *San Francisco Chronicle* about white-Filipino miscegenous relationships, Judge Lazarus comments that "girls of tender years are being ruined and led astray by the strange influence these men seem to have on women of a certain type." Pointing to the fact that Filipinos drove flashy cars and spent money on women, he decried a time when hundreds of "decent white youths can't find a job for love or money. . . . It's enough to make a man's blood boil, and mine is boiling at this minute!"[28] The allure of the Filipino male in this and many similar accounts, while seeming to make a point about Filipino sexuality, reveals instead a deep unease about the permeability of racial boundaries and the difficulty of policing women's sexuality during times of economic crisis. In other words, the Filipino male's sexual appeal was attributed to his primitive origins, but the dangers of this savage sensuality were refracted through the destabilization of class, race, and gender boundaries of the Depression era.

The U.S.-Filipino colonial encounter produced an extensive archive documenting the barbarity of Filipino people that supplemented and reworked colonial representations produced by the three centuries of Spanish imperial rule preceding American conquest. Western nations acknowledged the antiquity of Asian nations like Japan and China, although they simultaneously construed this antiquity as a sign of the decrepit or the tradition-bound; the Philippines, by contrast, was seen as primitive, nonliterate, and lacking in any claim to a continuous or unified culture. In addition, the circuits through which Orientalism emerged in Japan and China were more varied, consisting of aesthetic, missionary, commercial, intellectual, and political/diplomatic discourses and thus produced a greater melding of positive and negative representations. In the case of the Philippines, however, the relationship was not only a directly colonial one defined by exigencies of pacification and expropriation, but the United States annexed the country after a brutal and prolonged war of conquest (1899–1902) that required a monumental effort of censorship and justification in the American media and public discourse. Furthermore, the primary sources of representations of Filipinos were soldiers, colonial administrators, colonial educators, businessmen, missionaries, anthropologists, and medical scientists, thereby resulting in a narrower range of representations of the native subjects.[29]

American colonial accounts fixated on tribal populations as a metonym for the Filipino people and on the identification of the Philippines as a source of "raw materials" like sugar and rubber, rather than "luxury goods" like spices, silks, or porcelain (linked to the fabled civilizations of China, Persia, and India), thus producing a topography of Asia in which the Philippines emerged as its "darkest" region. Moreover, the apparatus of U.S. colonial rule furnished a panoply of methods and sites for the study of the native body in the Philippines and its museumization and display at exhibits, fairs, and sideshows in the United States. As Marlon Fuentes's autoethnographic film *Bontoc Eulogy* (1995) shows, the display of Filipino bodies at these venues used scientific methods and language to establish the primitive nature of Filipinos and justify U.S. colonialism as a modernizing force. The commentary that accompanied the visual presentation of Filipino tribal bodies effected the dismemberment of Filipino histories, communities, and bodies and their reconstruction within imperial ideologies.[30]

Colonial discourses furthered the characterization of Filipinos as civilizational and evolutionary throwbacks, or "little brown monkeys," as they were termed. They were perceived as subjects defined primarily by their physical being, and consequently as being deficient in the "higher faculties." While spirituality or aestheticism was attributed to other Oriental cultures such as the Japanese or the Chinese, Filipinos were portrayed as dog eaters or headhunters, and any propensity they displayed toward cultivation was attributed to their powers of mimicry. Vicente Rafael explains that the trope of Filipino mimicry functioned within imperial ideology to deny interiority, intellect, or spirituality to the Filipino by treating any intellectual or creative activity in the culture not as a reflection of an inner capacity but an imitation of more evolved cultures.[31]

The colonial archive of representations of the Filipino subject is defined by what I call the *hypercorporeality* of the native/migrant subject, or the reduction of Filipino subjectivity to primordial sensations, appetites, and propensities and the corresponding equation of Filipino culture with a primitive level of social and cultural development. It is against this archive of the hypercorporeality of the Filipino subject that Bulosan's reinscription of Filipino sexuality must be read to recover the momentum of its decolonizing project. Carlos Bulosan's use of narratives of interracial desire in *America Is in the Heart* and other writings was a complexly configured political project that sought, like the works of other postcolonial intellectuals such as Frantz Fanon and Jose Rizal, to decolonize and revolutionize the consciousness of the Filipino subject.[32] In order to read the complexity of the political dimensions of his work, it is crucial to situate it against the archive of colonial representations of native/migrant Filipino sexuality that it seeks to deconstruct and rewrite.

Hypercorporeality: Constituting the Filipino Native and (Im)migrant Subject

In immigration and colonial discourse, Filipino sexuality was defined against white bourgeois sexual norms as deviant and primitive. Thus, one might say, Filipino sexuality constituted an "unincorporated territory" of desire, designated as being under the jurisdiction of civilizing American norms but deemed unabsorbable within the American body politic. *America Is in the Heart* contains two "primal scenes" that depict the construction of the colonized and (im)migrant subject and illustrate Bulosan's awareness of the centrality of sexuality and embodiment to the racial subjection of Filipino/Americans. These "primal scenes" are comparable to those depicting black subject formation in Frantz Fanon's classic study, *Black Skin, White Masks* (1967). Ironically, although Fanon's text has elicited extensive commentary from postcolonial scholars, the scenes from *America Is in the Heart* have drawn little critical notice.[33]

The primal scenes of Filipino American subject formation occur at two pivotal moments—the first dramatizes the production of the native subject in the Philippines, and the second depicts the production of migrant subjectivity during the passage to the United States, when the native subject is reconstituted as the migrant subject. These scenes show the production of Filipino subjectivity through the colonial gaze and foreground the hypercorporeality associated with becoming Filipino American.

The first takes place when the young Carlos travels to Baguio to find work. Here, for the first time, he encounters white Americans and becomes conscious of a relationship between them and himself that differs from the version provided by his colonial schoolbooks.[34] Carlos observes that the Americans are quite literally looking for a certain kind of native subject, one defined primarily by a primitive sensuality. Young as he is, he becomes aware of the power of the colonial gaze to constitute Filipino identity and perceives the discriminatory effects of its scopic regime:

One day an American lady tourist asked me to undress before her camera, and gave me ten centavos for doing it. I had found a simple way to make a living. Whenever I saw a white person in the market with a camera, I made myself conspicuously ugly, hoping to earn ten centavos. But what interested the tourists more were the naked Igorot women and their children. Sometimes they took pictures of the old men with G-strings. They were not interested in Christian Filipinos like me. They seemed to take a particular delight in photographing young Igorot girls with large breasts and robust mountain men whose genitals were nearly exposed, their G-strings bulging large and alive. (Bulosan, *America Is in the Heart* [hereafter, *AIH*], 67)

Carlos highlights the selectivity in the construction of the colonial archive, within which signs of the Filipino's already-existing acculturation, like Christianity, are erased by the quest for a native subject who can represent the antithesis of American civilization. In Bulosan's critique, the camera becomes an instrument of power, and the lines of sight in the scene reproduce the circuits of power in the social structure. The young Carlos witnesses the manufacturing of Philippine identity under the gaze of American colonialism, a process in which his role is that of a silent spectator and in which he has been erased from the scene of national representation. Carlos's description highlights how the scene of power is also a scene of fantasy and desire; the cameras of the American tourists are trained on the breasts and genitalia of the tribal subjects and frame the Filipino subjects through the signs of sensuality and nakedness that are repressed by the constraints of American civilization. What we see here again, as in the representations of Oriental sexuality in Griffith's and Long's work, is the identification of Asian sexuality with forms of desire that are excluded from the parameters of a civilized moral order and, hence, the object of fascination because they are seen to represent that part of the self that must be surrendered to the exigencies of civilized life. Thus, this scene dramatizes the construction of colonial Filipino subjectivity as hypercorporeality, both through the erasures of other Filipino presences that it effects and through its revelations about the "particular interest" of the colonizer in this production.

The second "primal scene" represents colonial subject formation during the moment of passage, when the native subject metamorphoses into the migrant subject. This scene takes place on the ship that is carrying Carlos and other Filipino workers to the United States. Carlos discovers that the erasure of his presence by the colonial gaze in the Philippines is now repeated in a different register. Carlos and the other Filipinos who have been confined to the steerage hold of the ship for most of the journey are allowed out briefly onto the deck to sun themselves. As he and his friend Marcelo are lying out in the sun, they are spotted by a young white woman in a skimpy bathing suit who recoils in horror at the sight of the Filipino men and turns to her male escort in dismay:

> "Look at those half-naked savages from the Philippines, Roger! Haven't they any idea of decency?"
>
> "I don't blame them for coming into the sun," the young man said. "I know how it is below."
>
> "Roger!" said the terrified girl. "Don't tell me you have been down in that horrible place? I simply can't believe it!"
>
> The man said something, but they had already turned and the wind carried it away. I was to hear that girl's voice in many ways afterward in the United States. It became no longer her voice, but an angry chorus shouting:
>
> *"Why don't they ship those monkeys back where they came from?"* (*AIH*, 98–99)

Carlos, who was conscious of being seen as not "savage" enough when he was in the Philippines, realizes that as a migrant he is seen as only savage: in the first case, he is rendered invisible because his acculturation as a Christianzed Filipino conflicts with the alibi of the civilizing mission; in the second case, all differences between Filipinos are collapsed to define them as unassimilable and justify their exclusion from the United States. But the defining sign of being Filipino in both cases is Carlos's hypercorporeality, which is synonymous with savagery. The irony of this moment of subject constitution is that the white woman who recoils in horror is even more scantily clad than Carlos and his friend. In the moment of passage, the corporeal identity of the narrator is reduced to an epidermal schema, which becomes the site of a repetitive and relentless visibility imposed on the Filipino subject as a foreign presence in the United States.

Bulosan is careful to show that hypercorporeality is an interested colonial construct that begins with the production of colonial knowledges in the Philippines and is reworked in the context of Filipino migration. It is against this regime of visibility and surveillance that Bulosan offers his counternarrative of Filipino American becoming. Bulosan reveals that the degeneracy and pathology attributed to Filipino embodiment and sexuality is a metalepsis in colonial and race discourse, the substitution of a cause for an effect.

Becoming Filipino American: Allegories of Interracial Desire

> Rethinking intimacy calls out not only for redescription but for transformative analyses
> of the rhetorical and material conditions that enable hegemonic fantasies to thrive in
> the minds and on the bodies of subjects while, at the same time, attachments are developing
> that might redirect the different routes taken by history and biography.
>
> —Lauren Berlant, "Intimacy: A Special Issue"

In an essay on intimacy, Lauren Berlant highlights the power of heteronormativity to organize attachments and define social membership: "The love plot of intimacy and familialism . . . signifies belonging to society in a deep and normal way. Community is imagined through scenes of intimacy, coupling, and kinship; a historical relation to futurity is restricted to generational narrative and reproduction."[35] This form of sexual naturalization entails that desires that bypass the narrative of personhood and generation are marginalized or outlawed, driven outside the boundaries that encode belonging. Berlant's comments on heteronormativity illuminate the complex tension between the dynamics of rupture and recuperation that characterizes Bulosan's narratives of interracial desire. While Bulosan offers a powerful account of the outlawing of Filipino sexual and affective life within colonial regimes, his efforts to salvage the humanity of the Filipino subject depend on inscribing it within normalizing narratives of heterosexual love and family order. Bulosan's reliance on the "metacultural intelligibility" of the heterosexual romance in reinforcing his claim to America undermines the radical force of his decolonizing project because it leads him to ground his socialist vision of racial and class equality on a narrative of gender difference and sexual exclusion.[36]

Bulosan employs three key narrative elements to produce his counternarrative of becoming Filipino American: all three elements center on the reinscription of Filipino American sexuality, affective attachments, and affiliations in order to posit an alternative vision of community. First, he deploys the chronotope of the taxi-dance hall to symbolize the destruction of Filipino generativity through the commodified intimacies and illusory Americanization of purchased romance. According to Mikhail Bakhtin, "In the literary artistic chronotope, spatial and temporal indicators are fused into one carefully thought-out whole. Time, as it were, thickens, takes on flesh, becomes artistically visible; likewise, space becomes charged and responsive to the movements of time, plot, and history."[37] The fusion of temporal and spatial elements in Bulosan's depiction of the taxi-dance hall and its salience to his narrator's "discovery" of America render the taxi-dance hall a crucial site of Filipino American becoming. Second, Bulosan uses the trope of Filipino sexual purity to emblematize the humanity and revolutionary agency of the resistant Filipino subject and counter dominant accounts of Filipino sexual deviance. Third, Bulosan exposes the "racial lie" underlying colonial genealogies of white paternity and Filipino wardship and offers alternative models of affiliation to chart the genealogy of Filipino American identity.

The derangement of the "love plot of intimacy and familialism" represented in scenes of commercialized sex and intimacy in *America Is in the Heart* exposes the terms and scope of Filipino exclusion from national membership. By documenting the aberrant forms of intimacy and association that were produced and perpetuated in Filipino migrant communities through economic segregation and legal restrictions on interracial marriage and citizenship, Bulosan offered compelling testimony to the colonization of the lifeworld of Filipino subjects under their "special" status as wards and American "nationals." *America Is in the Heart* records the despair, frustration, and violence that result from the channeling of the energy of attachment into confined, dark, and life-denying spaces in American society. Carlos's wanderings across America chart out a geography of despair and illusory gratification within the segregated spaces of these migrant communities. In a pattern that is repeated many times over in the text, Carlos arrives in town and heads to the Filipino sections, traversing the all-too-familiar terrain where both spaces of work and spaces of leisure define the exploitation of the Filipino worker: "I arrived in Bakersfield and walked from poolrooms to gambling houses. The season for plucking grapes was still far off. The vines were just pruned. There was no work for the cold months of winter. From the gambling houses I went to the whorehouses. . . . There were no other places Filipinos could go. I sat in the living room and watched lonely Filipinos paw at the semi-nude girls" (*AIH*, 273). The topography of these spaces maps the depletion and degradation of the workers and the commodification of their leisure and sexuality.

Bulosan records these destructive effects as the result of a systematic effort to cut migrants off from incorporation into the generative life of the nation while extracting profit from their bodily labor and bodily pleasure. Thus, the Filipino is simultaneously positioned within the nation as a source of labor, while excluded from it as a potential citizen.[38] Their special status as American "nationals" dissimulates their exclusion and exploitation under a simulacrum of incorporation into America. In *America Is in the Heart* and several other writings, Bulosan uses the theme of interracial desire to represent this doubled strategy of "inclusive exclusion."

The pattern of exclusion and delusional participation is vividly staged in one of the inaugural moments of Carlos's "discovery" of America through the chronotope of the taxi-dance hall, the public space of interracial sexual commerce and intimacy. As an institution, the taxi-dance hall centered on "the traffic in romance and feminine society" and profited from the enormous demand for contact with white women among migrants forced to live within "bachelor" communities. As Paul Cressey notes in his classic study, *The Taxi-Dance Hall* (1932), "It is a mercenary and silent world—this world of the taxi-dance hall. Feminine society is for sale, and at a neat price. Dances are very short; seldom do they last more than ninety seconds."[39] The taxi-dance hall, which in dominant discourses operated as a sign of Filipino hypercorporeality and degeneracy, functions in Bulosan's text as a chronotope of Filipino exile in America.

The chronotope of the taxi-dance hall depicts a space that seems to be antithetical to the world of work because of its association with leisure, femininity, romance, and beauty, but it operates through the same principles of commodification and exploitation as the world of work, with the difference that in the world of work the exploitation is explicit, while here it operates through seduction. Time is continuously running out in the taxi-dance hall, revealing the relentless depreciation of labor converted to pleasure: one season's earnings buy one night's pleasure. The temporal and spatial logic of the taxi-dance hall makes manifest the illusory gratifications offered the Filipino in the name of Americanization. In a key initiation scene, Carlos returns to Seattle a second time after the first harrowing experience of being cheated and then sold to work in the Alaskan canneries:

> I was already in America, and I felt good and safe. I did not understand why. The gamblers, prostitutes and Chinese opium smokers did not excite me, but they aroused in me a feeling of flight. . . . I wanted to see other aspects of American life, for surely these destitute and vicious people were

merely a small part of it. Where would I begin this pilgrimage, this search for a door into America? . . .

I came to a building which brightly dressed white women were entering, lifting their diaphanous gowns as they climbed the stairs. I looked up and saw the huge sign: MANILA DANCE HALL. (*AIH*, 104–5)

The seductive and beautiful bodies of white dancers are full of the promise of romance and beauty and signify to the narrator and to the other Filipinos a certain vision of America and the possibility of possessing the American dream. The men fight and kill each other over the women, who, in Bulosan's account, fleece the men of their earnings while mesmerizing them with their charm and beauty: "Marcelo was unaware of what she was doing; he was spending his whole season's earnings on his first day in America" (*AIH*, 105). The dance ends for Marcelo with a quarrel with the other men competing for the dancer's attentions and one of his friends is killed in the ensuing violence. Carlos and the other spectators flee after the shooting. What begins for the narrator as a "pilgrimage" and a "search for a door into America" ends as a desperate flight from the delusion of Americanization that drains the meager earnings of the Filipinos, feeds a destructive cycle of violence in which they turn against each other, and traps them in the limbo of frustrated desire. The chronotope of the taxi-dance hall reveals the migrant's hunger for intimacy and the thwarting of that desire under the guise of fulfilling it. Bulosan's biographer P. C. Morantte observes that one of Bulosan's most pressing concerns about the situation of Filipinos in America was the inability of his countrymen to distinguish between a false sense of security and equality in America and the real thing: "Carlos knew it was an equality on the wrong side of the track: gambling, drinking, sleeping with prostitutes, dancing in taxi-dance halls, and 'dandying' in fashionable clothes. With visions warped the Pinoys mistook American excesses for Americanism."[40] While Filipino dandyism and sexual consumerism were markers of Filipino sexual pathology and theft of American jobs and white women in anti-immigrant and exclusionist discourse, Bulosan uses these signs as evidence of Filipino exploitation and delusion.

The chronotope of the taxi-dance hall reiterates the depletion of the Filipino worker in his misdirected quest for America. The pervasive experience of time in the taxi-dance hall is of a delirium produced through the incommensurability of time to desire. Desire is unassuaged while time is perpetually running out. The dwindling tickets, the brevity of the intimacy, and the fading youth and beauty of the dancers trace differing cycles of a relent-less spiral of desperation, futility, and exhaustion. The intense compression of time in the dance hall and the depletion associated with it also reveal the denial of "the basic human need to live in extended structures of temporal-ity."[41] In a finely calibrated calculus of license and repression aimed at gener-ating profit, the men can gaze at, hold, and dance with the women, but they cannot consummate desire. For Bulosan, the terms of exchange and contact in this site of casual intimacy, and the reckless, hedonistic participation of his countrymen, offered a graphic enactment of the Filipino's place in America.

Bulosan portrayed the dissimulation of the Filipino's special place in America in many of his writings using narratives of miscegenation to iden-tify the "racial lie" at the heart of the relationship. In a letter to a friend writ-ten shortly before his death, Bulosan outlined the plot of a novel he was then working on but never lived to complete. Bulosan's description of this story offers some important insights into the centrality of miscegenation in his work:

> I will probably start one of the most important books in my life soon. . . . It concerns racial lies: the relations between Pinoys and white Americans. Here it is: Suddenly in the night a Filipino houseboy kills a friend and in his attempt to escape from the law he stumbles into his dark room and bumps against the wall. When he wakes up he is confronted by a veiled image in the darkness who reveals to him that he has become white. It is true, of course, that he has become a white man. But the image tells him he will remain a white man so long as he will not fall in love with a white woman! And that is the tragedy because he has already fallen in love with a white woman. Get that? So long as he will not fall in love with a white woman! Then, according to the warning of the image, he would become a Filipino again, ugly, illiterate, monster-like, and vicious.
>
> This is a parable, of course, an American parable. Some elements in Amer-ica gave us a gift of speech, education, money, but they also wanted to take away our heart. They give you money but they deny your humanity.[42]

In this encapsulated version of Bulosan's American parable, the prohibi-tion on the white-Filipino romance emblematizes the ruse of the Pinoy's access to the American Dream and reveals how the appearance of access in economic terms masks the oppression of the Filipino worker. The prohibi-tion on miscegenous love reveals the contrast between the presumption of the Filipino's need for redemption from a condition of unalleviated savagery and brutality ("monsterlike") and the limits to the salvation proposed for him through his metaphorical conversion to whiteness (assimilation). The Filipino's entry into whiteness is a ruse because it is contingent on his meeting an impossible condition, since he is *already* in love with a white woman. The Filipino's love for the white woman is shown as an already-existing state of attachment since it is an effect of the colonial relationship itself where conquest is cathected as civilizing mission. Bulosan's parable highlights that the conditions that hem in the formulation of benevolent assimilation betray the promise it purports to fulfill. This is the racial lie to which Bulosan repeatedly refers in seeking to identify the causes for the failure of the American Dream in the lives of Filipinos and to come to terms with the violence, dissolution, and despair that marked the lives of so many in the Filipino American community.

The love of the Filipino man for the white woman in its creative and destructive aspects was one of the foundational fictions of Bulosan's work and offered a vehicle for revising colonial figurations of the native. The Filipino's desire for the white woman traverses the range of emotions from hopeless longing to inspired adoration to deluded idealism to carnal desire. In all these registers, Bulosan seems to be attempting to work out whether this love can be seen as autonomous of the worth of the beloved or whether this love is finally only as good as its object. In other words, is the colonial subject's love redeemed by the quality of his devotion or by the object of his devotion? Bulosan uses the trope of the purity of the Filipino's passion for the white woman to explore these questions. However, his use of this trope grew more sophisticated as he shifted from grounding it in romantic pathos to defining it within a socialist vision.

Bulosan's response to the dominant myth of the white woman's sexual purity (which also circumscribes the possibilities of interracial love in D. W. Griffith's *Broken Blossoms*) was to assert the sexual purity and devotion of the Filipino protagonist and to cast this purity as independent of the attributes of the white woman, who assumed a dual aspect in his writings: either unfaithful, avaricious, and manipulative or nurturing, tender, and self-sacrificing. Through the trope of purity, Bulosan overturned the colonial myth of the insane lust of the native for the white woman and simultaneously shifted the determination of the Filipino's worth to an internal sphere, turning his inner capacity for love and tenderness into a touchstone of his worth.

A particularly striking example of Filipino sexual idealism appears in the short story "The Romance of Magno Rubio."[43] At the center of the story is Magno Rubio, an ugly and uncouth Igorot farmworker, who earns twenty-five cents an hour doing stoop work on California farms while he keeps himself alive by corresponding with a white girl from Arkansas, whom he has never met. Illiterate himself, the simple Magno pays an exorbitant fee to a fellow farmworker, Claro, to write his love letters for him. When Magno complains about Claro's sentimental extortion to Nick, a college-educated farmworker, Nick assumes the task of scribe for Magno, free of cost. Claro scoffs at Magno for loving a woman "twice your size," but Nick counters by affirming the validity of Magno's love: "The object of love may be an idea, a dream, a reality. . . . The love is there. And it grows—depending, of course, on the ability of the lover to crystallize the beloved" (Bulosan, "The Romance of Magno Rubio" [hereafter, "RMR"], 34). The story focuses on Magno's trusting nature, his devotion to the unknown woman, and his transformation through the experience of love. His fascination with white women is stimulated by the girlie magazines he consumes, which form his only "reading" material. Nick notes his addiction to the fantasy images of white women and concludes: "I saw him looking with dreamy eyes at the pages of dime magazines. I knew he couldn't read, but the magazines were illustrated with the photographs of nude and semi-nude girls. I was tempted to teach him the alphabet, which I did for a few days, but he lacked concentration. And his memory was bad because his mind was taken up by the enticing photographs" ("RMR," 38–39). Yet despite the source of Magno's obsession with white women and his repulsive appearance and habits (which Bulosan catalogs in overpowering detail), the narrator focuses on his innocence, purity, and devotion, which seem incongruously housed in his unsightly body.

This innocence emerges in stark contrast to his love object, Claribelle, who fabricates stories about her family's desperate hardships to extract large amounts of money from Magno. In the end, after promising to marry Magno, she makes off with his money. But Magno is completely transformed by his love for Claribelle and works tirelessly to support her: "Magno Rubio never complained. Not one word of protest. The plight of the girl in Arkansas made him more industrious and frugal. He even cut down his expenses on chewing tobacco" ("RMR," 41).

Given that Claribelle is neither subtle nor skilled in her tactics and her mercenary motives are obvious to everyone but Magno, the representation of this romantic devotion raises and must resolve the issue of whether Magno's devotion is a manifestation of his sense of racial inferiority or whether it exceeds the colonialist fantasy from which it may very well have derived. Frantz Fanon, whose *Black Skin, White Masks* examines the pathologies of colonial interracial relationships, diagnoses the obsession of the black man for the white woman as a sign of twin desires, "a wish to be white" and "a lust for revenge." The desire for the white woman, according to Fanon, is the desire to be recognized as white:

> Out of the blackest part of my soul, across the zebra striping of my mind, surges this desire to be suddenly *white*.
>
> I wish to be acknowledged not as *black* but as *white*.
>
> Now—and this is a form of recognition that Hegel had not envisaged— who but a white woman can do this for me? By loving me she proves that I am worthy of white love. I am loved like a white man.
>
> I am a white man.
>
> Her love takes me onto the noble road that leads to total realization. . . .
>
> I marry white culture, white beauty, white whiteness.
>
> When my restless hands caress those white breasts, they grasp white civilization and dignity and make them mine.[44]

The question of the source of Magno's desire for Claribelle, addressed in Fanon's text, is also raised in Bulosan's story, but here it serves to open up a completely different set of concerns regarding the relationship between the colonizer and the colonized. After witnessing Magno's unquestioning faith in Claribelle, Nick is moved to ask: "What sustains a man to have such patience? What quality of soul does he possess to have so much faith in something he has never seen? . . . Where most men would have given up long ago, he kept on beyond belief and all reason" ("RMR," 41). The answer is that Magno's love for Claribelle enables him to survive the disintegrating and corrupting effects of a dehumanizing environment where he "worked like a carabao but lived like a dog." Magno tells the narrator, "You see, Nick, I'm clean in my soul thinking of her" ("RMR," 42). When Magno discovers that Claribelle has disappeared with his money, he accepts her betrayal with silent resignation, but Nick reacts with angry indignation: "Why does everybody make it difficult for an honest man like Magno Rubio to live in the world?" ("RMR," 50). Here, in some sense, Nick answers the question he had earlier raised about the nature of Magno's blind love for an unknown white woman. Nick's words clearly resonate beyond the specific relationship between Magno and Claribelle to the larger allegory within which it is framed—the Filipino subject's continuing faith in the promises of an American democracy that has betrayed him time and again. The problem, Bulosan seems to be suggesting through this allegory, is not with the nature of the colonial subject's belief but with the deception of colonial claims of benevolence. In addition, the purity of the Filipino's love is inscribed within the context of his powerlessness in the white man's world. The figure of Magno's purity operates within a discursive and material world in which the preservation of the capacity for love, trust, and idealism constitutes a crucial form of resistance and a mode of survival. Magno, like the Filipino taxi-dance hall patrons in *America Is in the Heart*, is fleeced by the white woman he consorts with, but Bulosan suggests that there is a qualitative difference in the nature of their desires for and illusions about white women. Although Magno and the taxi-dance hall patrons pay money to women in exchange for intimacy, Magno's attachment helps him transcend his circumstances and strengthen his character, while the taxi-dance hall setting breeds self-destructive violence and degradation. Nevertheless, although the trope of purity in "The Romance of Magno Rubio" articulates a mode of resistance to colonial oppression and labor exploitation, the political critique it offers is limited because Magno's purity emerges from an opposition between worldliness and purity. Thus, the purity of his affections operates through a transcendence of worldly contradictions rather than an engagement with them.

A more complex elaboration of the trope of the Filipino's sexual purity can be seen in Bulosan's later reworking of interracial desire in *America Is in the Heart*. Here again, the preservation of purity against the omnipresent threat of disintegration and dissolution drives the protagonist. In *America Is in the Heart*, unlike in "The Romance of Magno Rubio," the struggle to maintain purity is more self-conscious and is integrated into the larger socialist vision through the protagonist's involvement in the labor movement and the movement for Filipino American civil rights. In a pivotal episode in the text, Carlos works for a brief period as a "houseboy" for a famous Hollywood director. One morning when he enters the director's wife's bed-room to serve her breakfast, she steps out of the shower naked. Carlos is riv-eted by the spectacle of her glistening, naked white body. Catching him star-ing, she demands to know what he is looking at and is politely told that he is staring at her body. Infuriated, she orders him out of her room. The intensity of his gaze on the forbidden body of the white woman and his excruciating charge of desire are conveyed through the minuteness of the erotic details that register on his consciousness (*AIH*, 140–42).

Presented in isolation, this episode would seem to support the Fanonian allegory of the colonized subject's lust for the white woman. However, the bedroom scene is preceded by another exchange that refracts the meanings of the sexual encounter between the Filipino houseboy and the white mistress. The previous night, while serving dinner guests at the director's home, Carlos hears them discussing their Filipino servants. The guests remark to each other that Filipinos are "only too glad to work for white folks" and that they make dangerous house servants because they are "sex-starved" and crazy for white women. The following morning, two characters who are mere auditors during this exchange—the director's wife and Carlos—become actors in an interracial sexual encounter that revises the stereotype of the sex-starved Filipino house servant. The second scene highlights the perspective of the Filipino "houseboy" and renders visible the white woman's role in creating the myth of the sex-crazy Filipino. She is no longer the passive object of desire or an icon of purity as in the earlier dinner conversation. Instead, her agency is framed within the prerogatives of racial and gender privilege: She is shown as instigating his desire and negating his manhood by heedlessly displaying her body in front of him. As a white woman and his mistress, she has the power to emasculate and humiliate the Filipino man whose name bears the traces of the castrating effects of his domestic service—"houseboy." Carlos leaves town because he cannot submit to the degradation of domestic service on these terms, nor can he bear to be a witness to his brother's subservience. Carlos's sense of outrage is enunciated as an outcry against *his* bodily violation by his employers, thus reversing colonial narratives of Filipino hypercorporeality and sexual deviance. Here, his integrity and dignity as a human being and a worker is represented as a form of purity that has been defiled. In this powerful rereading of the myth of the Filipino man's desire for the white woman, Bulosan exposes the fiction of the white woman's purity and positions it against the servitude of the Filipino houseboy.

> I could not tell him [Macario] why I was running away. Not now. I could not bear to see him working for people who were less human and decent than he, and who believed because they were in the position to command, that they could treat him as though he were a domestic animal. . . .

I heard something shouting at the edge of my mind:
"I will never let them touch me with their filthy hands! I will never let them make a domestic animal out of me!" (*AIH*, 142)

In the Fanonian analysis of the white woman–black man dyad, the white woman's body represents the passive object over which the struggle between colonizer and colonized is played out and victory is defined through possession of that body. For Fanon, access to the prohibited body of the white woman symbolizes the fulfillment of a reverse fantasy of dominance and conquest. However, the colonial trope of the obsessive lust of the black man for the white woman is left intact within this reverse fantasy. By contrast, in Bulosan's narrative, the organizing figure of the purity of the colonial subject demarcates a psychic domain and a form of libidinal energy that has redemptive power because it can transcend the degradations of a brutalizing environment and evade the control of the oppressor. Miscegenous desire operates not through the negative dialectic of the Fanonian dyad but through the affirmation of an idealism that is irreducible to the immediate circumstances. Thus, when Bulosan asserts in the face of the overwhelming evidence of brutality and racism that "America is in the heart," he is referring to a political ideal engendered in this inviolable subjective realm within which he locates revolutionary agency and the transformative possibilities of the human soul.

Nevertheless, it is important to distinguish between the two forms of purity that Bulosan depicted in these stories. In the story of Magno Rubio, Magno's purity is a reflection of an inner simplicity and stoicism that is inimical to struggle and resistance; it does not contain the power to transform his situation, only to endure it. Thus, although Magno's story can serve as a vehicle for a political critique, he is not himself represented as an agent of transformation. On the other hand, the protagonist of *America Is in the Heart* invokes an idea of purity that is grounded in his dignity and worth as a worker and a human being. This coding of purity clearly emanates from a political consciousness that combines political idealism and activism. But more importantly, in this episode the purity of the protagonist is not produced within a normalizing narrative of heterosexual love. Unlike Magno Rubio's romantic idealism, Carlos's purity stems from his innate human dignity rather than the quality of his love for a white woman. Thus, while both forms of purity mobilize representations of the "human subject" or the "human type," the romantic pathos of the Magno Rubio story offers a more limited framework for critique. As we saw in the case of the Chinese man in Griffith's *Broken Blossoms*, the trope of the *pure* unreciprocated devotion of the Asian man for the white woman depends on a degree of abjection that renders such a subject a tenuous vehicle for a sustained political critique of domination. Similarly, in *America Is in the Heart*, when Bulosan frames the protagonist's purity within a narrative of heterosexual love, as he does in accounts of Carlos's relationships with several white women, his critique of colonialism and racial and class domination is short-circuited by its emotional transcendentalism. Thus, although the affirmation of purity offers a means of challenging colonial inscriptions of Filipino sexual degeneracy, certain narratives of purity in Bulosan's work offer only a sentimentalized counterforce to the oppression he documents.

If seduction and prostitution provided figures of Filipino disintegration and exploitation under American domination, the language of generation and kinship offered countervailing tropes for imagining the Filipino's place in "America." At a time when the racial subjection of the Filipino worker in the United States coincided with his enforced sexual and affective deprivation, the use of one condition as a metaphor for the other carried with it a certain inevitability: racial oppression as sexual oppression, sexual oppression as racial oppression. But if racial and sexual oppression were clearly inextricable in producing the subjection of Filipinos, how specifically was the relationship between the two to be represented? Furthermore, if the liberation of the Filipino was to be imagined and the Filipino's personhood established, in what discourses might it be enunciated?

The project of reclaiming the humanity of Filipinos is certainly an important rhetorical project in *America Is in the Heart*, but this project is riven with tension between locating a discourse with the "metacultural intelligibility" necessary to naturalize the Filipino's claim to America and the insurrectionary force necessary to transform the very meaning of "America." For Bulosan, the discourse of sexuality and family seemed to offer the matrix for articulating a new political vision of America.

However, its appeal lay in its power to naturalize and normalize a deviant subject and for that very reason these discourses curtailed the revolutionary scope of the narrative and reinscribed conventional understandings of gender and sexuality that underpinned the ideology of the family. The narrative impetus to produce the family as a natural expression of heterosexual love and a macrocosm of community rendered it impossible to represent the family as a historical and social construct. Thus, although the radical re-imaginings of national and transnational communities in *America Is in the Heart* represent these political forms as all-inclusive, these imagined communities are founded on an ideal of heteronormativity.[45] Accordingly, *America Is in the Heart* positions women as reproducers of the nation and custodians of national culture and by identifying masculinity with heterosexuality marginalizes queer sexualities as deviant (as seen in Bulosan's depictions of several scenes of homosexual panic when he flees the advances of other men).

Bulosan's use of miscegenous desire as an allegory of U.S.-Filipino relations was an attempt to reconstruct the "colonial family romance" that underscored ideologies of colonial wardship.[46] Françoise Vergès uses the term *colonial family romance* to identify the unconscious images of familial order that emerged in the process of French colonial domination of Réunion. She suggests that the Freudian notion of the family romance offers a narrative model for the projection of an idealized version of colonial authority over a subjugated population. In the Freudian account, the child creates a fantasy image of idealized, high-born, and all-powerful parents to console and avenge itself when confronted with the reality that its parents are imperfect and fallible. But Vergès argues for a reversal of this consoling fantasy in the colonial relationship, where the fiction of imaginary parents is developed by the colonial power to substitute its benign parental authority for "the real parents of the colonized, who were slaves, colonists and indentured workers."[47] Her account of the colonial family romance provides a paradigm for the reconstruction of conquest as civilizing mission that is especially applicable in the case of the United States.

The reconstruction of the "special relations" between the United States and the Philippines was particularly intense because U.S. imperial expansion flagrantly contravened the country's anticolonial origins and its avowed dissociation from the imperial practices of European colonial powers.[48] The policy of "benevolent assimilation" attempted to symbolically resolve these contradictions in American nationalism by proclaiming the purpose of U.S. rule as the substitution of justice for arbitrary rule. Benevolent assimilation posited the Filipino subject as a politically immature ward within "the U.S. policy of self-liquidating colonialism, in which the 'little brown brother' was permitted to achieve independence when he grew up, a maturation process that took forty-five years."[49]

The status of wardship conferred on Filipinos in the aftermath of American colonization was widely described, apprehended, and projected through models of filiality in an effort to naturalize relations of conquest as relations of affinity. The family romance created by the colonial power was disseminated through the educational system and ostensibly confirmed through the selective absorption of elite Filipinos into political office and their increased prosperity consequent to the creation of protected markets for Filipino agricultural products in the United States. Central to the American need to proclaim its paternal interest in its colonial wards was the need to distance itself not only from the practices of the Spanish colonial power it superseded but also, by extension, from imperial aspirations more generally. The flexibility and symbolic power of the family romance of wardship made it particularly serviceable to this American agenda.

Bulosan's writings, and *America Is in the Heart* in particular, offer a searching critique of this family romance of U.S.-Filipino relations from the doubled perspective of the male Filipino peasant and the male Filipino migrant worker. The trajectory of the protagonist in *America Is in the Heart* fuses these two perspectives, using them to expose the principal contradiction contained in the ideology of "special relations." Reflecting on the nature of this relationship, Bulosan wrote in 1937: "Western people are brought up to regard Orientals or colored peoples as inferior, but the mockery of it all is that Filipinos are taught to regard Americans as our equals. . . . The terrible truth in America shatters the Filipinos' dream of fraternity."[50] But while *America Is in the Heart* passionately repudiates the colonial family romance as emblematic of the political status of Filipinos in the present, it nevertheless embraces images of familial order as a utopian model of future equality.

America Is in the Heart opens with a scene that dramatizes the inevitability of departure from the home of the real parents at a time of colonial transition. The moment of migration marks the movement from the home of the real parents, which can no longer sustain the existence and aspirations of the protagonist, to another home that promises plenitude and enlightenment: "Then it came to me that my life there was too small to float the vessel of my desires. I wanted to cry out to all those who were left behind. . . . I knew that even if I went back to them, after many years of loneliness in another land, I would not be able to pick up where I had left off" (*AIH*, 65–66). However, the passage to America reveals the gap between the family romance of wardship and the racial oppression and servitude that confront the Filipino in the United States.

Carlos responds to this reality, as Sheng-mei Ma observes, by gendering his disillusionment with America, representing its benign aspect in the figure of the white woman/mother and identifying its cruelty and betrayal with the white man/father.[51] The figure of the white woman, the object of the protagonist's desire, is both a reiteration of the lost real mother and an embodiment of the lover through whom he can affirm his belonging in America by asserting a generative claim to its future.

The white woman's body is central to this fiction of a new America because it enables its conception as a hybrid nation. The recovery of the real mother through the figure of the white woman is paralleled by the recovery of the real father in the iconic figure of the Filipino worker who comes to signify the revolutionary agency through which a new America can be born. But the reinscription of the colonial family romance that enables Bulosan to represent his claim to America through alternative images of familial order also instantiates a crucial shift from a political community imagined as a patriarchal order (the Philippines and the United States) to a political community imagined as a fraternal order (a universal brotherhood).

Thus revolutionary social transformation comes to be imagined as a passage from a patriarchal to a fraternal order. But although the "America" that is in the heart and yet to be born is imagined as a universal community founded on equality, the foundational fiction of this brotherhood is of the role of women as reproducers of the polity, not its revolutionary agents. Therefore, although the fraternal order repudiates one aspect of patriarchy, the domination of fathers, it continues to preserve another, the subordination of women. In an astute reading of the fraternal social contract in political philosophy, Carole Pateman observes that while the shift from the rule of fathers to the rule of brothers is typically read as the founding of a civil society based on equality, individuality, and liberty, it might more fruitfully be read against the Freudian idea of the parricide that founds civilization and establishes the rule of law:

> The brothers' collective act is not merely to claim their natural liberty
> and right of self-government, but *to gain access to women*. . . . The parricide
> eliminates the father's political right, and also his *exclusive* sexual right.
> The brothers inherit his patriarchal, masculine right and share the women

among themselves. . . . they exercise the "original" political right of dominion over women that was once the prerogative of the father.[52]

Compelling as is Bulosan's vision of a utopian state of universal fraternity he
calls America, his reliance on images of familial order grounded in conventional gender ideologies undermines the egalitarian ideals he proclaims. The
gendering of the (trans)national imaginary in Bulosan's *America Is in the
Heart* clearly reveals that its imaginings of unity are founded on difference.
As Anne McClintock asks, the crucial question for progressive (trans)nation-
alisms is "whether the iconography of the family [can] be retained as the
figure for national unity, or must an alternative, radical iconography be
developed?"[53]

The earliest scenes of Carlos's life with his father are suffused with a recognition of his father's powerlessness. When Carlos leaves the village, his father
assures him lovingly of a permanent home on the land, an ideal that the narrative has shown the father cannot provide. Both the love and the failure
serve as a metonym for fatherhood and masculinity under colonialism:

> I took my father's hand and tried to tell him that it was goodbye. He
> leaned on his walking stick to keep himself from falling.
>   "Be sure to come back, son," he said weakly. "When you find it hard
> and there is no other way, you must come back to Binalonan and stay
> with us."
>   "I will come back, Father," I said. (*AIH*, 88–89)

The tender farewell between father and son preserves a fiction of paternal
strength that father and son have individually come to recognize is an illu-
sion. Carlos's desperate flight from home is propelled by the knowledge that
once his father has lost the land to the church, he is reduced to a "pathetic
little figure in the house," a man "completely broken in spirit" (*AIH*, 63).
The inability of the father to provide for the peasant son, a condition
endemic to colonial transition, transforms the peasant son into a migrant
worker, chasing the hope of survival first to the city, and then to America.
His accession to "sudden manhood," and his long journey into the
unknown, is compelled by the weakness of the real father, and this rupture
in his relationship with his father signals the end of childhood. Carlos's
father, for his part, has also recognized his own inability to stop the disintegration of his family:

> But I knew it was the end of my life in Mangusmana, the end of the bitter
> days of childhood. It was actually the end of my life with my father, the
> end of my farming life in the Philippines. . . . I knew I could not go back
> to Mangusmana, and my father knew it too because he had witnessed it
> before, when my other brothers went the way I was going, away from him
> and his earth forever. (*AIH*, 30)

Many months later, Carlos returns home to bid his final farewells before
leaving for America. But in Carlos's moment of homecoming, many changes
are in evidence. The family has lost all their land, his father is sick, unable to
work, and now his mother has taken her husband's place at the plow. The
signs of their dispossession are everywhere.

> I had come back to manhood, here in my native village. I had come
> back to myself and my roots, here in this narrow strip of land. *Back*
> *to my soil and to my father's faith.* I had not forgotten him limping through
> Mangusmana on his sore feet, going from house to house and asking the
> farmers if they could lend him a piece of land to cultivate or could hire
> him. I had not forgotten his love for the earth where his parents and their
> parents before him had lacerated their lives digging away the stones and
> trees to make the forest land of our village a fragrant and livable place.
> (*AIH*, 76, emphasis mine)

Carlos's need to look elsewhere for sustenance is compelled by his father's
inability to provide for the family. But while the narrator's remembrances of
his mother highlight her transcendence of her surroundings, the father is
very clearly shown as a social being whose place in-the-world will shape his
son's own coming of age. The homecoming is evoked simultaneously by the
mother's love (seen as timeless) and the failure of the father's faith (seen as
historical). The inability of the native father to support his son propels the
son into the land of the colonial father, whose authority the son resists by
seeking to establish a fraternal political community through his political
activism.

After Carlos arrives in America, his experiences are framed as a quest for
masculinity in a world in which antimiscegenation laws restrict his ability to
conceive a generative connection to the new land. Although Carlos seldom
refers to his memories of his father, he recognizes the stabilizing force of his
father's presence in his life at a climactic moment when he is driven to violence by racist brutality. The news that his father has died devastates him and

destroys his faith in himself and in America. This news arrives at a time when Carlos's exposure to the violence and hatred of white men demolishes the colonial family romance of benevolent white paternity. With the death of the real father, Carlos confronts the dread of attaining manhood without his father to strengthen him: "My father's death was the turning point of my life. I had tried to keep my faith in America, but now I could no longer. It was broken, trampled upon, driving me out into the dark nights with a gun in my hand. In the senseless days, in the tragic hours, I held tightly to the gun and stared at the world, hating it with all my power. And hating made me lonely, lonely for love, love that could resuscitate beauty and goodness. For it was life I aspired for, a life of goodness and beauty" (*AIH*, 164). Ironically, his ability to maintain his faith in America is attributed to the Filipino father while white paternity is seen as its betrayal.

But the full recovery of his masculinity can only take place after the imaginative recovery of his father's presence, which takes place toward the end of the text. This scene is framed as the moment of Carlos's "discovery of America," when he comes to a new understanding of the nature of his relationship to the land he lives in. He talks to a Filipino farmer who reminds him of his father, "He had the gentleness and the passion of my father when he spoke about the land." Carlos continues, "I felt this way when I talked to him. It was a discovery. I found myself in him, in the strange melody of his attachment to the land that did not belong to him, in his almost mystical belief in the fertility of the earth" (*AIH*, 273). The discovery of America is thus also the recovery of the lost figure of the father and a means of linking the father's experiences to his son's. The discovery reinscribes the father's experience of dispossession and the rootlessness of Carlos's experience of exile into a transfigured and empowering understanding of being at-home-in-the-world by belonging to the land rather than possessing it.

In marked contrast to the ambivalence that shadows recollections of the real father, maternal origin is eloquently affirmed. The associations around the mother's presence persist even long after Carlos has left his homeland and are invoked in his reunion with his brother Amado in the United States. Amado is unable to recognize Carlos after the long separation and demands irrefutable proof of their relationship. He asks Carlos the name of their mother, a symbolic request that elicits a lyrical outpouring from the narrator, "Yes, to him, and to me afterward, to know my mother's name was to know the password into the secrets of the past, into childhood and pleasant memories; but it was also a guiding star, a talisman, a charm that lights us to manhood and decency" (*AIH*, 123).

Interestingly enough, although the hardships of peasant life in the Philippines inflict suffering on Carlos's father and mother, his recollections of his childhood days gender these memories, connecting his mother's presence with tenderness and warmth and his father's with privation and strife. However, these associations run counter to the details of his childhood that he provides in the text and seem to be connected to a tendency to see women in a highly idealized way, belonging to the world and yet beyond it. On the other hand, the images of men render them as *worldly* figures, clearly located within networks of power and powerlessness, and unlike women, unable to transcend them. For instance, the narrator recounts the way in which poverty strips his mother of conventional feminine attributes; he describes her worn body, skirt tucked between her legs, as she pushes the plow across the land. Yet, in his mind, she remains the image of a transcendent feminine. His long journeys with his mother peddling salt fish to the villagers are etched in his memory, as are the meager returns for their labors, the dangers of the journey, and the pathetic rags that cover his mother's body. Yet the descriptions of Carlos's mother suggest that what she embodies is bigger than the sum of her possessions or her careworn appearance, and in his later years her identification with nurture, love, generosity, and dignity intensify, a reminder to her son of everything that is worth striving for and a symbol of the transcendent feminine principle in nature and society.

The transcendence associated with the mother and other feminine figures derives from their inscription within a cyclical, ahistorical conception of time that is linked with generativity and creativity. As such, it represents a paradisal world of oneness and belonging that can be temporarily achieved through sexual union but is impossible to sustain. Carlos captures it for a brief moment while dancing with a young woman near his village, experiencing a rapturous oceanic feeling, "When you dance for the first time, the world is like a cradle upon the biggest ocean in the universe," only to assert when the vision fades that his dancing partner is nothing but a "mud-smelling peasant girl" (*AIH*, 77). Later in America, when Carlos is forcibly initiated into sex by some Filipino workers, who push him into bed with a prostitute in the labor camp, he is transported by the sensuality to another realm beyond the sordid environment of their sexual exchange. The rhetoric is cloyingly poetic, and its strained tones suggest the exaggerated idealization underlying it: "It was like spring in an unknown land. There were roses everywhere, opening to a kind sun. I heard the sudden beating of waves upon rocks, the gentle fall of rain among palm leaves. Was this eternity? Was this the source of creation? Then I heard a thunderclap—and suddenly the sound and stench of humanity permeated the air, crushing the dream" (*AIH*, 159). This experience is tellingly located in an "unknown land" as if its remoteness from materiality alone can ensure its purity and perfection. The women themselves are not described in any detail, nor are they endowed with any agency in the exchange; instead, they symbolize a feminine principle of plenitude and union. Ironically, when the narrator comes back to reality, his first instinct is to run from these women, from any claims they may make on him, or any possibility of a continuing relationship with them.

How are we to understand the narrator's contradictory idealization of femininity as gratifying and rejuvenating and as containing and regressive? After the passage to America, Carlos symbolically resolves this contradiction by racializing the maternal principle, identifying its sustenance with white women and its regressive, constraining attributes with nonwhite women.

In one such instance, Teresa, José's wife, whom Carlos has just met, bursts into tears after escorting Carlos to his hotel room. Carlos, appalled, sees in her grief a generalized predicament rather than an individual response. His hysterical response to her seems to be disproportionate to the tenuousness of their contact and the brevity of their association. In an impassioned outpouring, he describes what her tears signify to him:

> Why were *the women in my world* always crying? Was there too much frustration in their lives? Were they hungry for compassion? I remembered my sisters: they, too, were always weeping. What was it that made them all cry? I remember my mother crying when my sister Irene died with the unfinished polka dot dress in her little hands.
>
> I was to run from crying women, because I was afraid they would evoke emotion in me. I was afraid of such emotions because they emanated from pity. I hardened myself against pity. And so in later years . . . I hurled contempt at women who tried to arouse deep emotions in me. I flung against them the tides of my hate, and when they started to weep, I only increased my bitterness. *I thought it was the only way for me to live: to stand free, to walk unhindered across the land.* (*AIH*, 258, emphasis mine)

Apart from the oblique reference to Teresa as representative of "the women of my world," Carlos's response seems on the surface to be only a reaction to feminine suffering. But the formulation "women of my world" codes a racial identification that is crucial to understanding the narrator's hysterical feelings of panic. Teresa's vulnerability is certainly less than that of some of the white women he encounters, such as the young girl who is raped in a box car. Yet in that situation, Carlos eagerly extends his protection to the helpless woman and actively identifies with her pain, even transmuting it into poetry through the plaintive rhetoric of his description: "There was a sudden rush of warm feeling in me, yearning to comfort her with the words I knew. This ravished girl and this lonely night, in a freight train bound for an unknown city" (*AIH*, 114). He continues in this vein after her departure: "Innocent-looking she was, and forlorn, and I felt there was a bond between us, a bond of fear and a common loneliness" (*AIH*, 115). In the incident with the white girl, Carlos gets hurt in the attempt to protect her yet is still able to conceive an intensely empathetic bond for her, a bond based on what he characterizes as their "common" loneliness and fear. It is as if by identifying with the white girl's predicament, Carlos gains access to a *universal* realm of suffering. But in the incident with Teresa, identification with the nonwhite woman's suffering signifies the reverse—relegation to a realm outside the universal. Carlos reveals that he has to actively dis-identify and sever connections with Teresa in order to attain "freedom," which he defines as individualism and self-sufficiency. Contrary to Carlos's assertion that he reacts to "women" who arouse pity in him by disdaining them, the text makes clear that he only reacts to some women like that, women who are nonwhite like himself. Is the racial dissociation with some women then a way of abjecting those attributes in himself that he thinks threaten his survival in America? Interestingly, the desire to dis-identify with the nonwhite woman is mythified as a fulfillment of a Crusoe-like ideal of manhood and solitariness, "to stand free, to walk unhindered across the land." The entry into a quintessentially American ideal of the "unencumbered self" is gained by leaving the nonwhite woman behind.

The representation of Carlos's relationships with women demarcates the possibilities of affinity through a racialized imaginary. In the above two instances, the women were nonwhite, the first a Filipina and the second a Mexican. In his relationships with white women, one notices a conspicuous reversal; the narrator's desire for these women renders them both of this world and not of this world, simultaneous embodiments of a feminine principle of compassion and tenderness that transcends the contaminations of worldliness and yet, as *white* women, guarantors of his masculinity and his belonging in America. Moreover, the white women incarnate the maternal principle, recalling the mother's presence and imaginatively enabling his naturalization in the alien land. Rather than expressing a hysterical desire to free himself of them, the protagonist yearns after the white women he encounters, pleading for their return even after they abandon him and offering himself as their protector when they are in need. The mother's presence is recollected not only in the ministrations of the almost otherworldly figures of Mary and Marian but also in the secular embodiments of maternity, women who serve as intellectual guides and muses in Carlos's journey through the world of politics and literature: Mary Strandon, Eileen and Alice Odell, Harriet Monroe, Dora Travers, Jean Doyle, Julia, and others.

The prohibition on miscegenation positioned white women both as the biological reproducers of the nation and as the reproducers of the boundary of their national group.[54] Thus, the sexuality of white women was harnessed legally and socially to the imperative to guarantee the future of America as a white nation. It appears that prohibitions on miscegenation create a profound ambivalence about racial and national identity in Bulosan's writing that is symbolically resolved through the deeply invested and idealized inscriptions of the white woman's body. The white woman's presence is so heavily charged with the force of these prohibitions that Carlos can only see her as a screen that reflects the meanings of his own racial identity. Carlos describes meeting Eileen Odell every week for three years, yet in spite of their proximity and intimacy over this extended period of time, she remains an elusive, hazily defined figure in his writings, more the creature of his fantasies and anxieties than a complex individual:

> I created for myself *an illusion of understanding* with Eileen, and in consequence, I yearned for *her* and *the world she represented*. The grass in the hospital yard spoke of her, and when it rained, the water rushed down the eaves calling her name. I told her these things in poems, and my mind became afire: could I get well for Eileen? Could I walk with her in the street without being ashamed because of my race? Could I see her always without fear? (*AIH*, 234, emphasis mine)

In summarizing the meaning of their relationship, Carlos recounts, "She was undeniably the America I had wanted to find in those frantic days of fear and flight, in those acute hours of hunger and loneliness. This America was human, good, real" (*AIH*, 235).

As a result of the racialization of maternity and nurture after the protagonist's arrival in America, the interracial romance comes to serve as the primary mechanism for naturalizing the Filipino's claim on America. But because this text was written at a time when miscegenation was outlawed, possibly as a built-in defense against misappropriations of his text, Bulosan insists upon the platonic nature of Carlos's relationships with white women. Hints of sensuality and eroticism are clearly repressed and often subsumed within an overarching maternity or intellectualism. Although Carlos describes women who are socially very different from one another, including prostitutes, farm girls, shop assistants, political activists, and intellectuals, they are all shown as sharing certain attributes of purity, gentleness, compassion, and self-sacrifice. They come to serve as a composite portrait of an ideal of femininity seen as synonymous with America. In this context, Marian's last words to Carlos before she dies are richly evocative: "And if you meet someone that you could like, take her with you and remember my face in hers" (*AIH*, 217). The series of white women whom Carlos comes to know and care for echo one another, not so much in particulars, as in a truth that they confirm about the capacity of the human heart. The white woman's responsiveness to him and recognition of him, then, not only guarantees his masculinity in a world that continually negates it, but interracial intimacy emerges as the utopian ground for alternative imaginings of community.

The maternal ideal is also displaced onto representations of the American landscape, which by association with maternity and fecundity becomes appropriable, a potential space of belonging for the exiled son. This displacement produces a reinscription of what Annette Kolodny has called the "American pastoral," a long masculine tradition of American writing about the land as feminine, maternal, and regenerative. Summarizing the pastoral impulses that were organized into this collective vision of America, Kolodny writes that within the American pastoral, "The soul's home . . . is that place where the conditions of exile—from Eden or from some primal harmony with the Mother—do not obtain; it is a realm of nurture, abundance, and unalienated labor within which all men are truly brothers."[55]

In *America Is in the Heart*, the pastoral is transformed into an impassioned political paean proclaiming the Filipino's home in America. In this postcolonial renarration of the American pastoral, the elemental tie between the migrant farmworkers and the land their labor makes fecund becomes emblematic of a new vision of fraternity and nationhood. The maternal associations with the land enable the exiled protagonist to assert belonging in America and alleviate the pain of alienation. In the text, the maternal associations of the land also appear to be unique to the American landscape and the bounty of its soil. Interestingly enough, while the land in the United States is represented as feminine and nurturing, the land in the Philippines is depicted in radically different terms. In his memory of the Philippines, the land is associated not with the mother but with the father and his lost patrimony: "The soil, and my father's faith." In the Philippines, the mother's labor on the land and her connection with it are emblematic of the emasculation of the father and their collective dispossession. Carlos leaves home because their tiny holding is lost to them, and his father is powerless to reclaim it. The beauty of the land is recollected with nostalgia and poignant longing in the text, but that beauty is not rendered in a specifically feminine way, as it is in the U.S. landscape.

The beauty of the American land is reiterated throughout the text, setting up a contrast between the eternal and timeless beauty of nature (emblematizing a feminine temporality) and the brutality and oppression of a *man*-made social world. Time and time again, Carlos escapes violence or degradation by taking a boxcar out of the city and heading to another destination. These moments of passage, ephemeral as they are, offer him a reprieve, opening up the vistas of nature, the vast darkness of the night sky, the calm magnificence of the moonlight, themselves visible manifestations of a natural order that offers a vision of harmony and peace. In one such instance, Carlos desperately flees from a shelter for destitute men. He boards a freight train and pushes the door open to look outside: "I wanted to shout with joy, but could not open my mouth, so awestruck I was by the moonlight. I looked into the bright night sky. . . . I heard the metallic cry of the freight train, and I knew that heaven could not be far from the earth" (*AIH*, 155). The contrast between the natural and the social world that is worked into the text builds on the gendered representation of American nationhood and reinforces the significance of the Filipino worker's labor, labor that emphasizes a closeness to a maternal nature and makes it fruitful. The elaboration of these associations over the course of the narrative allows for the transformation of the American pastoral into a vehicle for a radical political vision in which the Filipino worker's connection to the American soil renders him its *native* son and comes to symbolize a fraternal order based on noncompetitive and unalienated labor. It is fitting, then, that *America Is in the Heart* culminates with a vision of a crew of Filipino pea pickers hailing the narrator as he drives past on a bus:

> I wanted to shout good-bye to the Filipino pea pickers in the fields who stopped working when the bus came into view. . . . They looked toward the highway and raised their hands. One of them, who looked like my brother Amado, took off his hat. . . . There was a sweet fragrance in the air. . . .
>
> I glanced out of the window again to look at the broad land I had dreamed so much about, only to discover with astonishment that the American earth was like a huge heart unfolding warmly to receive me. (*AIH*, 326)

The idealized figures of the Filipino pea pickers become emblematic of a new vision of fraternity and nationhood that more fully embodies the American ideals of equality and democracy. Carlos characterizes this moment of recognition of his and his brothers' place in America as his "discovery" of America, and this discovery is experienced as a suffusion with the warmth of the maternal earth.

However, it is worth noting that although this passage emphasizes union with the earth, it eschews the association of union with possession and ownership and thus avoids what Annette Kolodny has called the "pastoral paradox": "Implicit in the metaphor of the land-as-woman was both the regressive pull of maternal containment *and* the seductive invitation to sexual assertion: if the Mother demands passivity, and threatens regression, the Virgin invites sexual assertion and awaits impregnation."[56] But perhaps because of Carlos's conscious desire to avoid the pitfalls of the "swamp of a culture based on property" his longing for intimacy with the land struggles to purge itself of possessiveness (*AIH*, 266). It is perhaps for this reason that one notices a discernible shift toward the end of *America Is in the Heart,* where Carlos distinguishes between his earlier longing to claim the land for his own and the more diffuse attachment he feels in his later years: "I also felt attached to the land, but it was now a different attachment. In the years long gone it was merely a desire to possess a plot of the earth and to draw nourishment from it. But now this desire to possess, after long years of flight and disease and want, had become an encompassing desire to *belong* to the land—perhaps to the whole world" (*AIH*, 273). Carlos's longing is reversed from a desire that the earth belong to him to a desire to belong to the earth.

The confident hubris of ownership is supplanted by a mature recognition of the primacy of the earth over any human claim to it. Exclusion and rootlessness, the two defining experiences in opposition to which Carlos asserts the right to place, are radically reconceptualized. Rather than providing a negative mode of being-in-the-world, a sign of powerlessness, they enable him to understand rootlessness as a form of freedom and potential community. The focus shifts from belonging to America to belonging to the whole world; the latter mode of belonging is sustained by Carlos's union organizing and reading. Carlos gives eloquent expression to this recognition in a conversation with his brother Macario: "It's much easier for us who have no roots to integrate ourselves in a universal ideal. Were we not exiles, were we not socially strangled in America, we would never have understood the significance of the Civil War in Spain" (*AIH*, 241). The protagonist, therefore, moves from a commitment to the nation as the primary locus of identification to a yearning for transnational forms of solidarity yet unborn, to which, however, he affixes the proper name America. The America that is in the heart is both a specific nation and an anticipation of an imagined political community that transcends the nation.

While Bulosan's idea of fraternity represents a universal ideal of equality and liberty, its production is structured on a gendered imaginary. Thus, Bulosan's reliance on the plot of the heterosexual romance as a framework for normalizing Filipino masculinity and asserting a generative claim to national belonging produces a vision of political community that reinforces conventional gender ideologies. Although some of the white women he writes about—such as Dora Travers and Harriet Monroe—are activists, poets, writers, and intellectuals, they assume passive roles as muses or guides in Bulosan's symbolic schema and are cut off from any agency in the republic of letters that is conceived as a fraternity, "the worlds of great men's living minds": "So from day to day I read, and reading widened my mental horizon, creating a spiritual kinship with other men who had pondered over the miseries of their countries" (*AIH*, 245).

Allegorized as symbolic bearers of the nation, women are denied any direct connection to national agency. The public political sphere, whether that is the world of revolutionary ideas or of political activism, is conceived as a fraternity in *America Is in the Heart*—the sphere of change, progress, and nation-making. By contrast, the feminine is associated with care, self-sacrifice, and love and identified with a timeless world of generation and renewal. In this dichotomous representation of the nation, Bulosan's vision of America reproduces the gender differences that undergird many other impassioned national imaginings of peoplehood. While vehemently asserting the symbolic centrality of women to the nation, this rhetoric relegates them to the margins of the polity. Drawing on Benedict Anderson's insights, Deniz Kandiyoti points out that "the very language of nationalism singles women out as the symbolic repository of group identity" because the nationalist project uses the language of kinship and home to highlight the "natural" affinities of national solidarity.[57]

As I have shown earlier, the spatial displacement experienced by the postcolonial protagonist is alleviated through the comforting continuity signified by the maternal principle first embodied in the Filipina peasant mother and later in the white women who supersede her, enabling Carlos to figure the alien land as a kind of "home." One could conjecture that for the migrant subject the investment in a quasi-mythical feminine principle of continuity in the face of spatial and temporal displacement is even more intense because this subject cannot draw on the nation's past to assert belonging in the new land—thus, the correspondingly greater investment in asserting a role in the nation's future. Speaking of how the bonds of national love are imagined, Nira Yuval-Davis foregrounds the importance of the future in securing the attachments of immigrants to their adopted homes: "People construct themselves as members of national collectivities not just because they and their forbears have shared a past, but also because they believe their futures are interdependent. It can explain the subjective sense of commitment of people into collectivities and nations . . . and can also explain individual and communal assimilations in other nations."[58]

However, to reclaim the humanity of the Filipino subject negated by colonial discourse, Bulosan represents it through ideas of subjectivity produced within hegemonic institutions, thereby engendering a desiring subject incorporated within the plot of interracial heterosexual familialism. The representation of his ideal of America through this desiring subject creates a gap between the desire for an egalitarian ideal called America and the emplotment of that desire through a gendered imaginary.[59]

FOUR

Sex Acts as Assimilation Acts: Female Power and Passing in Bharati Mukherjee's *Wife* and *Jasmine*

> There's a difference between exotic and foreign, isn't there? Exotic means you know how to use your foreignness, or you make yourself a little foreign in order to appear exotic.
>
> —Bharati Mukherjee, "Fighting for the Rebound"

Nearly a century separates John Luther Long's "Madame Butterfly" (1898) and Bharati Mukherjee's re-narrations of the white-Asian interracial romance in her novels *Wife* (1975) and *Jasmine* (1989).[1] Although Long's story was written when antmiscegenation laws and anti-Asian exclusion movements defined Asians as aliens, and Mukherjee's novels were published after racial restrictions on Asian immigration were lifted (1965) and antimiscegenation laws were declared unconstitutional (1968), both writers use the naturalizing discourse of sexuality to establish the legitimacy of the Asian claim to the United States. This suggests that despite the legal changes in the status of Asian Americans during this time, their place in America is still in need of validation.

In the development of the white-Asian interracial romance over the twentieth century, narratives of the white man—Asian woman dyad emerged as the dominant form of the interracial romance, while the white woman—Asian man narrative became the recessive form. Stories of interracial desire centered on the white man—Asian woman dyad lent themselves more readily to establishing the assimilability of Asians, thus revealing the gender hierarchies underlying fictional representations of racialized sexuality.

My analysis of Long's story and Mukherjee's novels shows how their Orientalist constructions of Asian women's exoticism mediate a cultural crisis in the bourgeois sexual order: in the former instance, by using the Japanese woman's pure desire for the American sailor to criticize male sexual license and immorality; and in the latter, by depicting Asian American femininity as an eroticized and domesticated alternative to white femininity and as embodying the archetypal American aspirations of desire and mobility.[2] However, while *Jasmine* appears to celebrate the emancipatory possibilities of self-Orientalizing eroticism—the idea that "exotic means you know how to use your foreignness"—the novel is riven with the strains of embracing the vision of sexualized racial impersonation as empowerment. Underneath the triumphalist Americanization of the heroine's manifest sentiments is a repressed narrative of the costs of assimilation. The contradictions in Mukherjee's novel *Jasmine* suggest that contrary to what critics and author have said, *Jasmine* is not a novel of assimilation but a novel of passing. However, in the postmodern, multicultural United States of the 1980s, passing does not involve looking white or even necessarily acting white. Rather, it involves acting out the dominant scripts of exotic otherness as an avenue to the American Dream.

A comparison between the trajectories of the two heroines dramatizes the connection Mukherjee makes between exoticism and sexual agency. The title of the earlier novel, *Wife,* establishes the parameters within which the heroine Dimple Dasgupta's emergence will be articulated. Dimple has an arranged marriage to a respectable Bengali man and lives briefly with her extended family in India before emigrating with her husband to New York. Dimple, who longed for marriage primarily because she thought it would bring her greater autonomy and a more glamorous existence, is bitter at the lack of privacy and the auxiliary role she plays in the extended family household. Hoping for freedom and escape in her new life in the United States, she finds that the constraints of the joint family are unexpectedly re-created in the suffocating proximity of the Indian immigrant community. To the oppressiveness of her derivative identity as wife is added the burden of preserving ethnic identity within the home and shoring up her insecure husband's masculinity in an alien culture. Her husband accompanies her on most of her excursions outside the home, and the only form in which America is allowed to enter her apartment is through the television screen or the avid consumerism that becomes the index of success among the immigrants. Through an outgoing Indian friend, Ina, Dimple meets an American man, Milt, with whom she has a brief affair; he sees Dimple as beautiful and sexy and appears to open up possibilities that she is too timid to pursue. At a party, she also meets an alluring couple, Marsha and Prodosh Mookerji.

Tantalized but intimidated by their intellectual sophistication, Dimple observes and converses with them but is too shy to develop the friendship. Lonely, bitter, and cut off from the outside world she yearns to explore, Dimple descends into madness and, in a fit of hallucinatory rage, murders her husband. At the end of the novel, she thinks wistfully of how the heroines on soap operas get away with murder.

Jasmine appears on the surface to be the antithesis of Dimple Dasgupta. She starts her life as Jyoti, a poor village girl who longs for the larger world outside Hasnapur, Punjab, where she lives. Instead of having an arranged marriage, Jyoti falls in love with and marries the idealistic Prakash, who calls his young wife Jasmine to urge her to outgrow her former village ways. They plan on emigrating to the United States, but Prakash is killed by Sukkhi, a Sikh terrorist, just before he leaves. Jasmine decides to complete Prakash's "mission" by traveling to America to commit sati by immolating herself. She travels with fake papers to Tampa, where she is raped on her first night in the United States by Half-Face, a Vietnam veteran who traffics in illegal immigrants. Jasmine, ritually assuming the aspect of the Hindu goddess, Kali, murders her rapist. Her violent rebirth in America transforms her understanding of her mission, and she rejects suicide for a new beginning. She finds her way to New York and lives briefly in the Indian ethnic enclave in Flushing but leaves to escape her tight, cloistered life there. She then works as a nanny for a white professional couple, Wylie and Taylor Hayes, and their adopted daughter, Duff. Wylie and Taylor separate, and Taylor falls in love with Jasmine, giving her a new name for her new life, Jase. She settles into her family life but is spotted by Sukkhi, the Sikh terrorist who killed her husband. She flees to Iowa and finds a bank job; there her boss, Bud Ripplemeyer, ravished by her exotic beauty, abandons his wife of many years, Karin, and moves in with her. He names her Jane Ripplemeyer. They adopt a Vietnamese boy named Du, but soon after, Bud is shot by a farmer, becomes paralyzed, and is confined to a wheelchair. A while later, Du leaves the Ripplemeyers to reunite with his sister in California. By this time, Taylor and Duff track down a now-pregnant Jase/Jane in Iowa and ask her to move with them to California. Jane lights out for the California frontier, carrying with her Bud's unborn child, exhilarated at the prospect of her new life with Taylor and Duff.

Both Mukherjee's novels explore the prospects for female power within the context of gender roles in the Indian immigrant community and the mainstream. In these narratives, interracial intimacy is contrasted to intrara-cial intimacy and emerges as a space for exploring new opportunities for female empowerment through the use of exotic sexuality. While Dimple allows herself only a brief tryst with a white lover, Jasmine embraces the pos-sibilities of immersion in the American mainstream through a series of rela-tionships with white men. The celebratory tone of *Jasmine* seems to affirm the sexual agency available to Asian American women within interracial relationships in the multicultural United States. The sexual agency that Mukherjee's *Jasmine* so headily seizes is identified with a cultural script of Asian American femininity that emerged in the late 1970s, and which I call the *sexual model minority*. What is revealing about the novel that celebrates this cultural script is that its affirmative discourse masks the psychological costs of assimilation that the text dare not name, but which erupt periodi-cally in episodes of seemingly agent-less violence.

The dynamics of the sexual model minority illuminate the contradictions of Mukherjee's overt celebration of assimilation. Cultural theorists have writ-ten extensively about the dominant construction of Asian Americans as model minorities in the 1970s as a counter to black charges of systematic and structural racism in the United States. They note that conservative critics used the economic success of some Asian American groups to deny the exis-tence of racial oppression in the United States, citing Asian American thrift, hard work, educational success, and family cohesiveness as proof that race was not an obstacle to achieving the American Dream.[3] The entry of many highly educated, middle-class Asians into the United States after the passage of the Immigration Act of 1965 (which privileged highly skilled immigrants) reinforced perceptions that Asian Americans were culturally equipped for success. Hitherto, analyses of the model minority stereotype have focused exclusively on the intersections of race and class. But I argue that changing meanings of Asian American gender and sexual identity and the growing sexual capital of Asian American women converged to produce an image of Asian American women as sexual model minorities. This was one of several images of Asian American femininity produced at the conjuncture of mul-ticulturalism and the reconstruction of family values in the 1970s, but it became pivotal because it served to mediate a cultural crisis in the bourgeois sexual order. John D'Emilio and Estelle B. Freedman identify the 1970s as the period of the collapse of sexual liberalism and the emergence of new con-servative proponents of marital and sexual propriety.[4] Mukherjee's *Jasmine* can be read as a complex negotiation with these changing racial and sexual values. As I have argued throughout this book, scripts of interracial desire do their cultural work by reconstructing racial boundaries *and* sexual norms and, in doing so, reformulate the meanings of national identity.

The genealogy of the sexual model minority can be traced to the century that separates John Luther Long's and Bharati Mukherjee's representations of the white man–Asian woman dyad. Cho-Cho-San, the Japanese geisha of Long's "Madame Butterfly," is a sexual commodity who exists outside the parameters of possible marriage or Americanization. Jasmine, by contrast, figures the sexual capital of the Asian American woman produced at the intersection of post-1965 new immigration, globalization, and multicultur-alism.[5] In the time span separating these two texts, the relative value of the Asian American woman's sexuality in comparison to the white woman's sex-uality has also changed: While Cho-Cho-San is seen as an inappropriate marriage partner for Pinkerton and is easily displaced by Adelaide, Jasmine is seen as more desirable and more marriageable than the white women she displaces in her several relationships with white men. Between these two texts, one can trace a particular trajectory in which the Asian American woman moves from being a sexual commodity to becoming the possessor of *sexual capital.*

By sexual capital, I refer to the aggregate of attributes that index desir-ability within the field of romantic or marital relationships in a given culture and thereby affect the life-chances and opportunities of an individual. Like the other forms of capital that Pierre Bourdieu calls social and cultural cap-ital, sexual capital involves certain nonmarket processes that have economic effects.[6] Sexual capital, like social and cultural capital, is linked but not reducible to economic capital. I coin the term *sexual capital* to highlight the impact of gender and sexuality on mobility and to identify a particular set of constraints within which individuals function as agents.

Social and political changes within the United States contributed toward the rearticulation of the meanings of Asian American femininity. The breakdown of overt racial barriers following civil rights struggles, the posi-tioning of Asian Americans as model minorities, the valorization of multi-culturalism, and the celebration of ethnic difference created a more varied terrain within which racial, sexual, and class difference produce the possi-bilities of Americanization. In addition, the women's movement effected

significant shifts in women's status and provided women greater sexual freedom; it opened up the public sphere to their participation and severed the
connection between domesticity and passionless femininity. Within this
transformed social landscape, Asian American femininity accrued sexual
capital because when white American men were assailed by growing demands for equality made by white American women, the Asian American
woman came to stand in for the more traditional model of family-centered
femininity challenged by feminists.[7] Furthermore, through her association
with the model minority, the Asian American woman was also differentiated
from the black woman, who was linked to matriarchal, emasculating, and
socially dysfunctional forms of femininity. The stereotypes of black femininity were reinforced by Daniel Patrick Moynihan's controversial study, *The
Negro Family: The Case for National Action*, which highlighted the prevalence
of black female-headed households, out-of-wedlock births, welfare dependency, and poverty.[8]

Thus, by a long and circuitous route we arrive at a postmodern American
moment when Asian American women's sexuality—earlier defined as extraterritorial because the sexual license it represented had to be excluded from
the moral order of the nation and marriage—is by the late twentieth century
domesticated to mediate a crisis for the white bourgeois sexual order. As a
result, a sexualized, gendered sign of racial difference (the Asian American
woman) comes to buttress and revive a besieged ideal of the *American* family.

Moreover, since contemporary ideals of companionate marriage celebrate
sexual vitality and eroticism *within* marriage, the Asian American woman,
once a figure for sexual freedom *outside* marriage, has now become emblematic of the perfect match between family-centrism and sex appeal. Thus, the
very racial difference that marks Cho-Cho-San as traditional represents, by
the end of the following century, a desirable feminine attribute that can
counter modern feminist challenges to white masculinity. I would describe
the structural position and function of this image of the Asian American
woman as that of a *sexual model minority*. As a sexual model minority, the
Asian American woman cannot entirely displace the white woman, whose
appeal is reinforced by racial privilege and the power of embodying the
norm, but she does, nevertheless, represent a powerfully seductive form of
femininity that can function as a mode of crisis management in the cultural
contest over different meanings of America. This is not to imply at all that

either the objectification of Asian American women has ended or to suggest that they are no longer subject to racism, but it does suggest that the meanings of race and sexuality have been recast.

The cultural script of the sexual model minority sheds light on the ambivalences in Mukherjee's celebration of assimilation. Despite Mukherjee's and the heroine's celebration of sexual agency, the novel *Jasmine* is riven with contradictions between its overt affirmation of assimilation and the violence that accompanies the heroine's progress through America.[9] The contradictions erupt from the tensions between the hunger for female power embodied in the heroine and the assimilationist context within which her strategies for power must be negotiated in the United States. In the U.S. context, Jasmine's earlier resistance to conventional gender roles has to be rearticulated to address the racialization of her identity in the New World. However, while Jasmine's defiance of traditional gender roles is clearly articulated in the Indian section of the novel, the clear-cut feminist critique of the constraints on women's freedom is repressed when Jasmine arrives in the United States, giving way to a rhetoric of optimism about the prospects for self-invention and power. The seemingly inexplicable violence that accompanies the heroine's progress through America, and which the novel attributes to the agency of Fate, is a displacement of the violence the heroine feels against the male figures who embody the expectations she enacts. Thus, I read *Jasmine* as a story of female rage against conformity to gender and racial roles that is repressed to produce a story of willing assimilation.

Viewing *Jasmine* as a novel of passing rather than of assimilation clarifies the shape-shifting strategy the heroine adopts as she literally tries to move through America undetected. The idea of passing also helps identify the strategy Mukherjee adopts in trying to position herself as an "American" writer and earn a place in the canon. Mukherjee has insistently and repeatedly claimed that *Jasmine* is an exuberantly assimilationist fable about contemporary Americanization: "I don't think about my fiction as being about alienation. On the contrary, I mean for it to be about assimilation."[10] Author and heroine both claim to embrace assimilation and represent assimilation through a discourse of consent, however, the textual ruptures clearly reveal the contradictions this entails. Rather than take these professions literally, they may be viewed as strategic affirmations of the dominant fiction of the immigrant's desire for America, itself an ideological construct for the reproduction of nationalism.

Interracial Romance and Female Power

> All the way on the subway to Queens she stared discreetly at black and brown girls in leather jackets. . . . Sometimes she put herself in their places, pretending that Amit with his oily hair and thin little mustache was a "dude" with a comb in his hip pocket, and making up stories that she would not have made up if she had thought of herself as Dimple Basu or even Dimple Dasgupta. When they arrived at the Sens' apartment, Dimple was still seeing herself as a high-breasted black woman in thick gold earrings and very short curly hair.
>
> —Bharati Mukherjee, *Wife*

Both *Wife* and *Jasmine* are structured around a contrast between interracial love and intraracial love and use the movement of the heroine from one space to the other to explore the possibilities for female power in both sites. *Wife* and *Jasmine* are structured around a double movement: on the one hand, an effort or compulsion toward erasing or shedding gendered ethnic identities, a desire *to move away from* a space of constraint; on the other hand, an effort or compulsion *to move toward* a less circumscribed space, a "frontier" or unbounded space of desire, identified as being outside the ethnic community and symbolized through sexual relationships with white men. But while the first movement inscribes a clear-cut trajectory because the sources of oppression are easily identifiable (Indian patriarchal traditions), the second movement is a heady yet uncertain one, sustained by the momentum of the flight from a prior identity and the will to imagine the existence of uninscribed spaces of pure possibility and yet continuously disrupted by sudden and seemingly irrational eruptions of violence.

Reading *Wife* and *Jasmine* as assimilation acts highlights the author's preoccupation with the indirect rather than direct acquisition of female power within ethnic communities or the mainstream. The two novels do not depict the struggles of women who forge their own identities in pursuit of independent goals; rather, they focus on women who acquire power through men by inhabiting roles produced by the desires of men. The emphasis is on the self-awareness of the women about the roles they play, their attempt to occupy these roles to gain power or wrest belonging, and the representation of a subjectivity that exceeds each role that Dimple or Jasmine assume. By contrast, the men in their lives see the heroines as being identical with the roles they play. This difference in perception opens up the possibility of wielding a limited power by allowing their true or other identities to remain undisclosed until the heroine so chooses. Thus, in *Jasmine*, although the heroine plays the role of the assimilated Jane Ripplemeyer to Bud's satisfaction, she is capable of suddenly and abruptly abandoning the identity when she is ready to move on with someone else. Her next identity remains uncertain, but assimilation is depicted as a provisional accommodation with necessity on the road to more extravagant possibilities. But while it lasts, "love" is what she and Bud call it. Thus, in *Jasmine*, passing enables a deferral, a way of choosing neither assimilation nor ethnic separatism after temporarily adopting both scripts. Mukherjee focuses keenly on the limitations or constraints of already existing gender and racial identities and often takes characters to a moment of rupture or crisis when existing roles have been outgrown, but she seldom depicts the process of constructing new selves in her fiction. Mukherjee's dramatization of the predicament of being between roles and of all roles as being provisional and contingent reinforces the affinities between her two novels and narratives of passing.

The contradiction between a triumphalist rhetoric of American self-invention and the necessity of occupying identities invented by others creates a paradox of power that the text struggles to contain—the paradox of producing willed submission to a particular role as an exercise of liberty. A strategy of passing in which the heroine consents to inhabiting roles for a limited time allows Mukherjee to avoid addressing the tensions of the paradox of willed submission by simply redefining coercion as consent. Thus, while most narratives of passing directly expose the enormous psychological cost of mimicry, Mukherjee's espousal of the archetypal American myths leads her to repress the acknowledgment of these costs in service of a fable of endless optimism and hope. But the tension imposed by a narrative of consent erupts again and again in disguised form, often as seemingly random and inexplicable violence. In an astute critique of perceptions that passing can be constituted as an act of choice, Cheryl Harris offers an eloquent reminder: "The economic coercion of white supremacy on self-definition nullifies any suggestion that passing is a logical exercise of liberty or self-identity. The decision to pass as white was not a choice, if by that word one means voluntarism or lack of compulsion. The fact of race subordination was coercive and circumscribed the liberty to self-define."[11] Harris's comments serve as a crucial counterpoint to the heady and exuberant discourse of self-invention that *Jasmine* embraces.

The negotiation of coercion and consent in the search for female power is the central theme of *Wife* and *Jasmine*. The complexity of these negotiations is compounded because they take place in the movement from the scene of intraracial desire to the scene of interracial desire and because of the charged ideology of romantic love, which treats such love as synonymous with choice. This becomes particularly clear in the contrast between the clarity of the feminist critique in *Wife* and the ambivalences of the "feminist" critique in *Jasmine*. I qualify the framing of *Jasmine* as a feminist critique despite Mukherjee's insistence that it is one. In *Jasmine*, the heroine's reliance on gaining power through men and through the use of her exotic sexuality make it problematic to define her empowerment as feminist.

It is also important to note that the idealized and successful representations of interracial love in Mukherjee's texts are between white women and Indian men (Prodosh and Marsha in *Wife*, Venn and Beagh in *The Holder of the World*); the scene of desire between the Indian woman and the white man, the subject of *Wife* and *Jasmine,* is a more ambivalent one.[12] That the interracial romance between the Indian woman and the white man offers the more fraught site in representations of interracial desire suggests that the tension arises from the conflict between feminist concerns and assimilationist maneuvers.

Wife and *Jasmine* are both stories about female rage at the constraints gender roles place on female desire, sexuality, and power. In both stories, when the object of critique is ethnic sexism, the depiction of these constraints is clear and graphic, as are the acts by which the heroine breaks free of these roles. In *Wife* and *Jasmine*, however, the critique of white patriarchy, which defines the space into which the heroines escape, is obscured by a rhetoric of consenting romantic love that celebrates the space of interracial desire as the space of freedom and emancipation for the Indian woman. But the movement into the mainstream should not be read as an assimilationist move but rather as a strategy of *passing as assimilationist* in order to secure a provisional foothold, from where other yearnings, camouflaged during the moment of passing, can be pursued. Thus, on the one hand, Jasmine's ostensible embrace of assimilation mutes the novel's critique of white patriarchy, but the heroine's repressed rage erupts in the violence that is inexplicably visited on all her male consorts. It is not a coincidence that the moment of Jasmine's initiation into America is symbolized by her incarnation as Kali, the uncontained divine female energy of destruction and creation. Kali is the dark double of the Asian American love goddess of white fantasy, in whose form Jasmine passes undetected through America and through whose sexuality the romance with America can be secured. The need to disguise the critique of white patriarchy and obscure the costs of assimilation is linked to the projection of *Jasmine* as an exuberant fable about contemporary Americanization.

Passing As a Wife: Cultural Purism and Transgressive Desire in Wife

Although on the surface *Wife* and *Jasmine* seem antithetical to each other, the former dealing with a narrative of "failed" Americanization and the latter dealing with a story of triumphalist Americanization, an analysis of the intersection of feminism and interracial desire in both stories reveals that the difference between the two texts may not be as clear-cut as it first appears. Interracial romance can be idealized only when it functions as a spectral presence, an ideal, discernible from within the text, but always lying outside it, a future destination, but by that very definition always elsewhere. Actually existing interracial romances, however, are a minefield in Mukherjee's texts, which celebrate their possibilities and repress their contradictions through the rhetoric of voluntarism or choice.

The struggles with self-transformation dramatized in *Wife* provide a dress rehearsal for the path into America elaborated in *Jasmine*. *Wife* follows a heroine who is cast into a completely passive role in the arrangements for her marriage and then moves to occupy a prescribed role as a wife. The conflict between what she desires and what she has is exacerbated by her emigration to the United States, where again she anticipates new freedoms only to find herself trapped within the rigid conformities of the Indian immigrant community. At Dimple's first party in New York, when she is offered a drink, she is acutely conscious that the appropriate response for her would be to refuse: "She felt that Amit was waiting for just the right answer, that it was up to her to uphold Bengali womanhood, marriage and male pride" (*Wife* [hereafter, *W*], 78). The pressure of constraints on Dimple's consciousness is intensified by her growing awareness of alternative possibilities for transformation and autonomy in the social world around her. But these alternatives are associated in her mind and in the minds of most of the others in the community with what is "alien" and "impure"; to pursue those possibilities would amount to a dangerous racial and sexual transgression, a betrayal of her Indianness and a repudiation of her role as a wife.

The interracial marriage between Marsha and Prodosh Mookerji serves as an emblem of the transgressive possibilities for desire, growth, and power, which Dimple cannot even articulate to herself at the beginning. The couple appear at the party when Dimple makes her first excursion "into" America, and their sophistication, intellectualism, and understated elegance serve primarily to expose the crude chauvinism of many of the Indian husbands and offer Dimple a seductive though frightening glimpse of alternatives that will take on progressively greater resonance. Their effect on Dimple is to bring to crisis her assumptions about womanhood, marriage, and duty: "Marsha, though she was taller than Amit and maybe as tall as Jyoti, was delicately built, with a face that Dimple thought of as intelligent before she could assess its beauty. Even this was troubling. Dimple had been brought up to think of women as only beautiful, pretty, or good mothers. Marsha was fair, tall and slim—the prerequisites for Indian beauty—but excessively so" (*W*, 80). Distressed by the threat to her worldview signified by this marriage, Dimple tries to dismiss Prodosh's decision to marry a white woman instead of an Indian woman chosen by his parents as a sign of gross selfishness.

The selective Americanization or gendered ghettoization practiced by the Indian immigrant community allows Amit access to American culture to further the couple's economic advancement while requiring Dimple to preserve the home as a space of pure Indianness.[13] This creates a split in Dimple that is manifested as an outward conformity to her prescribed role as a wife but as an internal rebellion against it, enacted through furtive, real, and imaginary forays into American culture, including wearing Western clothes, eating beef, and eventually committing adultery with a white man, who is, tellingly, Marsha's brother. As the split between Dimple's desires and her duty intensifies, and she is unable to challenge Amit openly in renegotiating the boundaries of her role, she identifies him as the absolute barrier to the realization of another identity: "But Amit would always be there beside her in his shiny, ill-fitting suits, acting as her conscience and common sense. It was sad she thought, how marriage cut off glittering alternatives" (*W*, 127). The masquerade of wifely devotion breaks intermittently when, in sudden hysterical rages, Dimple jabs her husband with a knife when he sneaks up on her in an amorous mood then pretends that the actions were accidental.

Even at the end, when Dimple murders Amit, she kills him in a hallucinatory state.

The marriages of Marsha and Prodosh and Dimple and Amit represent opposite modes of Americanization; the centrality of consent in figuring this difference is evident in the opposition between romantic love and arranged marriage. In the last section of *Wife*, Amit and Dimple move temporarily into Marsha and Prodosh's home. The gap between Dimple's desires and her familiar role is dramatized when she wears Marsha's clothes and glasses, enacting a furtive masquerade of an identity she cannot find the will or courage to claim. However, the masquerade as an "American" woman precipitates a consciousness that in her real life "she was so much worse off than ever, more lonely, more cut off from Amit, from the Indians, left only with borrowed disguises" (*W*, 200).

In Marsha's apartment, Dimple has a brief, adulterous affair with Milt. Her relationship with Milt clarifies for her what is missing in her own marriage: Milt's unselfconscious personality and playfulness offer a glaring contrast to the stolid, fractious, and condescending Amit. But Dimple also becomes aware of how their personality differences are linked to differences in power between the two men: Milt's confidence and ease in his own culture contrast with the strained, self-conscious gestures that cramp Amit's masculinity in a foreign country:

> When Milt called for the check (which he did without raising a finger, just a slight up-and-down motion of the neck) she realized how different he was from Amit. Amit did not like eating out in New York and the one time they had gone out for fried chicken, the waiter had kept him deliberately waiting though there had been only one other couple in the restaurant. She had wanted to scream, sitting patiently with a mustached man snapping his fingers. (*W*, 195)

Coupled with her awareness of the power difference between the two men is her consciousness of her relative sexual power over them. Early in their marriage, Amit reminds Dimple that she does not really fulfill his ideal of Indian feminine beauty. In his eyes, and by Indian standards of beauty, she lacks sexual capital. But in Milt's eyes, Dimple finds a heady and different vision of herself: "Dimple, you're the most gorgeous creature in New York—did anyone ever tell you that?" (*W*, 201). Interracial desire is connected to the possibility of greater power through access to mainstream American culture but also to the possibility of power over white American men through the force of an exotic sexuality. As such, the prospect of her increased sexual capital offers Dimple a seductive way out of confinement to the narrow and increasingly constricting gender roles defined by cultural purism. Thus, interracial desire offers an avenue for transforming racial disadvantages into racial assets and thus possessing America. But finally, despite the temptations represented by Milt and Marsha's world, Dimple cannot summon up the energy and strength to pursue an uncharted course. Instead, in rage and despair, she strikes out at the person she has identified as the source of her oppression.

Dimple's difficulties with empowerment extend to her inability to obtain an education. Marsha signifies this possibility, as well as the cosmopolitanism with which it is associated. Dimple's imagination is also haunted by a phantasmic figure who seems to embody this promise of feminist emergence and that resists the binary of assimilation and separatism; but the vision she signifies seems so removed from Dimple's lived reality as a housewife that Dimple is unable to finally embrace this possibility:

> She wished she could begin again, forget. . . . But she would not begin again, because you could build only on things you had already done. She had learned that simple lesson quite painfully in the last few months and she knew that, while there would be the desire for a hundred new starts, there would never be a real beginning. Sitting in the taxi with the window rolled up, she thought she saw the woman she might have been, a smart woman in pale make-up attending a lecture on Introductory Astrophysics. . . . But when the taxi came to a stop . . . the pale lady vanished and thirty plump women in Benarasee saris engulfed her. (*W*, 182)

The insecurities and passivity that hold Dimple back from realizing her desire for power and mobility are quickly shed by the heroine of Mukherjee's later novel, which revisits the questions of female empowerment that *Wife* temporarily resolves.

Karma Chameleon: Romantic Reincarnation in Jasmine

In *Jasmine*, Mukherjee returns to the problem of envisioning feminist emergence. The means of emancipation is the acquisition of power through others rather than the vision fleetingly glimpsed by Dimple, namely, the independent search for fulfillment and transformation. As a consequence, Mukherjee takes up again the negotiation of racial and gender power in the process of Americanization. But unlike in *Wife*, where interracial desire functions as a spectral alternative and briefly experienced counterreality, interracial romance in *Jasmine* provides the framework for the heroine's transformations. While the focus of critique in *Wife* was the gendered constraints of maintaining cultural purism, in *Jasmine* the focus on interracial relationships as the mode of the heroine's Americanization requires the author to confront the question that is elided in *Wife*—the question of the sexualized racial constraints of assimilation. In *Wife*, the relationship between Marsha and Prodosh is idealized presumably because Marsha's racial dominance neutralizes Prodosh's gender dominance, and the equality between them seems to be secured by his progressive ideas and her feminism. Additionally, the relationship between Dimple and Milt is only tangentially developed: It assumes significance for Dimple primarily because it represents an irreversible boundary transgression and because of the unsettling spaciousness, novelty, and indeterminacy it signifies in contrast to her "real" life.

But in *Jasmine*, the heroine works out her transformations within the spaces of interracial desire; the problem that *Wife* does not address has to be confronted in *Jasmine*: Is interracial desire a space of uncircumscribed possibility or does it create different constraints on female power and self-realization? What problems are raised by the coding of interracial eroticism as the medium for the Third World woman's liberation? Mukherjee herself acknowledges the problematic nature of negotiating feminism through sexual conquest but insists on its deployment as a feminist strategy appropriate for her heroine. Describing Jasmine as a "love goddess," in one of her interviews, Mukherjee explains the source and meaning of her sexual power:

> Jasmine is a woman who hopes. . . . I think that's probably what's attractive about her to the Americans around her. Also, she wants to please. That's the feminine quality in her that doesn't jibe with American feminist rhetoric. Yet she's the one who, unlike . . . or far more than Wylie, or any other American woman, manages to leave a futile world, make herself over, pick up men, discard men, and make money. She's an uneducated village girl who is bright and has a career going. She can move on and make a life for herself. So she's an activist—or a woman of action—who ends up being far more feminist than the women on Claremont Avenue who talk about feminism.[14]

The triangulated structure of this argument is revealing because it betrays the problematic articulation of Jasmine's "activism" and "feminism." Jasmine is more desirable than her white American feminist counterparts because her feminism accommodates the desire to "please," and yet by the criteria of autonomy established by American feminism—controlling men, making money, and having a career—Jasmine outperforms her American feminist counterparts. The focus here is on an exorbitant feminism defined *in comparison to* white American women and *in competition for* white men. It is no coincidence that every sexual relationship Jasmine has with a white man displaces a white woman (Mrs. Half-Face, Wylie, and Karin). This triangulated structure positions Jasmine as a sexual model minority, although Mukherjee invokes "Third World feminism" to define her location.

Mukherjee's representations of white American masculinity in *Jasmine* are dichotomous. They include a monstrous evil rapist, Half-Face, and two other white American lovers who are rendered abject by Jasmine's sexual power: Bud, a fifty-year old banker, who is shot in the back and, once handicapped, becomes dependent on her; and Taylor, a divorced professor, who is desperately in love with Jasmine/Jase and willing to follow her anywhere. After the exorcism of monstrous white masculinity through the murder of Half-Face at the moment of Jasmine's arrival in America, the country is represented as a relatively unbounded space for the fulfillment of her dreams through various white men. These representations of white masculinity are a metonym for a particular version of American history as it relates to the place of Asians in the American national imaginary. Half-Face is a Vietnam veteran, who embodies that history as a monstrous aberration, although Mukherjee suggests that the traces of it linger in sporadic bursts of violence and racism in the heart of whiteness. But the monstrous Vietnam veteran embodies a residual evil apart from which white American masculinity is marked by benevolence, even innocence. In an incident that reflects the dualistic representation of white masculinity, Jasmine is taunted by two white men, who seeing an Asian woman with a white man, call her a whore. Bud is outraged by their behavior and knocks them down: "His next words were in something foreign, but probably Japanese or Thai or Filipino, something bar girls responded to in places where he'd spent his rifle-toting youth. I wish I'd known America before it got perverted" (Mukherjee, *Jasmine* [hereafter, *J*], 179). Jasmine's nostalgia for a pre-Vietnam America suggests that the Vietnam War was an exceptional instance in American history. This nostalgia erases the long history of racial oppression in the United States by offering a vision of American innocence in the past and its continuity in the present through white liberalism. *Jasmine* explores the "romantic reincarnation" of the heroine in relation to this dualistic vision of white masculinity.[15]

Jasmine examines the avenues of female empowerment, but there is a fundamental tension between the script of assimilation, which requires conformity to certain sanctioned social roles, and the heroine's desire to rebel against the constraints of existing roles. Thus, the negotiation between gender power and racial power is a complex one in Mukherjee. The tension between feminist concerns and assimilationist maneuvers runs throughout her stories, and although one is never quite subsumed to the other, it is not as easily reconciled through positing a desire to "please," as Mukherjee's definition of an ec-centric feminism suggests. The attribution of a desire to please to the heroine becomes a way of containing a fundamental contradiction of power in Mukherjee's explorations of feminist emergence—the conflict between what her heroines want and what others want of them.

By the time Mukherjee wrote *Jasmine*, she had arrived at an unusual resolution for Dimple's problem. In a curious reversal, she suggests that strategies of oppression can be transformed into strategies of empowerment by an act of will and imagination. Role-playing need not be considered an act of coercion but one of consent, a paradoxical act of willed submission to a particular role. Thus, the heroine is transformed in accordance with the desires of various men through whom she gains power and mobility, and yet, paradoxically, she reiterates that she herself *wants* to fulfill these fantasies. Voluntarism is the key to the reversal that transforms oppression to liberation. For instance, Jasmine remembers her relationship with Prakash as a Pygmalion story: "He wanted to break down the Jyoti I'd been in Hasnapur and make me a new kind of city woman" (*J*, 70). Similarly, her first encounter with Taylor and Wylie is structured around her consciousness of what they imagine her to be: "I wanted to become the person they thought they saw: humorous, intelligent, refined, affectionate. Not illegal, not murderer, not widowed, raped, destitute, fearful" (*J*, 151–52). Her consciousness of the gap between who she is and the role she plays is perhaps most acute in her sexual role-playing with Bud, which reveals his incapacity either to know her fully or satisfy her: "After I prepare him for bed, undo the shoes, pull off the pants, sponge-bathe him, he likes me to change roles, from caregiver to temptress, and I try to do it convincingly, walking differently, frowning, smiling. . . . Now I must do all the playing, provide the surprises. I don't mind" (*J*, 31–32). But the matter-of-fact resignation with which she shrugs off the burden of passing—"I don't mind"—is undercut by the last sentence of this chapter. As a sexually gratified Bud sinks into sleep, Jane lies awake in a room heavy with "unacted drama": "This night I feel torn open like the hot dry soil, parched" (*J*, 33).

The difference between the heroine's perfunctory acknowledgments of her accommodation to role playing and the metaphorical inscriptions of her inner state are mirrored by the disjunction in the text between its overt rhetorical project of celebration and the recurrent eruptions of violence in the plot. Despite Jasmine's quick dismissal of feelings of pain, guilt, remorse, and sorrow throughout the narrative, her presence is associated with a cataclysmic violence. This violence has been explained by the author, by several critics, and by the heroine as endemic to the process of rebirth: "There are no harmless, compassionate ways to remake oneself. We murder who we were so that we can rebirth ourselves in the images of dreams" (*J*, 25). But this interpretation too easily reads the violence of transformation as directed exclusively at the self.

But the novel clearly demonstrates that all Jasmine's transformations are produced in response to the desires of her male consorts; they do not originate in her: "I have had a husband for each of the women I have been. Prakash for Jasmine, Taylor for Jase, Bud for Jane. Half-Face for Kali" (*J*, 175). So, can the violence of transformation then be read as solely self-directed? Or is it not directed, in disguised form, against those who create the roles that the heroine "willingly" inhabits? The conundrum the novel poses is how does a fiction of such ardent consenting produce eruptions of such agent-less and traumatic violence? Certainly, on the surface, the heroine appears deftly opportunistic, moving in and out of roles, relatively unscathed by the brutal ruptures, losses, and violations that accompany these transitions. But yet, with uncanny precision, all of Jasmine's male consorts are either killed, maimed, or rendered or shown as sexually incapacitated. Prakash is killed by a terrorist bomb, Bud is shot in the back, Half-Face is murdered, and Darrel, a neighboring farmer who becomes infatuated with Jane, commits suicide. Taylor, we discover rather quickly, has a low sperm count and cannot have a child. Jasmine's other white male consort also has difficulties with sexual performance. After Bud is shot, Jane, in her role as caretaker and temptress, offers graphic details of his difficulties with love-making. She has to wash him, clean him, sponge him; she has to administer massages so that on rare occasions he can ejaculate; she will always have to be on top. She feels pity; he cannot satisfy her sexually. The catalogue is clinical, spoken by the ever-dutiful caretaker, and yet it quietly exposes his transformation from a virile lover to an invalid. Furthermore, Jasmine's relations with both white men establish her sexual dominance and their abjection to her irresistible beauty. Eventually, their different physical incapacities enable Jasmine, ever seductive and fertile, to conceive and then take with her the child that Bud bears but Taylor will father. The theft of the paternity of the white republic and the imminent birth of a hybrid nation is dramatized at the end, although the symbolic significance of this transformation is eclipsed by the avowals of assimilatory ardor.

How do we explain this dissonance in *Jasmine* between the heroine's aura and her actions? *Jasmine* bears an uncanny resemblance to *Wife*, despite its diametrically opposed trajectory. In the earlier novel, the domesticated and passive Dimple, the most unlikely of murderesses, hacks off the head of the husband who forces her to play the traditional Indian wife. Both novels feature the conjunction of coercion and outward consent that is associated with female role-playing: the need felt by the heroine to pass as a certain kind of woman in order to belong, while deferring other longings and desires, or repressing a past; the inability of the heroine to create a role out of her own desires in relationships; a climactic conclusion that signals agency by the decision to abandon an exhausted role; and, most important, *a heroine who dreams of getting away with murder*. Dimple does not get away with murder and Jasmine does. Jasmine gets away with murder because she changes her identity after killing Half-Face and remembers to wipe off all incriminating fingerprints at the scene of the crime.

But what if one extends the metaphor dramatized in this climactic moment of violence and identity change to the constitutive contradictions in the novel's ec-centric feminism. What if Jasmine's strategy to avoid being linked to Half-Face's murder is mirrored by the author's attempts to dissociate her heroine from all the other acts of violence in the novel? In *Jasmine*, the author is forced to create a shape-changing heroine who embodies none of her identities; as an ostensibly "assimilationist" novel structured around the heroine's "desire to please," neither heroine nor author can acknowledge the rage or resistance engendered by living out roles dreamed by others. Voluntarism signals consent but violence is its dark Other. The corollary of this is that, unlike in *Wife*, the heroine cannot claim the rage as *hers*, and the author disguises the agency of violence directed against the creators of the images the heroine must inhabit. The myth of assimilation as willed is produced at an enormous psychological cost, but it is a cost that cannot be acknowledged within the novel if the myth is to be sustained. David Li astutely notes that the experiences of pain and suffering are pushed to the peripheries of Jasmine's existence and concludes that "this transcendent defiance . . . makes a mockery of material actualities."[16] In a powerful evocation of this contradiction, Jasmine, reflecting on the many identities she has passed through, emphasizes the disjuncture between these transformations: "Jyoti of Hasnapur was not Jasmine, Duff's day mummy and Taylor and Wylie's au pair in Manhattan; *that* Jasmine isn't *this* Jane Ripplemeyer having lunch with Mary Webb at the University Club today. And which of us is the undetected murderer of a half-faced monster, which of us has held a dying husband, which of us was raped and raped and raped in boats and cars and motel rooms?" (*J*, 114). This is the riddle that has baffled many Mukherjee critics. Who is Jasmine? Why is the agency of violence associated with her repeatedly obscured?[17] How can she be and not be who she is? How can a text that is so exuberantly optimistic about Americanization be so wracked with violence, incessant flight, and disruption? On her journey through America, Jasmine travels with forged papers and maneuvers to avoid detection: She is not who she seems to be. That is the defining condition of her movements and her access to Americanization. These dramatic elements function as metaphors of the phenomenology of passing.

How are we to understand violence and female agency in this chain of multiple displacements? The heroine of *Wife* struggles to persuade herself that she can adjust to her gendered role, but at the end she lays claim to her own murderous rage. The murder is a perverted act of assertion, but it turns Dimple from a woman who enacts her rage in fantasies or against substitute objects, like the mouse she kills or the fetus she aborts, into a public agent of violence.

But in *Jasmine* the link between the heroine and the violence that accompanies her is rendered more ambiguous. None of the violence (except in the case of Half-Face) appears to be attributable to Jyoti/Jasmine/Jase/Jane. Besides, as she repeatedly avers, she doesn't "do" anything, she simply is who she is: "I still think of myself as caregiver, recipe giver, preserver. I can honestly say all I wanted was to serve, be allowed to join, but I have created confusion and destruction wherever I go. As Karin says, I am a tornado" (*J,* 190). So Fate provides the alibi for the sudden and inexplicable calamities that befall the men with whom the heroine comes into contact. Yet, despite the repeated textual references to the inexorable operations of Fate, the story is rich with equivocation about the heroine's relationship to the violence that follows her. For instance, in a moment of guilty reflection, Jane recollects the events leading up to Bud's shooting and dwells at length on how she missed all the signs of impending trouble: Bud's urgent requests to her to inform the sheriff that he was leaving with Harlan Kroener; his quick, whispered warning to her that Harlan was going to shoot him (which she would understand only after the accident); her conviction that anyone else (Du or Karin) would have read the situation differently and averted the disaster. She concludes, "I feel responsible. For Prakash's death, Bud's maiming. I'm a tornado, blowing through Baden" (*J,* 183). In another instance, she links Bud's wounding to her own agency but, through a deft ambiguity, deflects blame and even asserts benevolence, suggesting that she may in effect have saved him in wounding him. Nevertheless, the crux of this statement is the link it establishes between Bud's wounding and Jane's power: "Bud was wounded in the war between my fate and my will. I think sometimes I saved his life by not marrying him. *I feel so potent, a goddess*" (*J,* 9, emphasis mine). One is reminded here that it is in her incarnation as a goddess, as Kali, that Jasmine enacts the only overt act of murder in the story. Furthermore, after Half-Face is murdered by "Kali," the narrator suddenly and unexpectedly links the event to another scene, the moment of Prakash's death, which we have been shown as being completely unlike it, except for the outcome—sudden, violent death. Yet Jasmine hauntingly draws the parallels between the two scenes, "For the second time in three months, I was in a room with a *slain* man, my body bloodied. I was walking death. Death Incarnate" (*J,* 106). The description zooms in on a classic tableaux of guilt, the blood of the victim on the body of another—but after presenting these charged visual associations, instead of shifting to a disavowal of guilt, the narrative moves unexpectedly to affirm the association as a manifestation of the heroine's goddesslike power to dispense death.

The riddle of *Jasmine* is where exactly does one draw the line between "Fate" and "will": The text, of course, marks a clear dichotomy between the two. But, the invocation of Fate in the novel functions as a displacement of the agency of violence because locating the violence at its real source would undercut the celebratory romance of Americanization in *Jasmine*. It would force the reader to confront the question that most novels of passing address: What does it cost psychologically to repress one identity in order to claim the power that attaches to another? *Jasmine* is a novel torn by the contradictions of reconciling female consciousness of oppressive gendered roles with a narrative of female empowerment through occupying male (white American and Indian) fantasies. Since a story about female rage at the conventional roles available to women (this is essentially what *Wife* is) is the antithesis of a plot of assimilation, *Jasmine* invents its "goddess ex-machina," Kali, who can absorb the rebellious furies that threaten the fiction of consent and empowerment *Jasmine* purports to be.[18] In *Wife*, as Dimple rapidly spirals into madness and her hatred of her husband overwhelms her, she envisions her self-transformation as a monstrous birth: "But the panic was still there. Also the hate. . . . It was as if some force was impelling her towards disaster; some monster had overtaken her body, a creature with serpentine curls and heaving bosom that would erupt indiscreetly through one of Dimple's orifices, leaving her, Dimple Basu, splattered like a bug on the living-room wall and rug" (*W*, 157). *Wife* turns on the internal split between the docile and domesticated wife and her monstrous double who commits murder. Might *Jasmine* then not be read as the double of *Wife*, as a novel in which the murderous feminine Other is recontained in the body of a domesticated woman, "caregiver, recipe giver, preserver"? Read in this light, *Jasmine* emerges as a novel of female rage and violence that appropriates the genre of domestic fiction—represented by the Jane Eyre story—to contain contradictory, unspeakable trajectories of self-assertion symbolized by Kali. Mukherjee repeatedly alludes to Brontë's novel in *Jasmine*; Jyoti's first encounter with the text proves prophetic of her later actions: "I remember *Great Expectations* and *Jane Eyre*, both of which I was forced to abandon because they were too difficult" (*J*, 35). Many years later in Iowa, Jasmine self-consciously adopts the identity of the white feminist heroine, including taking on her name, but eventually abandons this role when it proves too constraining. In the beginning, responding to Bud's desire to inscribe her as Tarzan's Jane, she counters that she would rather be another Jane, acknowledging, nevertheless, that Plain Jane can never represent who she is: "Bud calls me Jane. Me Bud, you Jane. I didn't get it at first. He kids. Calamity Jane. Jane as in Jane Russell, not Jane as in Plain Jane. But Plain Jane is all I want to be. Plain Jane is a role, like any other. . . . In Baden, I am Jane.

Almost" (*J*, 22). At the conclusion of the novel, the heroine cites the Jane Eyre love story as the prototype of her life in Iowa: "I think maybe I am Jane with my very own Mr. Rochester" (*J*, 210). But she decides soon after to abandon this domestication of her desire to claim something more. She lights out to start a new unorthodox family in California, to be reinscribed, it appears, into a newer more unorthodox family unit. The Victorian domestic fiction of desire seems about to be displaced by its postmodern, multicultural, American counterpart, located in the frontier territory. But suddenly and unexpectedly, the raw female energy the plot has struggled to contain erupts again. But the future trajectory of this force is unrepresentable within the text of simulated assimilation. The switch in tone in the last two paragraphs of the novel is striking: It begins with an emotional recapitulation of her prior incarnations and then moves suddenly from the imminent prospect of the heroine's domestic containment to an augury of her disruptive power. This power is defined as an implacable disavowal of responsibility for consequences:

> I cry into Taylor's shoulder, cry through all the lives I've given birth to, cry for all my dead.
>   Then there is nothing I can do. Time will tell if I am a tornado, rubble-maker, arising from nowhere and disappearing into a cloud. I am out the door and in the potholed and rutted driveway, *scrambling ahead of Taylor*, greedy with wants and reckless from hope. (*J*, 214, emphasis mine)

The last sentence suggests that Jasmine's desire outstrips and exceeds the white male consort who accompanies her into her next incarnation. She has already undermined Bud's paternity by abandoning him and carrying their unborn child with her to another life with another man. But the briefest glimpse of this future trajectory is all the novel can allow if it is to sustain its romance with America. Should we really be surprised, after the last we see of Jyoti/Jasmine/Jase/Jane, that the protagonist of the novel Mukherjee wrote soon after, *Leave It to Me*, is an avenging female killer?[19]

The ambivalence toward assimilation that is revealed in the repressed conflict between assimilation and feminist emergence in the interracial romances has been largely overlooked by reviewers of *Jasmine*, who have instead lauded the heroic tale of the remarkable Americanization of an Indian village girl. One of the reviews on the paperback Fawcett edition (1991) describes *Jasmine* as "the story of the transformation of an Indian village girl, whose grandmother wants to marry her off at 11, into an American woman who finally thinks for herself."[20] This is also the version of Jasmine's story that Mukherjee has herself insisted upon: the euphoric, if turbulent, fable of the making of the New American. In a revealing interview with Mukherjee, her interviewers, Michael Connell, Jessie Grearson, and Tom Grimes, astutely point out the discrepancy between Jasmine's actions and her aura, but Mukherjee seems to miss the point of the observation. While Mukherjee frames this discrepancy in terms of the difference between conventional and unconventional moral responses to her heroine, the interviewers gesture toward but never really articulate other reasons for readerly discomfort with the heroine:

> BM: What I've learned to do in *Jasmine*, I want to think, is create
>   a kind of novel form where there's an intimacy required between
>   reader and author. . . . Jasmine isn't necessarily a good person. . . .
>   She dumps a good, crippled man who loves her, and leaves with
>   someone else. So the reader is invited, is seduced—I want to
>   think—into a kind of relationship with not just the character,
>   but with the author.
> TIR [*The Iowa Review*]:That's a wonderful description. I think
>   people feel that discomfort produced by the intimacy. They
>   are seduced by Jasmine, and yet they resist her, too, because
>   she isn't an entirely lovable person.
> BM: I think she's lovable, but she's not moral in the conventional
>   sense.[21]

Mukherjee insists that the reader's intimacy with the heroine is sufficient to render her "lovable," but the interviewers makes the opposite claim, that the intimacy creates ambivalence, resistance, and attraction. The abruptness and remorselessness with which Jasmine vacates identities that she had warmly embraced or "loved," and the way in which her justifications for her decisions veer between necessity (coercion) and extravagance (wanting/desire), intensify this sense of ambivalence. Fundamentally, what is at issue is whether the euphoric rhetoric of Americanization spoken by Jasmine can be sustained over the trajectory of her many incarnations.

But, if instead of treating it as a story of assimilation, we view *Jasmine* as a story of passing, in which the heroine strategically inhabits names and identities created by others, then one might ask to what extent the act of passing might also define Jasmine's and her author's relationship to the reader. Is the interracial love story the single irrefutable instance of the minority's consent to the American nation? Do the readerly investments that sustain this myth of America as a love story of belonging shape the critical reception of this text as a classic narrative of assimilation?

Her many incarnations allow Jasmine to ventriloquize the limitless possibilities of the American Dream, yet her need to keep moving out of these roles suggests the disjunction between desire and its object: Each role is never quite enough, she wants more, but she can't say what she wants. "I know what I don't want to become," announces the narrator speaking as Jane and remembering a past life as Jyoti (*J*, 3). This sentence at the end of the first chapter seems to suggest that what she doesn't want to become refers only to her past life. But by the end of the novel, Jane too becomes an identity in the past tense, left behind among the debris of who she is not. Jyoti/Jasmine/Jase/Jane seems to make the passage into the mainstream that Dimple was too terrified to make, but she makes this passage by assuming various identities, not by becoming any one of them. Also, in the case of the white men with whom she has relationships, her "love" for them follows from a clear-eyed consciousness of the access they afford her to a world from which she is cut off: "The love I felt for Taylor that first day had nothing to do with sex. I fell in love with his world, its ease, its careless confidence and graceful self-absorption" (*J*, 151). Of Bud, Jasmine remarks that when she first knew him, she thought of him as "a secular god of Baden" (*J*, 174). The language of romantic desire is ironized by the transitional ties and identifications staged in its name.

Assimilation Acts: Passing and the Limits of Hybridity

The focus on passing in Mukherjee's two novels uncovers the ambivalence toward incorporation into the mainstream that the later novel represses through its euphoric rhetoric of self-making and conquest and through its reliance on the power of romance to ground the idea of consent to the Americanization it charts. In *Wife*, the division between the cloistered world of the Indian community and the "real" America that lies outside it is represented through the split between Dimple's role playing as an Indian wife and the vision of a "real" self asserted by shattering the earlier role. This dichotomous mapping of possibilities for female empowerment breaks down in

Jasmine. Jasmine's journey into America leads to the recognition that the passage through America is also defined by inhabiting existing roles rather than creating new ones—the recognition that, finally, role playing may be all that is possible. However, entry into America also marks entry into a space mythified as being the space of freedom and possibility. The author's and the heroine's investment in professing the ideal of assimilation is in part an ideological seduction of the reader and an attempt to solicit recognition from the reader of the heroine's and the author's irrefutable Americanness. As Kristin Carter-Sanborn comments, "The expectations of others—readers, listeners, lovers, and entire communities—do in fact provide one of the most important structural matrices on which *Jasmine* is plotted."[22] Mukherjee herself reiterates the complex intimacies that connect Jasmine, the reader, and the author: "The reader is invited, is seduced—I want to think—into a kind of relationship with not just the character, but with the author."[23]

But what are the politics of such assimilation acts? Do they enact subversive possibilities as some postcolonial theorists of hybridity and mimicry claim?[24] The form of postmodern passing that Jasmine performs through its depiction of Jasmine's ability to evade the fixities of patriarchal gender roles finally succeeds in only slightly modifying our vision of the mainstream. At the end of the novel, we are offered a glimpse of the new American family that has displaced the old one, "the perfect TV families of the fifties," which survive in the novel only in "black-and-white reruns" (*J*, 182). The new all-American family is reconstituted in Mukherjee's fiction as an amalgam of white liberalism and upwardly mobile Asian new-immigrant energies. This is the idealized scene of hybridity in her fiction and is represented through numerous white-Indian couples like Prodosh and Marsha Mookerji in *Wife*, Venn and Beah Masters in *The Holder of the World*, and in *Jasmine* through Jasmine's unorthodox family consisting of herself, a white American professor, an adopted Vietnamese computer-whiz son, an adopted white daughter, and an unborn biracial baby. But Mukherjee's multicultural vision of a New America produces only a transformation of the demography of the dominant group rather than an alternative vision of Americanness.

Both Mukherjee and the critics who defend her celebrate hybridity as a challenge to the postmodern regime of power represented in the American transnation, but they seemingly fail to consider that hybridity is no longer a mode of resistance but can also operate as a conduit of domination in postmodernity. Racial hierarchies, in particular, have been reconfigured in the post–civil rights era, and hybridity offers no surety of a resistant politics or a subversive effect. Indeed, in *Jasmine*, the hybrid category that is central to the maintenance of hegemonic accounts of Americanness is that of the sexual model minority, now metamorphosed as the myth of the new Americans. The theorists Michael Hardt and Antonio Negri point to a serious limitation in postmodernism's political project of celebrating hybridity:

> What if the dominating powers that are the intended object of critique have mutated in such a way as to depotentialize any such postmodernist challenge? In short, what if a new paradigm of power, a postmodern sovereignty, has come to rule . . . through differential hierarchies of the hybrid and fragmentary subjectivities . . . ? In this case . . . the postmodernist and postcolonialist strategies that appear to be liberatory would not challenge but in fact coincide with and even unwittingly reinforce the new strategies of rule![25]

The fable of Americanization constructed through *Jasmine* can be seen as producing a subversive fiction if one focuses only on particular hybrid tropes without considering their emplotment or their conflict with other manifestations of hybridity. Thus, one could argue that the multiracial America represented as the New America in *Jasmine* is subversive of racial homogeneity (whether spoken in the name of ethnic cultural nationalism or white nationalism). But the key question is, what does it install in their place?

Jasmine offers a multicultural vision of a hybrid America embodied in the union of upwardly mobile Asian new immigrants and white liberals. Certainly, *Jasmine* also celebrates the transformation of America by the presence of Hmong refugees, Mexican undocumented workers, Jamaican nannies, and Afghani cabdrivers, but the heroine clearly distances herself from these other New Americans, who live in ethnic ghettos or seem dissatisfied with their immigrant lot. They are shown as lacking the desire and the hope that are seen as prototypically American and which the heroine incarnates. Thus, even within the celebration of a hybrid America, subtle discriminations are elaborated and hierarchies are established between different forms of hybridity. New immigrants have been central to the rearticulation of ethnicity in U.S. racial formations, and contemporary multiculturalism obscures the continuing problem of racial stratification by celebrating ethnic diversity and plural forms of hyphenation: "In the updated version of the American Dream, underwritten by corporate and popular multiculturalism, ethnically diverse subjects aspire to success in a system that purports to reward the capitalist virtues of hard work, striving, and success in all alike. . . . Within the new multiculturalism, 'white' serves only as a modifier of ethnicity, and, simultaneously, nonwhite capital-compatible ethnicities are promised incorporation into the American Dream."[26]

The sexual model minority in *Jasmine* enables the construction of the plot of assimilation as a romance of consent. However, although the novel celebrates the sexual agency and sexual capital of the Asian American woman in an era of multiculturalism, the eruptions of violence in the text reveal the hidden costs of conformity. The focus on assimilation acts in *Jasmine* uncovers the contradictions that shape the heroine's decisions to inhabit the plot of interracial heterosexuality as a mode of empowerment.

As Foucault notes, rather than representing a stubbornly subversive drive, sexuality functions as "an especially dense transfer point for relations of power."[27] Writers and filmmakers have been drawn to representations of interracial intimacy because it seems to offer optimistic and life-affirming visions of an alternative imagined (trans)national community. But this promise of freedom and release through sexuality is itself one of the foundational fictions of Western modernity.

Reference Matter

Notes

Introduction

1. Act of Mar. 2, 1907, ch. 2534, 34 Stat. 1228–29, § 3. See Candice Lewis Bredbenner, *A Nationality of Her Own: Women, Marriage, and the Law of Citizenship* (Berkeley: University of California Press, 1998).

2. Michel Foucault, *The History of Sexuality*, vol. 1, trans. Robert Hurley (New York: Random House, 1978), 139, 26.

3. Ibid., 143.

4. See Mark Thomas Connelly, *The Response to Prostitution in the Progressive Era* (Chapel Hill: University of North Carolina Press, 1980); John D'Emilio and Estelle B. Freedman, *Intimate Matters: A History of Sexuality in America* (New York: Harper and Row, 1988); Michael Grossberg, *Governing the Hearth: Law and the Family in Nineteenth-Century America* (Chapel Hill: University of North Carolina Press, 1985); Martha Hodes, ed., *Sex, Love, Race: Crossing Boundaries in North American History* (New York: New York University Press, 1999); David J. Pivar, *Purity Crusade: Sexual Morality and Social Control, 1868–1900* (Westport, Conn.: Greenwood Press, 1973).

5. For a history of Asian immigration to the United States, see Sucheng Chan, *Asian Americans: An Interpretive History* (Boston: Twayne, 1991); and Ronald T. Takaki, *Strangers from a Different Shore: A History of Asian Americans* (New York: Penguin, 1989).

6. Takaki, *Strangers*, 309.

7. Paul G. Cressey, *The Taxi-Dance Hall: A Sociological Study in Commercialized Recreation and City Life* (Chicago: University of Illinois Press, 1932).

8. Peggy Pascoe, "Race, Gender, and Intercultural Relations: The Case of Interracial Marriage," *Frontiers* 12.1 (1991): 10.

9. Ibid.; Grossberg, *Governing the Hearth*, 136–40; Paul R. Spickard, *Mixed Blood: Intermarriage and Ethnic Identity in Twentieth-Century America* (Madison: University of Wisconsin Press, 1989), 374–75; Leti Volpp, "American Mestizo: Filipinos and Antimiscegenation Laws in California," *University of California Davis Law Review* 33 (2000): 798–99.

10. Pascoe, "Race, Gender, and Intercultural Relations"; Angela Y. Davis, *Women, Race, and Class* (New York: Random House, 1981); Volpp, "American Mestizo."

11. Freedman, *Intimate Matters*, 93–102; Rachel F. Moran, *Interracial Intimacy: The Regulation of Race and Romance* (Chicago: University of Chicago Press, 2002), 21.

12. Freedman, *Intimate Matters*, 102–103.

13. Ibid., 104–7; Grossberg, *Governing the Hearth*, 136.

14. Grossberg, *Governing the Hearth*, 138.

15. Freedman, *Intimate Matters*, 90.

16. Moran, *Interracial Intimacy*, 49.

17. Grossberg, *Governing the Hearth*, 139.

18. Freedman, *Intimate Matters*, 92.

19. Moran, *Interracial Intimacy*, 17.

20. Karen Isaksen Leonard, *Making Ethnic Choices: California's Punjabi Mexican Americans* (Philadelphia: Temple University Press, 1992), 68.

21. Leonard, *Making Ethnic Choices*; Takaki, *Strangers*, 341.

22. Moran, *Interracial Intimacy*, 50–51.

23. Freedman, *Intimate Matters*, 91.

24. Moran, *Interracial Intimacy*, 52–53.

25. Nellie Foster, "Legal Status of Filipino Intermarriage in California," in *Asian Indians, Filipinos, Other Asian Communities and the Law*, ed. Charles McClain (New York: Garland, 1994), 5–18; Megumi Dick Osumi, "Asians and California's Anti-Miscegenation Laws," in *Asian and Pacific American Experiences: Women's Perspectives*, ed. Nobuya Tsuchida (Minneapolis: Asian/Pacific American Learning Resource Center, University of Minnesota, 1982), 1–37; Volpp, "American Mestizo"; and Henry Yu, "Mixing Bodies and Cultures: The Meaning of America's Fascination with Sex between 'Orientals' and 'Whites,' " in *Sex, Love, Race: Crossing Boundaries in North American History*, ed. Martha Hodes (New York: New York University Press, 1999), 444–63.

26. Bredbenner, *A Nationality of Her Own*, ch. 2 and ch. 3.

27. Sucheng Chan, "The Exclusion of Chinese Women, 1870–1943," in

Chinese Immigrants and American Law, ed. Charles J. McClain (New York: Garland, 1994), 36; Bredbenner, *A Nationality of Her Own*, ch. 4.

28. It should be noted that state efforts to regulate heterosexual reproduction led to the creation of complex homosocial networks and homosexual ties within these largely male ethnic communities. While these same-sex relationships were pathologized in mainstream accounts of Asian American communities, they offer a rich ground of investigation for the production of alternative subjectivities and social units that enabled immigrants to survive the economic and social pressures of poverty and displacement. Similarly, Asian American immigrants often arrived with and formed "fictive" kin networks within the United States, whether these were "paper sons," godparents, village partnerships, or "uncles." Of course the fictiveness of these networks lay in their distinctness from the normative "natural" heterosexual family. For research that opens up some of these questions, see Nayan Shah, *Contagious Divides: Epidemics and Race in San Francisco's Chinatown* (Berkeley: University of California Press, 2001); Dana Y. Takagi, "Maiden Voyage: Excursion into Sexuality and Identity Politics in Asian America," in *Asian American Sexualities: Dimensions of the Gay and Lesbian Experience*, ed. Russell Leong (New York: Routledge, 1996), 21–35; and Jennifer Ting, "Bachelor Society: Deviant Heterosexuality and Asian American Historiography," in *Privileging Positions: The Sites of Asian American Studies*, ed. Gary Y. Okihiro et al. (Pullman, Wash.: Washington State University Press, 1995), 271–80.

29. For discussions of the labor regime of early Asian immigration and its gendered effects, see Chan, *Asian Americans*, 104; and Yen Le Espiritu, *Asian American Women and Men: Labor, Laws, and Love* (Thousand Oaks, Calif.: Sage, 1997), 17.

30. Takaki, *Strangers*, 47, 234–35, 256.

31. Percentage of Filipinas calculated from U.S. Census figures provided by Osumi, "Anti-Miscegenation Laws," 23; Takaki, *Strangers*, 308.

32. Osumi, "Anti-Miscegenation Laws," 14–16.

33. *United States v. Bhagat Singh Thind*, 261 U.S. 204, 210 (1923). For a history of the Asian Indian naturalization cases, see Joan M. Jensen, *Passage from India: Asian Indian Immigrants in North America* (New Haven: Yale University Press, 1988). For an analysis of the racial strategies adopted in the Asian Indian naturalization cases, see Susan Koshy, "Category Crisis: South Asian Americans and Questions of Race and Ethnicity," *Diaspora* 7.3 (1998): 285–320.

34. Leonard, *Making Ethnic Choices*.

35. Osumi, "Anti-Miscegenation Laws," 16–22; Moran, *Interracial Intimacy*, 39; Takaki, *Strangers*, 341–42; and Volpp, "American Mestizo," 803–24.

36. Susan Koshy, "Morphing Race into Ethnicity: Asian Americans and Critical Transformations of Whiteness," *Boundary 2* 28.1 (2001): 153–94; James W. Loewen,

The Mississippi Chinese: Between Black and White, 2d ed. (Prospect Heights, Ill.:
Waveland, 1988); Robert Seto Quan with Julian B. Roebuck, *Lotus Among the Magnolias: The Mississippi Chinese* (Jackson: University of Mississippi Press, 1982).

37. Chan, *Asian Americans*, 105–6; and Chan, "Exclusion of Chinese Women,"
3–5, 13, 46.

38. Espiritu, *Asian American Women and Men*, 54–56.

39. For discussions of Asian American gender identities, see King-Kok Cheung,
Articulate Silences (Ithaca: Cornell University Press, 1993); David L. Eng, *Racial
Castration: Managing Masculinity in Asian America* (Durham: Duke University
Press, 2001); Espiritu, *Asian American Women and Men*, 93–98; Laura Hyun Yi
Kang, *Compositional Subjects: Enfiguring Asian/American Women* (Durham: Duke
University Press, 2002); Elaine H. Kim, "'Such Opposite Creatures': Men and
Women in Asian American Literature," *Michigan Quarterly Review* 29 (1990): 68–
93; Rachel C. Lee, *The Americas of Asian American Literature: Gendered Fictions of
Nation and Transnation* (Princeton: Princeton University Press, 1999); Robert G.
Lee, *Orientals: Asian Americans in Popular Culture* (Philadelphia: Temple University
Press, 1999); Renee Tajima, "Lotus Blossoms Don't Bleed: Images of Asian
Women," in *Making Waves: An Anthology of Writings by and about Asian American
Women*, ed. Asian Women United of California (Boston: Beacon, 1989), 308–17.

40. Chan, *Asian Americans*, 104; Espiritu, *Asian American Women and Men*,
ch. 2.

41. The often-cited truism of the effeminacy of the Asian American male in
popular culture gained currency through the polemics of Frank Chin's revisionist
project to reclaim Chinese American manhood. See Frank Chin and Jeffrey Paul
Chan, "Racist Love," in *Seeing through Shuck,* ed. Richard Kostelanetz (New York:
Ballantine, 1972), 65–79.

42. Pierre Bourdieu and Jean-Claude Passeron, *Reproduction in Education,
Society, and Culture*, trans. Richard Nice (London: Sage in association with
Theory, Culture, and Society, Department of Administrative and Social Studies,
Teesside Polytechnic, 1990).

43. While sexual capital also defines the position of Asian American men,
in their case it appears to be more closely connected to economic power. Popular
antagonism to Filipino immigrants dating white women frequently connected
Filipino attractiveness to their consumerism and their willingness to spend money
on white women. During the Depression, the alleged Filipino theft of white men's
jobs and women emblematizes the convergence of sexual and economic power
(real or imaginary) in defining Filipino male sexual capital. I should also note
that although this book focuses on the heterosexual economy, the value of the
Asian American woman operates quite differently in a homosexual economy.

44. This is one of several trajectories of racialized feminine sexuality and is in no way representative of all Asian American women; it does, however, offer a useful critical model for mapping how cultural transformations recast the meanings of race and gender.

45. See Espiritu, *Asian American Women and Men*.

46. U.S. Department of Labor, *The Negro Family: The Case for National Action* (Washington D.C.: U.S. Government Printing Office, 1965), 29.

47. The term *cultural work* was coined by Jane Tompkins to indicate the importance of popular texts that are often excluded from the canon because they do not have the literary complexity or sophistication of the "classics." Tompkins contends that popular texts have nevertheless played a critical role in organizing and addressing the cultural preoccupations of their time, and therefore their popularity requires a rereading of these texts as central cultural documents of a particular period. Jane Tompkins, *Sensational Designs: The Cultural Work of American Fiction, 1790–1860* (New York: Oxford University Press, 1985). For other discussions of the white-Asian interracial romance, see Gina Marchetti, *Romance and the "Yellow Peril": Race, Sex, and Discursive Strategies in Hollywood Fiction* (Berkeley: University of California Press, 1993); and Sheng-mei Ma, *Immigrant Subjectivities in Asian American and Asian Diaspora Literatures* (Albany, N.Y.: State University of New York Press, 1998). For discussions of the nation-making powers of desire, see Nancy Armstrong, *Desire and Domestic Fiction: A Political History of the Novel* (New York: Oxford University Press, 1987); Doris Sommer, *Foundational Fictions: The National Romances of Latin America* (Berkeley: University of California Press, 1991); and Ann Laura Stoler, *Race and the Education of Desire: Foucault's History of Sexuality and the Colonial Order of Things* (Durham: Duke University Press, 1995).

48. Joel Williamson, *New People: Miscegenation and Mulattoes in the United States* (New York: Free Press, 1980), 109–14.

49. Foucault, *History of Sexuality*, vol. 1, 12.

50. Yu, "Mixing Bodies and Cultures," 449.

51. Uday S. Mehta, "Liberal Strategies of Exclusion," in *Tensions of Empire: Colonial Cultures in a Bourgeois World*, ed. Frederick Cooper and Ann Laura Stoler (Berkeley: University of California Press, 1997), 63, 61.

52. Sommer, *Foundational Fictions*, 32.

53. Lauren Berlant and Michael Warner, "Sex in Public," in "Intimacy," ed. Lauren Berlant, special issue, *Critical Inquiry* 24.2 (1998): 317.

54. Kobena Mercer, "Reading Racial Fetishism: The Photographs of Robert Mapplethorpe," in *Fetishism as Cultural Discourse*, ed. Emily Apter and William Pietz (Ithaca: Cornell University Press, 1993), 324.

Chapter 1

1. Pierre Loti, *Madame Chrysanthemum* (1887; reprint, London: KPI, 1985); John Luther Long, "Madame Butterfly," in *Madame Butterfly, Purple Eyes, etc.* (1898; reprint, New York: Garrett Press, 1969), 1–86; David Belasco, *Madame Butterfly*, in *Six Plays* (Boston: Little, Brown and Co., 1928); Giacomo Puccini, *Madam Butterfly,* English National Opera Guide Series, no. 26 (London: John Calder, 1984); Richard Lakin Mason, *The World of Suzie Wong* (Cleveland: World Publishing Company, 1957); and *Miss Saigon*, music, Claude-Michel Schönberg, lyrics, Richard Maltby Jr. and Alain Boubil, Drury Lane Theater, London, Sept. 20, 1989. It is commonly assumed that John Luther Long collaborated with David Belasco in producing the Broadway play, but Montrose J. Moses explains that their work together was not technically a collaboration since Belasco drew heavily on Long's story but authored the piece himself. Montrose J. Moses, introduction to *Madame Butterfly*, in Belasco, *Six Plays*.

2. David Henry Hwang, *M. Butterfly* (New York: Plume, 1989), afterword, 95.

3. For discussions of alterations made to the opera, see Arthur Groos, "Lieutenant F. B. Pinkerton: Problems in the Genesis of an Operatic Hero," *Italica* 64.4 (1987): 654–75; Julian Smith, "'Madame Butterfly': The Paris Première of 1906," in *Werk und Wiedergabe: Musiktheater Exemplarisch Interpretiert*, ed. Sigrid Wiesmann (Bayreuth: Fehr, 1980): 229–38; and Julian Smith, "A Metamorphic Tragedy," *Proceedings of the Royal Music Association* 106 (1980): 105–14.

4. Groos, "Genesis," 658.

5. Irene L. Szyliowicz, *Pierre Loti and the Oriental Woman* (New York: St. Martin's Press, 1988), 75.

6. Jeanne-Pierre Lehmann, "Images of the Orient," in *Madame Butterfly*, English National Opera Guide, no. 26, 10.

7. See Carl Dawson, *Lafcadio Hearn and the Vision of Japan* (Baltimore: Johns Hopkins University Press, 1992); Groos, "Genesis"; and Smith, "Paris Première."

8. Amy Kaplan, "Romancing the Empire: The Embodiment of American Masculinity in the Popular Historical Novel of the 1890s," *American Literary History* 2.4 (winter 1990): 661.

9. Colleen Lye, "*M. Butterfly* and the Rhetoric of Antiessentialism: Minority Discourse in an International Frame," in *The Ethnic Canon*, ed. David Palumbo-Liu (Minneapolis: University of Minnesota Press, 1995), 260–89.

10. Eva Saks, "Representing Miscegenation Law," *Raritan* 8.2 (1988): 46.

11. For a discussion of the reworking of nationalism and masculinity in the popular historical novels that appeared in the same decade as "Madame Butterfly," see Kaplan, "Romancing the Empire."

12. Amy Kaplan and Donald E. Pease, ed., *Cultures of United States Imperialism*

(Durham: Duke University Press, 1993); and Oscar V. Campomanes, "The New Empire's Forgetful and Forgotten Citizens: Unrepresentability and Unassimilability in Filipino-American Postcolonialities," *Hitting Critical Mass* 2.2 (1995): 145–200.

13. Philip Fisher, *Hard Facts: Setting and Form in the American Novel* (New York: Oxford University Press, 1985), 9–10.

14. See Tomás Almaguer, *Racial Fault Lines: The Historical Origins of White Supremacy in California* (Berkeley: University of California Press, 1994); Sucheng Chan, *Asian Americans: An Interpretive History* (Boston: Twayne, 1991); Roger Daniels, "U.S. Policy Toward Asian Immigrants: Contemporary Developments in Historical Perspective," *International Journal* 63.2 (1993): 310–34; Bill Ong Hing, *Making and Remaking Asian America Through Immigration Policy, 1850–1990* (Stanford: Stanford University Press, 1993); Harold R. Isaacs, *Scratches on Our Minds: American Images of China and India* (New York: John Day, 1958); Elaine H. Kim, *Asian American Literature: An Introduction to the Writings and Their Social Context* (Philadelphia: Temple University Press, 1982); Lisa Lowe, *Immigrant Acts* (Durham: Duke University Press, 1996); Gary Y. Okihiro, *Margins and Mainstreams: Asians in American History and Culture* (Seattle: University of Washington Press, 1994); Ronald T. Takaki, *Iron Cages: Race and Culture in Nineteenth-Century America* (New York: Knopf, 1979); Ronald T. Takaki, *Strangers from a Different Shore: A History of Asian Americans* (New York: Penguin, 1989).

15. For an excellent discussion of informal empire, see Thomas J. McCormick, *China Market: America's Quest for Informal Empire, 1893–1901* (Chicago: Quadrangle, 1967); Walter LaFeber, *The New Empire: An Interpretation of American Expansion, 1860–1898* (Ithaca: Cornell University Press, 1963); and William Appleman Williams, "The Age of Corporate Capitalism," in *The Contours of American History* (Chicago: Quadrangle, 1966), 343–478.

16. Johannes Fabian, *Time and the Other: How Anthropology Makes Its Object* (New York: Columbia University Press, 1983).

17. Homi K. Bhabha, "Of Mimicry and Man: The Ambivalence of Colonial Discourse," *October* 28 (1984): 126.

18. Bette London, "Of Mimicry and English Men: E. M. Forster and the Performance of Masculinity," in *A Passage to India*, ed. Tony Davies and Nigel Wood (Buckingham, England: Open University Press, 1994), 90–120; and Parama Roy, *Indian Traffic: Identities in Question in Colonial and Postcolonial India* (Berkeley: University of California Press, 1998).

19. Akira Iriye, "Japan as a Competitor, 1895–1917," in *Mutual Images: Essays in American-Japanese Relations*, ed. Iriye (Cambridge, Mass.: Harvard University Press, 1975), 98. See also Akira Iriye, *Across the Pacific: An Inner History of American-East Asian Relations* (New York: Harcourt, 1967).

20. Mrs. Irvin H. Correl, "Madame Butterfly: Her Long Secret Revealed," *Japan Magazine* (May 1931): 341–45.

21. Ibid., 345.

22. Kenton J. Clymer, *Protestant Missionaries in the Philippines, 1898–1916: An Inquiry into the American Colonial Mentality* (Urbana, Ill.: University of Illinois Press, 1986), 8.

23. Quoted in ibid., 182.

24. Patricia Grimshaw, *Paths of Duty: American Missionary Wives in Nineteenth-Century Hawaii* (Honolulu: University of Hawaii Press, 1989); James Reed, *The Missionary Mind and American East Asia Policy: 1911–1915* (Cambridge, Mass.: Harvard University Press, 1983); Irwin Scheiner, *Christian Converts and Social Protest in Meiji Japan* (Berkeley: University of California Press, 1970); and Robert S. Schwantes, *Japanese and Americans: A Century of Cultural Relations* (New York: Harper, 1955).

25. Grimshaw, *Paths of Duty*, 63.

26. According to Reed, China quickly superseded Japan as the most important and promising mission destination. One prominent missionary noted in a report that "the problems of Christian work in Japan much more closely resemble those in Great Britain or in the United States of America than do those in any other country to which missionaries have gone." Reed, *The Missionary Mind*, 27–30; quoted in 30–31.

27. Ibid., 31–32.

28. Schwantes, *Japanese and Americans*, 259.

29. Ibid., 268–69. Jane Correl explains that when she and her husband first arrived in Japan at the very early stages of the mission movement, they were prohibited from preaching and consequently concentrated their efforts on learning Japanese. It was only after a while that they "opened schools, and were able to have meeting-houses; and thus the good was sown." Correl, "Madame Butterfly: Her Long Secret Revealed," 344.

30. Interestingly, the Japanese customary law that governs the action of the story was reformed in the 1898 civil code resulting in the introduction of a fault-based system available to both parties, whereas the earlier law had only allowed for the possibility of the man terminating the relationship. This law was then clearly the site of contestation in efforts to modernize the Japanese legal system in the time period immediately preceding the publication of the story. See Rebecca Bailey-Harris, "Madame Butterfly and the Conflict of Laws," *American Journal of Comparative Law* 39.1 (1991): 157–77.

31. In a detailed discussion of Long's Japanese stories, Charles B. Wordell points to their infantile representation of Japanese women, their preoccupation with American-style romance, their portrayal of Japanese men as grotesque and

morally defective, and their focus on Westernization as cultural defilement. He explains these weaknesses, however, as a sign of Long's limitations as a writer and his lack of knowledge of the country. Wordell, *Japan's Image in America: Popular Writing about Japan, 1800–1941* (Kyoto: Yamaguchi Publishing House, 1998), 110.

32. For discussions of the Japanese vogue in the arts, see Elizabeth Aslin, *The Aesthetic Movement: Prelude to Art Nouveau* (New York: Praeger, 1969); Warren I. Cohen, *East Asian Art and American Culture* (New York: Columbia University Press, 1992); Julia Meech and Gabriel Weisberg, *Japonisme Comes to America: The Japanese Impact on the Graphic Arts, 1876–1925* (New York: Abrams, 1990); and Siegfried Wichman, *Japonisme: The Japanese Influence in Western Art Since 1858* (London: Thames and Hudson, 1981).

33. Neil Harris, "All the World a Melting Pot? Japan at American Fairs, 1876–1904," in *Mutual Images*, ed. Iriye, 31.

34. T. J. Jackson Lears, *No Place of Grace: Antimodernism and the Transformation of American Culture, 1880–1920* (Chicago: University of Chicago Press, 1994), 4–6, xv.

35. Mari Yoshihara, "Women's Asia: American Women and the Gendering of American Orientalism, 1870s–WWII" (Ph.D. diss., Brown University, 1997), 42, 47, 100.

36. Ibid.

37. Dawson, *Lafcadio Hearn*, 136.

38. James C. Thomson Jr., Peter W. Stanley, and John Curtis Perry, *Sentimental Imperialists: The American Experience in East Asia* (New York: Harper and Row, 1981), 70–71.

39. Carol Weisbrod suggests that this passage contains an implicit reference to the growing flexibility of divorce laws in the United States that had drawn censure from many commentators who decried these changes for weakening marriage ties and replacing monogamy with serial polygamy. Weisbrod, *Butterfly, the Bride: Essays on Law, Narrative, and the Family* (Ann Arbor, Mich.: University of Michigan Press, 1999), 25–26.

40. Jane Hunter, *The Gospel of Gentility: American Women Missionaries in Turn-of-the-Century China* (New Haven: Yale University Press, 1984), xiii; Reed, *The Missionary Mind*, 20.

41. Grimshaw, *Paths of Duty*, xiv.

42. Hunter, *Gospel of Gentility*, 175–79.

Chapter 2

1. D. W. Griffith, dir., *Broken Blossoms*. Scenario by Griffith, based on "The Chink and the Child" by Thomas Burke. Perf. Lillian Gish, Richard Barthelmess, and Donald Crisp. Photography, G. W. Bitzer; "Special Effects," Henrik Sartov.

United Artists. Premiere, George M. Cohan Theater, New York, May 13, 1919; general release, October 20, 1920.

2. D. W. Griffith, dir., *The Birth of a Nation*, 1915. Scenario by Griffith and Frank Woods, based on the play and novel *The Clansman: An Historical Romance of the Ku Klux Klan* (1905), by Thomas Dixon Jr., with additional material from Dixon's *The Leopard's Spots: A Romance of the White Man's Burden, 1865–1900* (1902).

3. Michael Rogin, "'The Sword Became a Flashing Vision': D. W. Griffith's *The Birth of a Nation*," in *The New American Studies: Essays from Representations,* ed. Philip Fisher (Berkeley: University of California Press, 1991), 384–85. D. W. Griffith, dir., *Hearts of the World* (Paramount-Artcraft, 1918).

4. Lillian Gish, with Ann Pinchot, *Lillian Gish: The Movies, Mr. Griffith, and Me* (Englewood Cliffs, N.J.; Prentice-Hall, 1969), 201. For a detailed account of the making of the film, see Richard Schickel, *D. W. Griffith: An American Life* (New York: Simon and Schuster, 1984).

5. Rogin, "The Sword," 385.

6. Schickel, *D. W. Griffith*, 343.

7. Ibid., 340–60.

8. Quoted in Rogin, "The Sword," 382.

9. Quoted in ibid., 385.

10. Quoted in ibid., 381.

11. Miriam Hansen, "Universal Language and Democratic Culture: Myths of Origin in Early American Cinema," in *Mythos und Aufklärung in der Amerikanis-chen Literatur* [Myth and Enlightenment in American Literature], ed. Dieter Meindl and Friedrich W. Horlacher (Erlangen: Universitätsbund Erlangen-Nürnberg, 1985), 321–51.

12. Joseph S. Nye Jr., *The Paradox of American Power: Why the World's Only Superpower Can't Go It Alone* (New York: Oxford University Press, 2002).

13. Joseph S. Nye Jr., "U.S. Power and the Strategy After Iraq," op-ed, *Foreign Affairs*, July 1, 2003.

14. As quoted in Dorothy B. Jones, *The Portrayal of China and India on the American Screen, 1896–1955: The Evolution of Chinese and Indian Themes, Locales, and Characters as Portrayed on the American Screen* (Cambridge, Mass.: Center for International Studies, MIT, 1955), 2.

15. As quoted in ibid., 2–3.

16. Paul M. Kennedy, *The Rise and Fall of the Great Powers: Economic Change and Military Conflict from 1500–2000* (New York: Vintage, 1989); and Corelli Barnett, *The Collapse of British Power* (London: Eyre Methuen, 1972), 232.

17. Patrick Karl O'Brien and Armand Klesse, *Two Hegemonies: Britain 1846–1914 and the United States 1941–2001* (Aldershot, Hants: Ashgate, 2002).

18. Charles P. Kindleberger, *World Economic Primacy: 1500–1990* (New York: Oxford University Press, 1990).

19. Thomas Burke, "The Chink and the Child," in *Limehouse Nights* (London: Grant Richards, 1917), 15–37. The Chinese protagonist of Burke's story and Griffith's film is named Cheng Huan, but he is referred to in the title and narrative of Burke's story as "the Chink." Griffith wanted to avoid the derogatory connotations of the term *chink* and substituted it with the generic label "the Yellow Man" because it was less freighted with negative associations. In discussing the characters in the story and film, I refer to Burke's protagonist as Cheng Huan rather than as "the Chink," and to Griffith's protagonist as "the Yellow Man."

20. James C. Thomson Jr., Peter W. Stanley, and John Curtis Perry, *Sentimental Imperialists: The American Experience in East Asia* (New York: Harper and Row, 1981), 70–71.

21. Gareth Stedman Jones, *Outcast London: A Study of the Relationship between Classes in Victorian Society* (Oxford: Clarendon, 1971).

22. Anne McClintock, *Imperial Leather: Race, Gender, and Sexuality in the Colonial Conquest* (New York: Routledge, 1995), 48.

23. Daniel J. Kevles, *In the Name of Eugenics: Genetics and the Uses of Human Heredity* (New York: Knopf, 1985); George L. Mosse, *Nationalism and Sexuality: Respectability and Abnormal Sexuality in Modern Europe* (New York: Fertig, 1985), 34–36.

24. Michel Foucault, *The History of Sexuality*, vol. 1, trans. Robert Hurley (New York: Random House, 1978), 140.

25. Quoted in Ann Laura Stoler, *Race and the Education of Desire: Foucault's History of Sexuality and the Colonial Order of Things* (Durham: Duke University Press, 1995), 35. See also Foucault, *History of Sexuality*, vol. 1, 140–44.

26. Foucault, *History of Sexuality*, vol. 1, 118.

27. Stoler, *Race and the Education of Desire*, 36–37.

28. See Jones, *Outcast London*; and Pick, *Faces of Degeneration*.

29. Pick, *Faces of Degeneration*, 200.

30. Kevles, *In the Name of Eugenics*, 72.

31. Pick, *Faces of Degeneration*, 10.

32. Quoted in Kevles, *In the Name of Eugenics*, 47.

33. Ibid., 72–75.

34. Ibid., 76.

35. Quoted in ibid., 97.

36. Uday S. Mehta, "Liberal Strategies of Exclusion," in *Tensions of Empire: Colonial Cultures in a Bourgeois World*, ed. Frederick Cooper and Ann Laura Stoler (Berkeley: University of California Press, 1997), 63.

37. Ibid., 61.

38. Ibid.

39. Evolutionary theorists and race scientists frequently entered into discussions of the advantages and disadvantages of migration. Charles Darwin himself hypothesized that American success could be attributed to a process of natural selection since only the most energetic individuals would be likely to emigrate, thus bringing the fittest Europeans to the New World. Similarly, Herbert Spencer suggested that immigration and amalgamation produced a finer, more adaptable breed of men. However, Francis Walker, a eugenicist, contended that the new immigrants were "beaten men from beaten races; representing the worst failures in the struggle for existence." John Higham, *Strangers in the Land: Patterns of American Nativism, 1860–1925* (New Brunswick, N.J.: Rutgers University Press, 1955), 142; quoted in 22.

40. George Mosse notes that stereotypes of sexual degeneracy often attributed a feminized sexuality to those racial groups characterized as degenerate, such as blacks, Jews, and Asians. The femininity, in this instance, stood for an excessive sensuousness and lack of self-discipline. Mosse, *Nationalism and Sexuality*, 36.

41. McClintock, *Imperial Leather*, 359.

42. I develop this argument in greater detail in the context of contemporary racial politics in "Category Crisis: South Asian Americans and the Questions of Race and Ethnicity," *Diaspora* 7.3 (1998): 285–320; and "Morphing Race into Ethnicity: Asian Americans and Critical Transformations of Whiteness," *Boundary 2* 28.1 (2001): 153–94.

43. Quoted in Schickel, *D. W. Griffith*, 405.

44. Gish, with Pinchot, *Lillian Gish*, 163.

45. Rogin, "Sword," 362.

46. For discussions of race and representation in *The Birth of a Nation*, see Donald Bogle, "Black Beginnings: From *Uncle Tom's Cabin* to *The Birth of a Nation*," in *Representing Blackness: Issues in Film and Video*, ed. Valerie Smith (New Brunswick, N.J.: Rutgers University Press, 1997), 13–24; Donald Bogle, *Toms, Coons, Mulattoes, and Bucks: An Interpretive History of Blacks in American Films* (New York: Continuum, 1994); Gerald R. Butters Jr., "African-American Cinema and *The Birth of a Nation*," in *Black Manhood on the Silent Screen* (Lawrence, Kans.: University Press of Kansas, 2002); Terry Christensen, *Reel Politics: American Political Movies from "Birth of a Nation" to "Platoon"* (Oxford, England: Blackwell, 1987); Thomas Cripps, *Slow Fade to Black: The Negro in American Film, 1900–1942* (New York: Oxford University Press, 1993); Manthia Diawara, "Black Spectatorship: Problems of Identification and Resistance," *Screen* 29.4 (1988): 66–

76; Richard Dyer, "Into the Light: The Whiteness of the South in *The Birth of a Nation*," in *Dixie Debates: Perspectives on Southern Cultures*, ed. Richard H. King and Helen Taylor (New York: New York University Press, 1996), 165–76; Janet Staiger, "*The Birth of a Nation*: Reconsidering Its Reception," in *Interpreting Films: Studies in the Historical Reception of American Cinema*, ed. Staiger (Princeton: Princeton University Press, 1992), 139–53; Mason Boyd Stokes, "Becoming Visible: I'm White, Therefore I'm Anxious," in *The Color of Sex: Whiteness, Heterosexuality, and the Fictions of White Supremacy*, ed. Stokes (Durham: Duke University Press, 2001), 158–77; Charles Taylor, "The Re-birth of the Aesthetic in Cinema," *Wide Angle* 13.3–4 (1991): 12–30.

47. Schickel, *D. W. Griffith*, 29, 390.

48. Kenneth S. Lynn, "The Torment of D. W. Griffith," *American Scholar* (Spring 1990): 255–64.

49. This is the gist of Jack Kirby's study of racial representation in Griffith's films, namely, that in comparison to the racist representations of his contemporaries, Griffith's depictions are often less harsh. Jack Temple Kirby, "D. W. Griffith's Racial Portraiture," *Phylon* 39.2 (1978): 118–27.

50. Elaine H. Kim, *Asian American Literature: An Introduction to the Writings and Their Social Context* (Philadelphia: Temple University Press, 1982), 4.

51. See Gina Marchetti, *Romance and the "Yellow Peril": Race, Sex, and Discursive Strategies in Hollywood Fiction* (Berkeley: University of California Press, 1993); Eugene Franklin Wong, *On Visual Media Racism: Asians in the American Motion Pictures* (New York: Arno Press, 1978); and Dorothy B. Jones, *Portrayal of China and India*.

52. Vance Kepley Jr., "Griffith's 'Broken Blossoms' and the Problem of Historical Specificity," *Quarterly Review of Film Studies* 3.1 (winter 1978): 40.

53. Ibid. 42, 42–43.

54. Sergei Eisenstein, "Dickens, Griffith, and the Film Today," in *Film Form: Essays in Film Theory*, ed. and trans. Jay Leyda (San Diego: Harvest, 1977), 234.

55. Ibid., 235.

56. In the tenuousness with which the Asian was positioned within American modernity, the Yellow Man resembled the native American more closely than he did the black man and hence the similarity in Griffith's representation of white-Indian and white-Asian miscegenation. Anatomizing the pathos elicited by the Indian in Griffith's films of white-Indian miscegenation, such as *The Call of the Wild* (1908) and *A Romance of the Western Hills* (1910), Gregory S. Jay observes, "This sympathy appears directed toward a creature considered doomed by its very nature, its nobility a primitive defense against the complexity of modernity."

Jay, "'White Man's Book No Good': D. W. Griffith and the American Indian," *Cinema Journal* 39.4 (2000): 10. The conjunction of nobility and vulnerability are reprised in the portrayal of the Yellow Man.

57. I differ from Gina Marchetti, who suggests that *Broken Blossoms* is constructed as "a rape-lynching fantasy" and is in this respect comparable to *The Birth of a Nation* and to Cecil B. DeMille's film *The Cheat* (1915). While the threat of rape surfaces briefly in *Broken Blossoms*, the ideology of romance, shown as transcending animalistic lust, allows Griffith to rework the rape fantasy projected in *The Birth of a Nation*. See Marchetti, *Romance*, 34.

58. Sandy Flitterman-Lewis, "The Blossom and the Bole: Narrative and Visual Spectacle in Early Film Melodrama," *Cinema Journal* 33.3 (1994): 5, emphasis mine.

59. Julia Lesage, "Artful Racism, Artful Rape: Griffith's *Broken Blossoms*," in *Home Is Where the Heart Is: Studies in Melodrama and the Woman's Film*, ed. Christine Gledhill (London: BFI Books, 1987), 236, 244–47.

60. John Kuo Wei Tchen, "Modernizing White Patriarchy: Re-Viewing D. W. Griffith's *Broken Blossoms*," in *Moving the Image: Independent Asian Pacific American Media Arts*, ed. Russell Leong (Los Angeles: UCLA Asian American Studies Center and Visual Communications, Southern California Asian American Studies Central, Inc., 1991), 141, 137.

61. Marchetti, *Romance*, 34.

62. Ibid., 34, 10.

63. Marchetti, *Romance*, 32.

64. Tchen, "Modernizing White Patriarchy," 136.

65. Burke, "The Chink and the Child," 15.

66. Ibid., 20.

67. Ibid., 27–29.

68. When first approached by Griffith, the twenty-three-year-old Lillian Gish was reluctant to play a fifteen-year-old. She was finally persuaded by Griffith's insistence that a younger actress would simply not have the experience or range to play the harrowing scenes of Lucy's brutalization. Gish, with Pinchot, *Lillian Gish*, 218.

69. Richard Dyer, *White* (London: Routledge, 1997), 6.

70. I borrow this term from Robert Tilton, who uses it to describe white-native American miscegenation in James Fenimore Cooper's *The Last of the Mohicans* (1826). Robert S. Tilton, *Pocohontas: The Evolution of an American Narrative* (Cambridge: Cambridge University Press, 1994), 63.

71. Frank Chin and Jeffrey Paul Chan, "Racist Love," in *Seeing through Shuck*, ed. Richard Kostelanetz (New York: Ballantine, 1972), 68.

72. According to Karl Brown, the overly feminine associations of the film's "sickly sweet" title prompted the male film crew to unofficially retitle it *Busted Posies*. Karl Brown, *Adventures with D. W. Griffith* (New York: Farrar, 1973), 227.

73. Burke, "The Chink and the Child," 19.

74. McClintock, *Imperial Leather*, 54.

75. Ibid, 49–56.

76. Burke, "The Chink and the Child," 22.

77. Brown, *Adventures*, 224, emphasis mine.

78. Burke's Chinatown stories were bestsellers when Griffith, on Mary Pickford's and Douglas Fairbanks's recommendation, decided to film one of the stories. Karl Brown writes that the stories were very much in vogue: "I'd read all of them. So had everyone else. You might as well confess at once that you were utterly behind the times if you were not intimately acquainted with Burke's stories of Limehouse. The whole English-reading world knew every dark and dangerous alley of Limehouse as well as they knew the way to the corner grocery." *Adventures*, 224.

79. James L. Smith, *Melodrama* (London: Methuen, 1973), 56.

80. Geoffrey Nowell-Smith, "Minnelli and Melodrama," *Screen* 18.2 (1977): 115.

81. Charles Affron, *Star Acting: Gish, Garbo, Davis* (New York: Dutton, 1977), 14.

82. Griffith reportedly took Barthelmess to the Los Angeles Chinatown on several evenings to observe its Chinese residents in preparation for playing the role of Cheng. It is rather remarkable that, in spite of this, Barthelmess gives such a stylized rendition of his role. His exaggerated gestures also stand in marked contrast to the acting of the many Asian extras in the early Chinese port scenes.

83. Jay, "'White Man's Book No Good,'" 10.

84. Dudley Andrew, *Film in the Aura of Art* (Princeton: Princeton University Press, 1984), 20–21.

85. McClintock, *Imperial Leather*, 40.

86. Andrew, *Film in the Aura of Art*, 21.

87. Edwin Björkman, *Thomas Burke: A Critical Appreciation of the Man of Limehouse* (New York: Doran, n.d.), 5.

88. Nayan Shah, *Contagious Divides: Epidemics and Race in San Francisco's Chinatown* (Berkeley: University of California Press, 2001), 13.

89. See Mae M. Ngai, "The Architecture of Race in American Immigration Law: A Reexamination of the Immigration Act of 1924," *Journal of American History* 86 (1999): 67–92.

90. The term *not-yet-white* was coined by John Bukowczyk and is quoted in David R. Roediger, "Whiteness and Ethnicity in the History of 'White Ethnics'

in the United States," in *Toward the Abolition of Whiteness: Essays on Race, Politics, and Working Class History*, ed. Roediger (London: Verso, 1994), 184. See Noel Ignatiev, *How the Irish Became White* (New York: Routledge, 1995); Dale T. Knobel, *Paddy and the Republic: Ethnicity and Nationality in Ante-Bellum America* (Middletown: Wesleyan University Press, 1986); David R. Roediger, *The Wages of Whiteness: Race and the Making of the American Working Class* (London: Verso, 1991); Alexander Saxton, *The Indispensable Enemy: Labor and the Anti-Chinese Movement in California,* (Berkeley: University of California Press, 1971); and Richard Williams, *Hierarchical Structures and Social Value: The Creation of Black and Irish Identities in the United States* (Cambridge: Cambridge University Press, 1990).

91. This crucial difference between U.S. and British racial formation is nowhere better illustrated than in the case of the Irish. The Irish were seen as racially separate from Anglo-Saxons in England but slowly came to be amalgamated with them within the United States. Roediger writes that the "simian" and "savage" Irish "only gradually fought, worked and voted their ways into the white race in the U.S." Roediger, "Whiteness and Ethnicity," 184.

92. It is worth noting, too, that while Battling Burrows is definitely ascribed a working-class identity, Griffith's embourgeoisment of Lucy is unmistakable. Although her racial identity suffices to render her unattainable to the Yellow Man, Griffith nevertheless makes subtle changes to her class associations by presenting her as a bourgeois soul trapped in the body of a working-class girl, an evolutionary accident in the London slums. In the film, her sensibility is airbrushed. Hence, her love of flowers, beautiful objects, and dreams of a future wedding in silk and ribbons.

93. Griffith, like John Luther Long, uses the treaty port as a "privileged setting" for developing the meanings of American national identity in relation to its emerging global role.

94. Andrew, *Film in the Aura of Art,* 20.

Chapter 3

1. For a discussion of Asian American alienation and abjection, see David Leiwei Li, *Imagining the Nation: Asian American Literature and Cultural Consent* (Stanford: Stanford University Press, 1998).

2. See Oscar V. Campomanes, "New Formations of Asian American Studies and the Question of U.S. Imperialism," *positions: east asia cultures critique* 5.2 (1997): 523–50; King-Kok Cheung, ed., *An Interethnic Companion to Asian American Literature* (New York: Cambridge University Press, 1997); Tomo Hattori, "Model Minority Discourse and Asian American Jouis-Sense," *differences: A Journal of Feminist Criticism* 11.2 (1999): 228–47; Elaine H. Kim and Lisa Lowe, eds.,

positions: east asia cultures critique 5.2 (1997); Susan Koshy, "The Fiction of Asian American Literature," *Yale Journal of Criticism* 9.2 (1996): 315–46; Françoise Lionnet and Shu-mei Shih, eds., *Minor Transnationalism* (Durham: Duke University Press, 2005); Viet Thanh Nguyen, *Race and Resistance: Literature and Politics in Asian America* (Oxford: Oxford University Press, 2002); David Palumbo-Liu, *Asian/American: Historical Crossings of a Racial Frontier* (Stanford: Stanford University Press, 1999); and Epifanio San Juan Jr., *Racial Formations/Critical Transformations: Articulations of Power in Ethnic Studies and Racial Studies in the United States* (Atlantic Highland, N.J.: Humanities Press, 1992).

3. Carlos Bulosan, *America Is in the Heart: A Personal History* (1946; reprint, Seattle: University of Washington Press, 1973).

4. Quoted in Elaine Kim, *Asian American Literature: An Introduction to the Writings and Their Social Context* (Philadelphia: Temple University Press, 1988), 44.

5. In order to differentiate between the narrator and author of the quasi-autobiographical *America Is in the Heart*, I refer to the former as "Carlos" and to the latter as "Bulosan."

6. For some fine readings of the anticolonial dimensions of Bulosan's work, see Epifanio San Juan Jr., *Carlos Bulosan and the Imagination of the Class Struggle* (Quezon City: University of the Philippines Press, 1972); Epifanio San Juan Jr., "Filipino Writing in the United States: Reclaiming Whose America?" *Philippine Studies* 41 (1993): 141–66; Epifanio San Juan Jr., introduction to *On Becoming Filipino: Selected Writings of Carlos Bulosan*, by Carlos Bulosan (Philadelphia: Temple University Press, 1995); and Tim Libretti, "First and Third Worlds in U.S. Literature: Rethinking Carlos Bulosan," *MELUS Journal* 23.4 (1998): 135–55.

7. Rachel C. Lee, *The Americas of Asian American Literature: Gendered Fictions of Nation and Transnation* (Princeton: Princeton University Press, 1999).

8. Sheng-mei Ma, *Immigrant Subjectivities in Asian American and Asian Diaspora Literatures* (Albany, N.Y.: State University of New York Press, 1998), 78.

9. Epifanio San Juan, Jr., "Searching for the Heart of 'America,' " in *Teaching American Ethnic Literatures*, ed. John R. Maitino and David R. Peck (Albuquerque: University of New Mexico Press, 1996), 260.

10. Michel Foucault, *The History of Sexuality*, vol. 1, trans. Robert Hurley (New York: Random House, 1978), 143.

11. Foucault, *The History of Sexuality*, vol. 1, 140.

12. Ibid., 144.

13. See Dorothy B. Fujita-Rony, *American Workers, Colonial Power: Philippine Seattle and the Transpacific West, 1919–1941* (Berkeley: University of California Press, 2003). My use of the pronoun *he* in referring to the worker in Bulosan's writings is deliberate. Although Bulosan often used a universalist rhetoric to represent the worker, his conceptualization of workers' struggles was clearly gendered.

14. Lauren Berlant and Michael Warner, "Sex in Public," in "Intimacy," ed. Lauren Berlant, special issue, *Critical Inquiry* 24.2 (1998): 323.

15. Ronald T. Takaki, *Strangers from a Different Shore: A History of Asian Americans* (New York: Penguin, 1990), 341–43; and Leti Volpp, "American Mestizo: Filipinos and Antimiscegenation Laws in California," University of California Davis Law Review 33 (2000): 795–835.

16. Rachel F. Moran, *Interracial Intimacy: The Regulation of Race and Romance* (Chicago: University of Chicago Press, 2002), 41.

17. H. Brett Melendy, "Filipinos in the United States," in *Asian Indians, Filipinos, Other Asian Communities and the Law*, ed. Charles McClain (New York: Garland, 1994), 20–47; S. E. Wallovitts, *The Filipinos in California* (San Francisco: R and E Associates, 1972); and Bruno Lasker, *Filipino Immigration to the United States and to Hawaii* (New York: Arno, 1969).

18. Ibid.

19. The unique position of the Philippines as the only Asian nation with which the United States had a history of colonial and neocolonial domination calls for different paradigms from those applied to other Asian American groups. N. V. M. Gonzalez and Oscar V. Campomanes note that the "historical engagement with the legacy of colonialism . . . charges the Filipino (American) literary tradition with its constitutive tensions." N. V. M. Gonzalez and Oscar V. Campomanes, "Filipino American Literature," in *An Interethnic Companion to Asian American Literature*, 62. For a vigorous call for rethinking Filipino American literature, see Oscar V. Campomanes, "The New Empire's Forgetful and Forgotten Citizens: Unrepresentability and Unassimilability in Filipino-American Postcolonialities," *Hitting Critical Mass* 2.2 (1995): 145–200; and Campomanes, "New Formations of Asian American Studies," 523–50.

20. José A. Cabranes, *Citizenship and the American Empire* (New Haven: Yale University Press, 1979).

21. Volpp, "American Mestizo," 822–23.

22. Ibid., 799.

23. Paul G. Cressey, *The Taxi-Dance Hall: A Sociological Study in Commercialized Recreation and City Life* (Chicago: University of Illinois Press, 1932); and Rhacel Salazar Parreñas, " 'White Trash' Meets the 'Little Brown Monkeys': The Taxi Dance Hall as a Site of Interracial and Gender Alliances between White Working Class Women and Filipino Immigrant Men in the 1920s and 30s," *Amerasia Journal* 24.2 (1998): 115–34.

24. U.S. Congress Committee on Immigration and Naturalization, *Exclusion of Immigration from the Philippine Islands* (Washington, D.C.: Government Printing Office, 1930).

25. Justice of the Peace D. W. Rohrback, quoted in H. Brett Melendy, *Asians in America: Filipinos, Koreans, and East Indians* (New York: Hippocrene, 1977), 55.

26. Emory Bogardus notes that competition over scarce jobs in the months preceding the riots intensified white hostility to Filipinos. In addition, the passage of a resolution condemning Filipinos and calling for their exclusion by the Northern Monterey Chamber of Commerce fuelled local resentment toward them. Bogardus, "Anti-Filipino Race Riots," in *The Philippines Reader*, ed. Daniel B. Schirmer and Stephen Rosskamm Shalom (Boston: South End Press, 1987), 58–62.

27. Volpp, "American Mestizo," 812–13.

28. As quoted in "Filipinos' White Girls: Waitress Tells of Mixed Race Parties," *San Francisco Chronicle*, Feb. 22, 1936: 13.

29. For an analysis of medical discourse in representations of the Philippines, see Warwick Anderson, "'Where Every Prospect Pleases and Only Man is Vile': Laboratory Medicine and Colonial Discourse," in *Discrepant Histories: Translocal Essays on Filipino Cultures*, ed. Vicente L. Rafael (Philadelphia: Temple University Press, 1995), 83–112. See also Reynaldo C. Ileto, "Cholera and the Origins of the American Sanitary Order in the Philippines," in *Discrepant Histories*, ed. Rafael, 51–82.

30. Marlon Fuentes, dir., *Bontoc Eulogy*, produced, written, and edited by Fuentes (New York: Cinema Guild, 1995).

31. Vicente L. Rafael, *White Love and Other Events in Filipino History* (Durham: Duke University Press, 2000), 34. Rafael's study of the first census of Philippine populations administered by the U.S. government shows how the population was classified by linguistic divisions, skin color, citizenship, and birthplace, but then these disparate categories were collapsed into two primary divisions between "wild" and "civilized" groups. All those groups who shared a Christian culture fell into the "civilized" category, while all those who were Muslim or animists were labeled "wild." Rafael, *White Love*, 33. This classification denied non-Christian faiths or indigenous religious practices the status of religious or spiritual expression. In part, the erasure of local religions was possible because the majority of the population was Catholic, unlike in larger Asian countries such as China and India, where Christian converts formed a tiny fraction of the total population. In the latter instances, native religions comprised a larger, more widespread, and socially dense structural feature of native societies and hence could not be written out of colonial accounts as "wild" social forms. The almost reflexive attribution of spirituality or religiosity to these other Asian groups, albeit often in conjunction with heathenism and decadence, stands in contrast to the emptying out of indigenous spirituality in the Philippine case.

32. As a form of postcolonial critique, Bulosan's text might usefully be read

alongside Jose Rizal's "The Indolence of Filipinos" or S. H. Alatas's magisterial *The Myth of the Lazy Native*, which offer sustained rebuttals of colonial images of the native in Southeast Asia. Jose Rizal, "The Indolence of the Filipinos," in *Selected Essays and Letters of Jose Rizal*, ed. and trans. E. Alzona (Manila: Rangel and Sons, 1964); S. H. Alatas, *The Myth of the Lazy Native* (London: Frank Cass, 1977).

33. Frantz Fanon, *Black Skin, White Masks* (1967; reprint, New York: Grove Press, 1982), 63.

34. For discussions of the role of education in furthering imperialist ideologies, see Barbara S. Gaerlan, "The Pursuit of Modernity: Trinidad H. Pardo de Tavera and the Educational Legacy of the Philippine Revolution," *Amerasia Journal* 24.2 (1998): 87–108; and Renato Constantino, with the collaboration of Letizia R. Constantino, *The Philippines: A Past Revisited* (Quezon City: Tala Publishing Services, 1975).

35. Lauren Berlant and Michael Warner, "Sex in Public,' in "Intimacy," ed. Lauren Berlant, special issue, *Critical Inquiry* 24.2 (1998): 318.

36. Ibid., 317.

37. M. M. Bakhtin, *The Dialogic Imagination*, ed. Michael Holquist and trans. Caryl Emerson and Michael Holquist (Austin, Tex.: University of Texas Press, 1981), 84.

38. For further discussions of this strategy of inclusive exclusion, see the work of Sucheng Chan, Gordon Chang, Yen Le Espiritu, Lisa Lowe, Gary Okihiro, David Palumbo-Liu, and Ronald Takaki.

39. Cressey, *The Taxi-Dance Hall*, 11.

40. P. C. Morantte, *Remembering Carlos Bulosan: His Heart Affair with America* (Quezon City: New Day, 1984), 66.

41. Andreas Huyssen, *Twilight Memories: Marking Time in a Culture of Amnesia* (New York: Routledge, 1995), 35.

42. Quoted in Epifanio San Juan Jr., *From Exile to Diaspora: Versions of the Filipino Experience in the United States* (Boulder, Colo.: Westview Press, 1998), 34–35.

43. Carlos Bulosan, "The Romance of Magno Rubio," *Amerasia Journal* 6.1 (1979): 33–50.

44. Fanon, *Black Skin, White Masks*, 63.

45. The plot of interracial desire provided Bulosan a narrative framework for representing the incorporation of the Filipino subject into "America." However, the process of incorporation he represents is not commensurate with assimilation; rather, what he attempts to explore is how the Filipino experience of colonization and racial oppression reopens the question of what America has come to mean in the present and how the struggles of Filipinos in the Philippines and the United

States, in resonating with struggles against fascism, colonialism, and capitalism worldwide, call for more expansive conceptions of solidarity than those circumscribed by the nation-state.

46. Françoise Vergès, *Monsters and Revolutionaries: Colonial Family Romance and Métissage* (Durham: Duke University Press, 1999).

47. Ibid., 3–7.

48. Steffi San Buenaventura points out that "granting the Filipino natives 'ward status' without citizenship rights was a very convenient solution to the problem of not having to assimilate a 'barbarous' people living in a distant U.S. territory in the Pacific." San Buenaventura, "The Colors of Manifest Destiny: Filipinos and the American Other(s)," *Amerasia Journal* 24.3 (1998): 7.

49. David Joel Steinberg, quoted in Epifanio San Juan Jr., "One Hundred Years of Producing and Reproducing the 'Filipino,' " *Amerasia Journal* 24.2 (1998): 10.

50. Quoted in San Juan, *From Exile to Diaspora*, 96.

51. Ma, *Immigrant Subjectivities*, 81–82.

52. Carole Pateman, "The Fraternal Social Contract," in *The Disorder of Women: Democracy, Feminism, and Political Theory*, ed. Pateman (Stanford: Stanford University Press, 1989), 43.

53. Anne McClintock, "Family Feuds: Gender, Nationalism, and the Family," *Feminist Review* 44 (1993): 78.

54. Nira Yuval-Davis lists these as two of the characteristic roles played by women in nationalist discourse. Nira Yuval-Davis, "Gender and Nation," *Ethnic and Racial Studies* 16.4 (1993): 620–32.

55. Annette Kolodny, *The Lay of the Land: Metaphor as Experience and History in American Life and Letters* (Chapel Hill: University of North Carolina Press, 1975), 4.

56. Ibid., 67.

57. Deniz Kandiyoti, "Identity and Its Discontents: Women and the Nation," *Millennium: Journal of International Studies* 20.3 (1991): 434.

58. Nira Yuval-Davis, "Gender and Nation," 623.

59. For scholarship on the intersections of race and sexuality, see José Quiroga, *Tropics of Desire: Interventions from Queer Latino America* (New York: New York University Press, 2000); Arnaldo Cruz-Malavé and Martin F. Manalansan, eds., *Queer Globalizations: Citizenship and the Afterlife of Colonialism* (New York: New York University Press, 2002); José Esteban Muñoz, *Disidentifications: Queers of Color and the Performance of Politics* (Minneapolis: University of Minnesota Press, 1999); Siobhan B. Somerville, *Queering the Color Line: Race and the Invention of Homosexuality in American Culture* (Durham: Duke University Press, 2000); and

Urvashi Vaid, "Inclusion, Exclusion, and Occlusion: The Queer Idea of Asian Pacific American-ness," *Amerasia Journal* 25.3 (1999–2000): 1–16.

Chapter 4

1. John Luther Long, "Madame Butterfly," in *Madame Butterfly, Purple Eyes, etc.* (1898; reprint, New York: Garrett Press, 1969), 1–86; Bharati Mukherjee, *Wife* (1975; reprint, New York: Fawcett Crest-Ballantine, 1993); Bharati Mukherjee, *Jasmine* (1989; reprint, New York: Fawcett Crest-Ballantine, 1991).

2. For discussions of American Orientalism, see James Moy, *Marginal Sights: Staging the Chinese in America* (Iowa City: University of Iowa Press, 1993); Malini Johar Schueller, *U.S. Orientalisms: Race, Nation, and Gender in Literature, 1790–1890* (Ann Arbor: University of Michigan Press, 1998); John Kuo Wei Tchen, *New York before Chinatown: Orientalism and the Shaping of American Culture, 1776–1882* (Baltimore: Johns Hopkins University Press, 1999); William F. Wu, *The Yellow Peril: Chinese Americans in American Fiction 1850–1940* (Hamden, Conn.: Archon Books, 1982); Mari Yoshihara, *Embracing the East: White Women and American Orientalism* (New York: Oxford University Press, 2003); and Henry Yu, *Thinking Orientals: Migration, Contact, and Exoticism in Modern America* (New York: Oxford University Press, 2001).

3. For further analysis, see Tomo Hattori, "Model Minority Discourse and Asian American Jouis-Sense," *differences: A Journal of Feminist Criticism* 11.2 (1999): 228–47; Bob H. Suzuki, "Education and the Socialization of Asian Americans: A Revisionist Analysis of the 'Model Minority' Thesis," *Amerasia* 4.2 (1977): 23–51.

4. John D'Emilio and Estelle B. Freedman, *Intimate Matters: A History of Sexuality in America* (New York: Harper and Row, 1988), 343.

5. For further elaborations of this argument, see Susan Koshy, "The Geography of Female Subjectivity: Ethnicity, Gender, and Diaspora in Mukherjee's Fiction," *Diaspora* 3 (1994): 69–84; and Koshy, "Bharati Mukherjee's Jasmine," in *Resource Guide to Asian American Literature*, ed. Stephen Sumida and Sau-ling Cynthia Wong (New York: Modern Language Association, 2001), 165–77.

6. Pierre Bourdieu and Jean-Claude Passeron, *Reproduction in Education, Society, and Culture*, trans. Richard Nice (London: Sage in association with Theory, Culture, and Society, Department of Administrative and Social Studies, Teesside Polytechnic, 1990).

7. See Yen Le Espiritu, *Asian American Women and Men: Labor, Laws, and Love* (Thousand Oaks, Calif.: Sage, 1997).

8. U.S. Department of Labor, *The Negro Family: The Case for National Action* (Washington D.C.: U.S. Government Printing Office, 1965), 29.

9. I'm especially grateful to filmmaker Gurinder Chadha for her provocative questions about the violence in Mukherjee's stories.

10. Bharati Mukherjee, "An Interview with Bharati Mukherjee," by Geoff Hancock, *Canadian Fiction Magazine* 59 (1987): 37.

11. Cheryl I. Harris, "Whiteness as Property," *Harvard Law Review* 106.8 (1993): 1743–44.

12. Bharati Mukherjee, *The Holder of the World* (New York: Knopf, 1993).

13. On the gendering of cultural purism in the Indian immigrant community, see Anannya Bhattacharjee, "The Habit of Ex-Nomination: Nation, Woman, and the Indian Immigrant Bourgeoisie," *Public Culture* 5.1 (1992): 19–44.

14. Bharati Mukherjee, "An Interview with Bharati Mukherjee," by Michael Connell, Jessie Grearson, and Tom Grimes, *Iowa Review* 20.3 (1990): 25–26.

15. Ibid., 11.

16. David Leiwei Li, *Imagining the Nation: Asian American Literature and Cultural Consent* (Stanford: Stanford University Press, 1998), 96.

17. This question is raised by Kristin Carter-Sanborn, "'We Murder Who We Were': *Jasmine* and the Violence of Identity," *American Literature* 66.3 (1994): 573–93. Other important discussions of Mukherjee's work include Anindyo Roy and Gurleen Grewal in *Bharati Mukherjee: Critical Perspectives*, ed. Emmanuel S. Nelson (New York: Garland, 1993); Lavina Dhingra Shankar, "Activism, 'Feminisms,' and Americanization in Bharati Mukherjee's *Wife* and *Jasmine*," *Hitting Critical Mass: A Journal of Asian American Cultural Criticism* 3.1 (1995): 61–84; John C. Hawley, "Assimilation and Resistance in Female Fiction of Immigration: Bharati Mukherjee, Amy Tan, and Christine Bell," in *Rediscovering America, 1492–1992: National, Cultural, and Disciplinary Boundaries Re-examined* (Baton Rouge: Louisiana State University Press, 1992), 226–34; and Patricia Chu, *Gendered Strategies of Assimilation* (Durham: Duke University Press, 2000).

18. Sarah Curtis, "All American Indian," book review of Bharati Mukherjee's *Jasmine*, *Times Literary Supplement*, Apr. 27, 1990: 436. Quoted in Carter-Sanborn, "'We Murder Who We Were,'" 589.

19. Bharati Mukherjee, *Leave It to Me* (New York: Knopf, 1997). In a similar representation of contrasting images of female power in Maxine Hong Kingston's *The Woman Warrior*, the narrator contrasts the story of the mythical woman warrior Fa Mu Lan to that of the avenging Amazons, former concubines of the dead baron, who turn their experience of oppression into a crusade to rescue outcaste women in their society and kill their male tormentors. This tale is appended to Fa Mu Lan's story, which is a story of a woman who enacts a desire for a non-traditional role in the guise of a man and then returns after the war to her proper position as wife, mother, and daughter-in-law. The story of the Amazons enacts

empowerment as a revenge fantasy of power, but this desire turns the women into outlaws and conflicts with the narrator Maxine's profound desire to create an empowering female persona that will not obstruct her acceptance within the Chinese American community. In *Jasmine* and *The Woman Warrior*, the tension is between outlaw female power expressed as rage against male oppression and female power secured through heterosexual relations with men. Maxine Hong Kingston, *The Woman Warrior* (1975; reprint, New York: Vintage, 1989), 44–45.

20. Review of *Jasmine* from *The Baltimore Sun*, quoted on paperback cover of Bharati Mukherjee, *Jasmine* (New York: Fawcett Crest, 1989).

21. Bharati Mukherjee, "An Interview," by Connell, Grearson, and Grimes, 25.

22. Carter-Sanborn, " 'We Murder Who We Were,' " 576.

23. Bharati Mukherjee, "An Interview," by Connell, Grearson, and Grimes, 25.

24. See Suzanne Kehde, "Colonial Discourse and Female Identity: Bharati Mukherjee's *Jasmine*," in *International Women's Writing: New Landscapes of Identity*, ed. Anne E. Brown (Westport: Greenwood, 1995), 70–77.

25. Michael Hardt and Antonio Negri, *Empire* (Cambridge: Harvard University Press, 2000), 138.

26. Susan Koshy, "Morphing Race into Ethnicity: Asian Americans and Critical Transformations of Whiteness," *Boundary* 2 28.1 (2001): 194.

27. Michel Foucault, *The History of Sexuality*, vol. 1, trans. Robert Hurley (New York: Random House, 1978), 103.

Bibliography

Affron, Charles. *Star Acting: Gish, Garbo, Davis.* New York: Dutton, 1977.

Alatas, S. H. *The Myth of the Lazy Native.* London: Frank Cass, 1977.

Almaguer, Tomás. *Racial Fault Lines: The Historical Origins of White Supremacy in California.* Berkeley: University of California Press, 1994.

Anderson, Benedict. *Imagined Communities: Reflections on the Origin and Spread of Nationalism.* Rev. ed. London: Verso, 1992.

Anderson, Warwick. " 'Where Every Prospect Pleases and Only Man is Vile' ": Laboratory Medicine and Colonial Discourse." In *Discrepant Histories: Translocal Essays on Filipino Cultures,* ed. Vicente L. Rafael, 83–112. Philadelphia: Temple University Press, 1995.

Andrew, Dudley. *Film in the Aura of Art.* Princeton: Princeton University Press, 1984.

Armstrong, Nancy. *Desire and Domestic Fiction: A Political History of the Novel.* New York: Oxford University Press, 1987.

Aslin, Elizabeth. *The Aesthetic Movement: Prelude to Art Nouveau.* New York: Praeger, 1969.

Bailey-Harris, Rebecca. "Madame Butterfly and the Conflict of Laws." *The American Journal of Comparative Law* 39.1 (1991): 157–77.

Bakhtin, M. M. *The Dialogic Imagination.* Ed. Michael Holquist, trans. Caryl Emerson and Michael Holquist. Austin, Tex.: University of Texas Press, 1981.

Barnett, Corelli. *The Collapse of British Power.* London: Eyre Methuen, 1972.

Belasco, David. *Madame Butterfly.* In *Six Plays.* Boston: Little, Brown and Co., 1928.

Berlant, Lauren. "Intimacy: A Special Issue." In "Intimacy," ed. Lauren Berlant, special issue, *Critical Inquiry* 24.2 (1998): 1–8.

Berlant, Lauren, and Michael Warner. "Sex in Public." In "Intimacy," ed. Lauren Berlant, special issue, *Critical Inquiry* 24.2 (1998): 311–30.

Bhabha, Homi K. "DissemiNation: Time, Narrative, and the Margins of the Modern Nation." In *Nation and Narration,* ed. Homi K. Bhabha, 291–322. London: Routledge, 1990.

———. "Of Mimicry and Man: The Ambivalence of Colonial Discourse." *October* 28 (1984): 125–33.

Bhattacharjee, Anannya. "The Habit of Ex-Nomination: Nation, Woman, and the Indian Immigrant Bourgeoisie." *Public Culture* 5.1 (1992): 19–44.

Björkman, Edwin. *Thomas Burke: A Critical Appreciation of the Man of Limehouse.* New York: Doran, n.d.

Bogardus, Emory S. "Anti-Filipino Race Riots." In *The Philippines Reader,* ed. Daniel B. Schirmer and Stephen Rosskamm Shalom, 58–62. Boston: South End Press, 1987.

Bogle, Donald. "Black Beginnings: From *Uncle Tom's Cabin* to *The Birth of a Nation.*" In *Representing Blackness: Issues in Film and Video,* ed. Valerie Smith, 13–24. New Brunswick: Rutgers University Press, 1997.

———. *Toms, Coons, Mulattoes, and Bucks: An Interpretive History of Blacks in American Films.* New York: Continuum, 1994.

Bourdieu, Pierre, and Jean-Claude Passeron. *Reproduction in Education, Society, and Culture.* Trans. Richard Nice. London: Sage in association with Theory, Culture, and Society, Department of Administrative and Social Studies, Teesside Polytechnic, 1990.

Bredbenner, Candice Lewis. *A Nationality of Her Own: Women, Marriage, and the Law of Citizenship.* Berkeley: University of California Press, 1998.

Brown, Karl. *Adventures with D. W. Griffith.* New York: Farrar, 1973.

Browne, Nick. "Orientalism as an Ideological Form: American Film Theory in the Silent Period." *Wide Angle: Film Quarterly of Theory, Criticism, and Practice* 11.4 (1989): 23–31.

Bulosan, Carlos. *America Is in the Heart.* 1946. Reprint, Seattle: University of Washington Press, 1973.

———. "The Romance of Magno Rubio." *Amerasia Journal* 6.1 (1979): 33–50.

Burke, Thomas. "The Chink and the Child." *Limehouse Nights,* 15–37. London: Grant Richards, 1917.

———. *The London Spy: A Book of Town Travels.* New York: George H. Doran Company, 1922.

———. *Nights in Town: A London Autobiography.* London: G. Allen and Unwin, 1915.

———. *Out and about London.* New York: H. Holt and Company, 1919.

———. *Son of London.* London: Herbert Jenkins Limited, 1946.

Butler, Judith. *Bodies That Matter: On the Discursive Limits of "Sex."* New York: Routledge, 1993.

Butters, Gerald R., Jr. "African-American Cinema and *The Birth of a Nation.*" In *Black Manhood on the Silent Screen.* Lawrence, Kans.: University Press of Kansas, 2002.

Cabranes, José A. *Citizenship and the American Empire.* New Haven: Yale University Press, 1979.

Campomanes, Oscar V. "The New Empire's Forgetful and Forgotten Citizens: Unrepresentability and Unassimilability in Filipino-American Postcolonialities." *Hitting Critical Mass* 2.2 (1995): 145–200.

———. "New Formations of Asian American Studies and the Question of U.S. Imperialism." *positions: east asia cultures critique* 5.2 (1997): 523–50.

Carter-Sanborn, Kristin. "'We Murder Who We Were': *Jasmine* and the Violence of Identity." *American Literature* 66.3 (1994): 573–93.

Chan, Sucheng. *Asian Americans: An Interpretive History.* Boston: Twayne, 1991.

———. "The Exclusion of Chinese Women, 1870–1943." In *Chinese Immigrants and American Law,* ed. Charles J. McClain, 2–54. New York: Garland, 1994.

Chang, Gordon H. Introduction to *Asian Americans and Politics: Perspectives, Experiences, Prospects,* ed. Chang, 1–10. Stanford: Stanford University Press, 2001.

Cheung, King-Kok. *Articulate Silences.* Ithaca: Cornell University Press, 1993.

———, ed. *An Interethnic Companion to Asian American Literature.* New York: Cambridge University Press, 1997.

———. "The Woman Warrior versus The Chinaman Pacific: Must a Chinese American Critic Choose between Feminism and Heroism?" In *Conflicts in Feminism,* ed. Marianne Hirsch and Evelyn Fox Keller, 234–51. New York: Routledge, 1990.

Chin, Frank, and Jeffrey Paul Chan. "Racist Love." In *Seeing through Shuck,* ed. Richard Kostelanetz, 65–79. New York: Ballantine, 1972.

Chisholm, Brad. "Reading Intertitles." *Journal of Popular Film and Television* 15 (1987): 137–42.

Christensen, Terry. *Reel Politics: American Political Movies from "Birth of a Nation" to "Platoon."* New York: Blackwell, 1987.

Chu, Patricia. *Gendered Strategies of Assimilation.* Durham: Duke University Press, 2000.

Clymer, Kenton J. *Protestant Missionaries in the Philippines, 1898–1916: An Inquiry into the American Colonial Mentality.* Urbana, Ill.: University of Illinois Press, 1986.

Cohen, Warren I. *East Asian Art and American Culture.* New York: Columbia University Press, 1992.

Connelly, Mark Thomas. *The Response to Prostitution in the Progressive Era.* Chapel Hill: University of North Carolina Press, 1980.

Constantino, Renato, with the collaboration of Letizia R. Constantino. *The Philippines: A Past Revisited.* Quezon City: Tala Publishing Services, 1975.

Cooper, Frederick, and Ann Laura Stoler, ed. *Tensions of Empire: Colonial Cultures in a Bourgeois World.* Berkeley: University of California Press, 1997.

Correl, Irvin H., Mrs. "Madame Butterfly: Her Long Secret Revealed." *Japan Magazine* (May 1931): 341–45.

Cressey, Paul G. *The Taxi-Dance Hall: A Sociological Study in Commercialized Recreation and City Life.* Chicago: University of Illinois Press, 1932.

Cripps, Thomas. *Slow Fade to Black: The Negro in American Film, 1900–1942.* New York: Oxford University Press, 1993.

Cruz-Malavé, Arnaldo, and Martin F. Manalansan, eds. *Queer Globalizations: Citizenship and the Afterlife of Colonialism.* New York: New York University Press, 2002.

Daniels, Roger. "U.S. Policy toward Asian Immigrants: Contemporary Developments in Historical Perspective." *International Journal* 63.2 (1993): 310–34.

Davis, Angela Y. *Women, Race, and Class.* New York: Random House, 1981.

Dawson, Carl. *Lafcadio Hearn and the Vision of Japan.* Baltimore: Johns Hopkins University Press, 1992.

D'Emilio, John, and Estelle B. Freedman. *Intimate Matters: A History of Sexuality in America.* New York: Harper and Row, 1988.

Derrida, Jacques. *Of Grammatology.* Trans. Gayatri Chakravorty Spivak. Baltimore: Johns Hopkins University Press, 1976.

Diawara, Manthia. "Black Spectatorship: Problems of Identification and Resistance." *Screen* 29.4 (1988): 66–76.

Dixon, Thomas, Jr. *The Clansman: An Historical Romance of the Ku Klux Klan.* New York: Doubleday, Page and Company, 1905.

———. *The Leopard's Spots: A Romance of the White Man's Burden, 1865–1900.* New York: Doubleday, Page and Company, 1902.

Dyer, Richard. "Into the Light: The Whiteness of the South in *The Birth of a Nation.*" In *Dixie Debates: Perspectives on Southern Cultures,* ed. Richard H. King and Helen Taylor, 165–76. New York: New York University Press, 1996.

———. *White.* London: Routledge, 1997.

Eagleton, Terry. *The Ideology of the Aesthetic.* Oxford: Blackwell, 1990.

Eisenstein, Sergei. "Dickens, Griffith, and the Film Today." *Film Form: Essays in Film Theory.* Ed. and trans. Jay Leyda, 195–255. San Diego: Harvest, 1977.

Eng, David L. *Racial Castration: Managing Masculinity in Asian America.* Durham: Duke University Press, 2001.

Enloe, Cynthia. *Bananas, Beaches and Bases: Making Feminist Sense of International Politics*. Berkeley: University of California Press, 1989.

Espiritu, Yen Le. *Asian American Women and Men: Labor, Laws, and Love*. Thousand Oaks, Calif.: Sage, 1997.

Fabian, Johannes. *Time and the Other: How Anthropology Makes Its Object*. New York: Columbia University Press, 1983.

Fanon, Frantz. *Black Skin, White Masks*. 1967. Reprint, New York: Grove Press, 1982.

"Filipinos' White Girls: Waitress Tells of Mixed Race Parties," *San Francisco Chronicle*, Feb. 22, 1936: 13.

Fisher, Philip. *Hard Facts: Setting and Form in the American Novel*. New York: Oxford University Press, 1985.

Flitterman-Lewis, Sandy. "The Blossom and the Bole: Narrative and Visual Spectacle in Early Film Melodrama." *Cinema Journal* 33.3 (1994): 3–15.

Foster, Nellie. "Legal Status of Filipino Intermarriage in California." In *Asian Indians, Filipinos, Other Asian Communities and the Law*, ed. Charles McClain, 5–18. New York: Garland, 1994.

Foucault, Michel. *The History of Sexuality*. Vol. 1. Trans. Robert Hurley. New York: Random House, 1978.

Fuentes, Marlon E., dir. *Bontoc Eulogy*. Produced, written, and edited by Fuentes. New York: Cinema Guild, 1995.

Fujita-Rony, Dorothy B. *American Workers, Colonial Power: Philippine Seattle and the Transpacific West, 1919–1941*. Berkeley: University of California Press, 2003.

Gaerlan, Barbara S. "The Pursuit of Modernity: Trinidad H. Pardo de Tavera and the Educational Legacy of the Philippine Revolution," *Amerasia Journal* 24.2 (1998): 87–108.

Gish, Lillian, with Ann Pinchot. *Lillian Gish: The Movies, Mr. Griffith, and Me*. Englewood Cliffs, N.J.: Prentice-Hall, 1969.

Gonzalez, N. V. M., and Oscar V. Campomanes. "Filipino American Literature." In *An Interethnic Companion to Asian American Literature*, ed. King-Kok Cheung, 62–124. New York: Cambridge University Press, 1997.

Grewal, Gurleen. "Born Again American: The Immigrant Consciousness in *Jasmine*." In *Bharati Mukherjee: Critical Perspectives*, ed. Emmanuel S. Nelson, 181–96. New York: Garland, 1993.

Griffith, D. W., dir. *The Birth of a Nation*, 1915. Scenario by Griffith and Frank Woods, based on the play and the novel *The Clansman: An Historical Romance of the Ku Klux Klan*, by Thomas Dixon Jr., with additional material from Dixon's *The Leopard's Spots: A Romance of the White Man's Burden, 1865–1900*.
———, dir. *Hearts of the World*. Paramount-Artcraft, 1918.

——, dir. *The Greatest Thing in Life*. Paramount-Artcraft, 1918. No prints known to exist.

——, dir. *Way Down East*. United Artists, 1920.

——, dir. *Broken Blossoms*. Scenario by Griffith, based on "The Chink and the Child" by Thomas Burke. Perf. Lillian Gish, Richard Barthelmess, and Donald Crisp. Photography, Bitzer; "Special Effects," Henrik Sartov. United Artists. Premiere, George M. Cohan Theater, New York, May 13, 1919; general release, October 20, 1920.

Grimshaw, Patricia. *Paths of Duty: American Missionary Wives in Nineteenth-Century Hawaii*. Honolulu: University of Hawaii Press, 1989.

Groos, Arthur. "Lieutenant F. B. Pinkerton: Problems in the Genesis of an Operatic Hero." *Italica* 64.4 (1987): 654–75.

Grossberg, Michael. *Governing the Hearth: Law and the Family in Nineteenth-Century America*. Chapel Hill: University of North Carolina Press, 1985.

Hall, Ben. *The Best Remaining Seats: The Story of the Golden Age of the Movie Palace*. New York: Clarkson N. Potter, 1961.

Hansen, Miriam. "Universal Language and Democratic Culture: Myths of Origin in Early American Cinema." In *Mythos und Aufklärung in der Amerikanischen Literatur* [Myth and Enlightenment in American Literature], ed. Dieter Meindl and Friedrich W. Horlacher, 321–51. Erlangen: Universitätsbund Erlangen-Nürnberg, 1985.

Hardt, Michael, and Antonio Negri. *Empire*. Cambridge: Harvard University Press, 2000.

Harris, Cheryl I. "Whiteness as Property." *Harvard Law Review* 106.8 (1993): 1709–91.

Harris, Neil. "All the World a Melting Pot? Japan at American Fairs, 1876–1904." In *Mutual Images: Essays in American-Japanese Relations,* ed. Akira Iriye, 24–54. Cambridge, Mass.: Harvard University Press, 1975.

Hattori, Tomo. "Model Minority Discourse and Asian American Jouis-Sense." *differences: A Journal of Feminist Criticism* 11.2 (1999): 228–47.

Hawley, John C. "Assimilation and Resistance in Female Fiction of Immigration: Bharati Mukherjee, Amy Tan, and Christine Bell." In *Rediscovering America, 1492–1992: National, Cultural, and Disciplinary Boundaries Re-examined*, 226–34. Baton Rouge: Louisiana State University Press, 1992.

Henderson, Robert M. *D. W. Griffith: His Life and Work*. New York: Oxford University Press, 1972.

Higham, John. *Strangers in the Land: Patterns of American Nativism, 1860–1925*. New Brunswick, N.J.: Rutgers University Press, 1955.

Hing, Bill Ong. *Making and Remaking Asian America Through Immigration Policy, 1850–1990*. Stanford: Stanford University Press, 1993.

Hunter, Jane. *The Gospel of Gentility: American Women Missionaries in Turn-of-the-Century China.* New Haven: Yale University Press, 1984.

Huyssen, Andreas. *Twilight Memories: Marking Time in a Culture of Amnesia.* New York: Routledge, 1995.

Hwang, David Henry. *M. Butterfly.* New York: Plume, 1989.

Ignatiev, Noel. *How the Irish Became White.* New York: Routledge, 1995.

Ileto, Reynaldo C. "Cholera and the Origins of the American Sanitary Order in the Philippines." In *Discrepant Histories: Translocal Essays on Filipino Cultures,* ed. Vicente L. Rafael, 51–82. Philadelphia: Temple University Press, 1995.

Iriye, Akira. *Across the Pacific: An Inner History of American-East Asian Relations.* New York: Harcourt, 1967.

———. "Japan as a Competitor, 1895–1917." In *Mutual Images: Essays in American-Japanese Relations,* ed. Akira Iriye, 73–99. Cambridge, Mass.: Harvard University Press, 1975.

Isaacs, Harold R. *Scratches on Our Minds: American Images of China and India.* New York: John Day, 1958.

Jacobson, Matthew Frye. *Whiteness of a Different Color: European Immigrants and the Alchemy of Race.* Cambridge, Mass.: Harvard University Press, 1998.

Jay, Gregory S. "'White Man's Book No Good': D. W. Griffith and the American Indian." *Cinema Journal* 39.4 (2000): 3–26.

Jensen, Joan M. *Passage from India: Asian Indian Immigrants in North America.* New Haven: Yale University Press, 1988.

Jones, Dorothy B. *The Portrayal of China and India on the American Screen, 1896–1955: The Evolution of Chinese and Indian Themes, Locales, and Characters as Portrayed on the American Screen.* Cambridge, Mass.: Center for International Studies, MIT, 1955.

Jones, Gareth Stedman. *Outcast London: A Study of the Relationship between Classes in Victorian Society.* Oxford: Clarendon, 1971.

Kandiyoti, Deniz. "Identity and Its Discontents: Women and the Nation." *Millennium: Journal of International Studies* 20.3 (1991): 429–43.

Kang, Laura Hyun Yi. *Compositional Subjects: Enfiguring Asian/American Women.* Durham: Duke University Press, 2000.

Kaplan, Amy. "Romancing the Empire: The Embodiment of American Masculinity in the Popular Historical Novel of the 1890s." *American Literary History* 2.4 (1990): 659–90.

Kaplan, Amy, and Donald E. Pease, ed. *Cultures of United States Imperialism.* Durham: Duke University Press, 1993.

Kehde, Suzanne. "Colonial Discourse and Female Identity: Bharati Mukherjee's *Jasmine.*" In *International Women's Writing: New Landscapes of Identity,* ed. Anne E. Brown, 70–77. Westport: Greenwood, 1995.

Kennedy, Paul M. *The Rise and Fall of the Great Powers: Economic Change and Military Conflict from 1500–2000.* New York: Vintage, 1989.

Kepley, Vance, Jr. "Griffith's 'Broken Blossoms' and the Problem of Historical Specificity." *Quarterly Review of Film Studies* 3.1 (1978): 37–47.

Kern, Robert. *Orientalism, Modernism, and the American Poem.* Cambridge: Cambridge University Press, 1996.

Kevles, Daniel J. *In the Name of Eugenics: Genetics and the Uses of Human Heredity.* New York: Knopf, 1985.

Kim, Elaine H. *Asian American Literature: An Introduction to the Writings and Their Social Context.* Philadelphia: Temple University Press, 1982.

———. "'Such Opposite Creatures': Men and Women in Asian American Literature." *Michigan Quarterly Review* 29 (1990): 68–93.

Kim, Elaine H., and Lisa Lowe, eds. *positions: east asia cultures critique* 5.2 (1997).

Kindleberger, Charles P. *World Economic Primacy: 1500–1990.* New York: Oxford University Press, 1990.

Kingston, Maxine Hong. *The Woman Warrior.* 1975. Reprint, New York: Vintage, 1989.

Kirby, Jack Temple. "D. W. Griffith's Racial Portraiture." *Phylon* 39.2 (1978): 118–27.

Kolodny, Annette. *The Lay of the Land: Metaphor as Experience and History in American Life and Letters.* Chapel Hill: University of North Carolina Press, 1975.

Koshy, Susan. "Bharati Mukherjee's *Jasmine.*" In *Resource Guide to Asian American Literature,* ed. Stephen Sumida and Sau-ling Cynthia Wong, 165–77. New York: Modern Languages Association, 2001.

———. "Category Crisis: South Asian Americans and Questions of Race and Ethnicity." *Diaspora* 7.3 (1998): 285–320.

———.. "The Fiction of Asian American Literature." *Yale Journal of Criticism* 9.2 (1996): 315–46.

———. "The Geography of Female Subjectivity: Ethnicity, Gender, and Diaspora in Mukherjee's Fiction." *Diaspora* 3 (1994): 69–84.

———. "Morphing Race into Ethnicity: Asian Americans and Critical Transformations of Whiteness." *Boundary 2* 28.1 (2001): 153–94.

Knobel, Dale T. *Paddy and the Republic: Ethnicity and Nationality in Ante-Bellum America.* Middletown, Conn.: Wesleyan University Press, 1986.

LaFeber, Walter. *The New Empire: An Interpretation of American Expansion, 1860–1898.* Ithaca: Cornell University Press, 1963.

Lang, Robert. *American Film Melodrama: Griffith, Vidor, Minnelli.* Princeton: Princeton University Press, 1989.

Lasker, Bruno. *Filipino Immigration to the United States and to Hawaii.* New York: Arno, 1969.

Lears, T. J. Jackson. *No Place of Grace: Antimodernism and the Transformation of American Culture, 1880–1920.* Chicago: University of Chicago Press, 1994.

Lee, Rachel C. *The Americas of Asian American Literature: Gendered Fictions of Nation and Transnation.* Princeton: Princeton University Press, 1999.

Lee, Robert G. *Orientals: Asian Americans in Popular Culture.* Philadelphia: Temple University Press, 1999.

Lehmann, Jeanne-Pierre. "Images of the Orient." In *Madam Butterfly*, English National Opera Guide, no. 26, 7–14.

Leonard, Karen Isaksen. *Making Ethnic Choices: California's Punjabi Mexican Americans.* Philadelphia: Temple University Press, 1992.

Lesage, Julia. "Artful Racism, Artful Rape: Griffith's *Broken Blossoms*." In *Home Is Where the Heart Is: Studies in Melodrama and the Woman's Film*, ed. Christine Gledhill, 235–54. London: BFI Books, 1987.

Li, David Leiwei. *Imagining the Nation: Asian American Literature and Cultural Consent.* Stanford: Stanford University Press, 1998.

Libretti, Tim. "First and Third Worlds in U.S. Literature: Rethinking Carlos Bulosan," *MELUS Journal* 23.4 (1998): 135–55.

Lindsay, Vachel. *The Art of the Moving Picture.* New York: Liverright, 1915.

Ling, Jinqi. *Narrating Nationalisms: Ideology and Form in Asian American Literature.* New York: Oxford University Press, 1998.

Lionnet, Françoise, and Shu-mei Shih, eds. *Minor Transnationalism.* Durham: Duke University Press, 2005.

Loewen, James W. *The Mississippi Chinese: Between Black and White*, 2d ed. Prospect Heights, Ill.: Waveland, 1988.

London, Bette. "Of Mimicry and English Men: E. M. Forster and the Performance of Masculinity" In *A Passage to India*, ed. Tony Davies and Nigel Wood, 90–120. Buckingham, England: Open University Press, 1994.

Long, John Luther. "Madame Butterfly." 1898. Reprint in *Madame Butterfly, Purple Eyes, etc.* The American Short Story Series 25, 1–86. New York: Garrett, 1969.

Loti, Pierre. *Madame Chrysanthemum.* London: KPI, 1985.

Lowe, Lisa. *Immigrant Acts.* Durham: Duke University Press, 1996.

Lye, Colleen. "*M. Butterfly* and the Rhetoric of Antiessentialism: Minority Discourse in an International Frame." In *The Ethnic Canon*, ed. David Palumbo-Liu, 260–89. Minneapolis: University of Minnesota Press, 1995.

Lynn, Kenneth S. "The Torment of D. W. Griffith." *American Scholar* (spring 1990): 255–64.

Ma, Sheng-mei. *Immigrant Subjectivities in Asian American and Asian Diaspora Literatures.* Albany, N.Y.: SUNY Press, 1998.

Marchetti, Gina. *Romance and the "Yellow Peril": Race, Sex, and Discursive Strategies in Hollywood Fiction.* Berkeley: University of California Press, 1993.

Mason, Richard Lakin. *The World of Suzie Wong.* Cleveland, Ohio: World Publishing Company, 1957.

May, Lary. *Screening Out the Past: The Birth of Mass Culture and the Motion Picture Industry.* New York: Oxford University Press, 1980.

McClintock, Anne. "Family Feuds: Gender, Nationalism, and the Family." *Feminist Review* 44 (summer 1993): 61–80.

———. *Imperial Leather: Race, Gender, and Sexuality in the Colonial Contest.* New York: Routledge, 1995.

McCormick, Thomas J. *China Market: America's Quest for Informal Empire, 1893–1901.* Chicago: Quadrangle, 1967.

Meech, Julia, and Gabriel Weisberg. *Japonisme Comes to America: The Japanese Impact on the Graphic Arts, 1876–1925.* New York: Abrams, 1990.

Mehta, Uday S. "Liberal Strategies of Exclusion." In *Tensions of Empire: Colonial Cultures in a Bourgeois World,* ed. Frederick Cooper and Ann Laura Stoler, 59–86. Berkeley: University of California Press, 1997.

Melendy, H. Brett. *Asians in America: Filipinos, Koreans, and East Indians.* New York: Hippocrene, 1977.

———. "Filipinos in the United States." In *Asian Indians, Filipinos, Other Asian Communities and the Law,* ed. Charles McClain, 20–47. New York: Garland, 1994.

Mercer, Kobena. "Reading Racial Fetishism: The Photographs of Robert Mapplethorpe." In *Fetishism as Cultural Discourse,* ed. Emily Apter and William Pietz, 307–29. Ithaca: Cornell University Press, 1993.

Merritt, Russell. "Nickelodeon Theaters 1905–1914: Building an Audience for the Movies." In *The American Film Industry,* ed. Tino Balio, 59–79. Madison: University of Wisconsin Press, 1976.

Metz, Christian. *Language and Cinema.* Trans. Donna Jean Umiker-Sebeok. The Hague: Mouton, 1974.

Miss Saigon. Dir. Nicholas Hytner. Prod. Cameron Mackintosh. Composer, Claude-Michel Schönberg. Lyrics, Alain Boublil and Richard Maltby, Jr. Premiere, Drury Lane Theater, London, Sept. 29, 1989.

Moon, Katherine. *Sex Among Allies: Military Prostitution in U.S.-Korea Relations.* New York: Columbia University Press, 1997.

Moran, Rachel F. *Interracial Intimacy: The Regulation of Race and Romance.* Chicago: University of Chicago Press, 2002.

Morantte, P. C. *Remembering Carlos Bulosan: His Heart Affair with America.* Quezon City: New Day, 1984.

Moses, Montrose J. Introduction to *Madame Butterfly*, by David Belasco. In *Six Plays*. Boston: Little, Brown and Co., 1928.

Mosse, George L. *Nationalism and Sexuality: Respectability and Abnormal Sexuality in Modern Europe*. New York: Fertig, 1985.

Moy, James. *Marginal Sights: Staging the Chinese in America*. Iowa City: University of Iowa Press, 1993.

Mukherjee, Bharati. *Darkness.* Markham, Ont.: Penguin, 1985.

———. "Fighting for the Rebound." In *The Middleman and Other Stories*, 77–94. New York: Fawcett Crest-Ballantine, 1988.

———. *The Holder of the World*. New York: Knopf, 1993.

———. "An Interview with Bharati Mukherjee." By Michael Connell, Jessie Grearson, and Tom Grimes. *Iowa Review* 20.3 (1990): 7–32.

———. "An Interview with Bharati Mukherjee." By Geoff Hancock. *Canadian Fiction Magazine* 59 (1987): 30–44.

———. *Jasmine.* 1989. Reprint, New York: Fawcett Crest-Ballantine, 1991.

———. *Leave It to Me.* New York: Knopf, 1997.

———. *Wife.* 1975. Reprint, New York: Fawcett Crest-Ballantine, 1993.

Muñoz, José Esteban. *Disidentifications: Queers of Color and the Performance of Politics*. Minneapolis: University of Minnesota Press, 1999.

Naylor, David. *American Picture Palaces: The Architecture of Fantasy.* New York: Van Nostrand Reinhold Company, 1981.

Ngai, Mae M. "The Architecture of Race in American Immigration Law: A Re-examination of the Immigration Act of 1924." *Journal of American History* 86 (1999): 67–92.

Nguyen, Viet Thanh. *Race and Resistance: Literature and Politics in Asian America.* Oxford: Oxford University Press, 2002.

Nowell-Smith, Geoffrey. "Minnelli and Melodrama." *Screen* 18.2 (1977): 113–18.

Nye, Joseph S., Jr. *The Paradox of American Power: Why the World's Only Superpower Can't Go It Alone*. New York: Oxford University Press, 2002.

———. "U.S. Power and Strategy After Iraq." Op-Ed. *Foreign Affairs*, July 1, 2003.

O'Brien, Patrick Karl, and Armand Klesse. *Two Hegemonies: Britain 1846–1914 and the United States 1941–2001*. Aldershot, Hants: Ashgate, 2002.

Okihiro, Gary Y. *Margins and Mainstreams: Asians in American History and Culture*. Seattle: University of Washington Press, 1994.

Osumi, Megumi Dick. "Asians and California's Anti-Miscegenation Laws." In *Asian and Pacific American Experiences: Women's Perspectives,* ed. Nobuya

Tsuchida, 1–37. Minneapolis: Asian/Pacific American Learning Resource Center, University of Minnesota, 1982.

Palumbo-Liu, David. *Asian/American: Historical Crossings of a Racial Frontier.* Stanford: Stanford University Press, 1999.

Pascoe, Peggy. "Race, Gender, and Intercultural Relations: The Case of Interracial Marriage." *Frontiers* 12.1 (1991): 5–18.

Parreñas, Rhacel Salazar. "'White Trash' Meets the 'Little Brown Monkeys': The Taxi Dance Hall as a Site of Interracial and Gender Alliances between White Working Class Women and Filipino Immigrant Men in the 1920s and 30s." *Amerasia Journal* 24.2 (1998): 115–34.

Pateman, Carole. "The Fraternal Social Contract." In *The Disorder of Women: Democracy, Feminism, and Political Theory*, 33–57. Stanford: Stanford University Press, 1989.

Pick, Daniel. *Faces of Degeneration: A European Disorder, c. 1848–c. 1918.* Cambridge: Cambridge University Press, 1989.

Pivar, David J. *Purity Crusade: Sexual Morality and Social Control, 1868–1900.* Westport, Conn.: Greenwood Press, 1973.

Puccini, Giacomo. *Madam Butterfly.* English National Opera Guide Series, no. 26. London: John Calder, 1984.

Qian, Zhaoming. *The Modernist Response to Chinese Art: Pound, Moore, Stevens.* Charlottesville: University of Virginia Press, 2003.

Quan, Robert Seto, with Julian B. Roebuck. *Lotus Among the Magnolias: The Mississippi Chinese.* Jackson, Miss.: University of Mississippi Press, 1982.

Quiroga, José. *Tropics of Desire: Interventions from Queer Latino America.* New York: New York University Press, 2000.

Rafael, Vicente L. *White Love and Other Events in Filipino History.* Durham: Duke University Press, 2000.

Reed, James. *The Missionary Mind and American East Asia Policy: 1911–1915.* Cambridge, Mass.: Harvard University Press, 1983.

Rizal, Jose. "The Indolence of the Filipinos." In *Selected Essays and Letters of Jose Rizal,* ed. and trans. E. Alzona. Manila: Rangel and Sons, 1964.

Roediger, David. *The Wages of Whiteness: Race and the Making of the American Working Class.* London: Verso, 1991.

———. "Whiteness and Ethnicity in the History of 'White Ethnics' in the United States." *Toward the Abolition of Whiteness: Essays on Race, Politics, and Working Class History*, ed. Roediger, 181–98. London: Verso, 1994.

Rogin, Michael. "'The Sword Became a Flashing Vision': D. W. Griffith's *The Birth of a Nation.*" *The New American Studies: Essays from Representations*, ed. Philip Fisher, 346–91. Berkeley: University of California Press, 1991.

Roy, Anindyo. "The Aesthetics of an (Un)willing Immigrant: Bharati Mukherjee's

Days and Nights in Calcutta and *Jasmine*." In *Bharati Mukherjee: Critical Perspectives,* ed. Emmanuel S. Nelson, 127–41. New York: Garland, 1993.

Roy, Parama. *Indian Traffic: Identities in Question in Colonial and Postcolonial India.* Berkeley: University of California Press, 1998.

Said, Edward W. *Orientalism.* New York: Vintage, 1979.

Saks, Eva. "Representing Miscegenation Law." *Raritan* 8.2 (1988): 39–69.

San Buenaventura, Steffi. "The Colors of Manifest Destiny: Filipinos and the American Other(s)." *Amerasia Journal* 24.3 (1998): 1–26.

San Juan, Epifiano, Jr. *Carlos Bulosan and the Imagination of the Class Struggle.* Quezon City: University of the Philippines Press, 1972.

———. "Filipino Writing in the United States: Reclaiming Whose America?" *Philippine Studies* 41 (1993): 141–66.

———. *From Exile to Diaspora: Versions of the Filipino Experience in the United States.* Boulder, Colo.: Westview Press, 1998.

———. Introduction to *On Becoming Filipino: Selected Writings of Carlos Bulosan,* by Carlos Bulosan. Philadelphia: Temple University Press, 1995.

———. "One Hundred Years of Producing and Reproducing the 'Filipino.'" *Amerasia Journal* 24.2 (1998): 1–33.

———. *Racial Formations/Critical Transformations: Articulations of Power in Ethnic Studies and Racial Studies in the United States.* Atlantic Highland, N.J.: Humanities Press, 1992.

———. "Searching for the Heart of 'America.'" In *Teaching American Ethnic Literatures,* ed. John R. Maitino and David R. Peck, 259–72. Albuquerque: University of New Mexico Press, 1996.

Saxton, Alexander. *The Indispensable Enemy: Labor and the Anti-Chinese Movement in California.* Berkeley: University of California Press, 1971.

Scheiner, Irwin. *Christian Converts and Social Protest in Meiji Japan.* Berkeley: University of California Press, 1970.

Schickel, Richard. *D. W. Griffith: An American Life.* New York: Simon and Schuster, 1984.

Schueller, Malini Johar. *U.S. Orientalisms: Race, Nation, and Gender in Literature, 1790–1890.* Ann Arbor: University of Michigan Press, 1998.

Schwantes, Robert S. *Japanese and Americans: A Century of Cultural Relations.* New York: Harper, 1955.

Shah, Nayan. *Contagious Divides: Epidemics and Race in San Francisco's Chinatown.* Berkeley: University of California Press, 2001.

Shankar, Lavina Dhingra. "Activism, 'Feminisms,' and Americanization in Bharati Mukherjee's *Wife* and *Jasmine*." *Hitting Critical Mass: A Journal of Asian American Cultural Criticism* 3.1 (1995): 61–84.

Shankar, Lavina Dhingra, and Rajini Srikanth, eds. *A Part and Yet Apart: South Asians in Asian America.* Philadelphia: Temple University Press, 1998.

Smith, James L. *Melodrama.* London: Methuen, 1973.

Smith, Julian. "'Madame Butterfly': The Paris Première of 1906." In *Werk und Wiedergabe: Musiktheater Exemplarisch Interpretiert,* ed. Sigrid Wiesmann, 229–38. Bayreuth: Fehr, 1980.

———. "A Metamorphic Tragedy." *Proceedings of the Royal Music Association* 106 (1980): 105–14.

———. "Tribulations of a Score." In *Madam Butterfly*, English National Opera Series, no. 26, 15–23.

Somerville, Siobhan B. *Queering the Color Line: Race and the Invention of Homosexuality in American Culture.* Durham: Duke University Press, 2000.

Sommer, Doris. *Foundational Fictions: The National Romances of Latin America.* Berkeley: University of California Press, 1991.

Sonza, Jorshinelle T. "The Stranger in Paradise: Portrait of the 'Filipino' in Bulosan's 'America.'" *Journal of English Studies* 2.1 (1994): 84–102.

Spickard, Paul R. *Mixed Blood: Intermarriage and Ethnic Identity in Twentieth-Century America.* Madison: University of Wisconsin Press, 1989.

Staiger, Janet. "*The Birth of a Nation*: Reconsidering Its Reception." In *Interpreting Films: Studies in the Historical Reception of American Cinema.* Princeton: Princeton University Press, 1992.

Stokes, Mason Boyd. "Becoming Visible: I'm White, Therefore I'm Anxious." In *The Color of Sex: Whiteness, Heterosexuality, and the Fictions of White Supremacy,* ed. Stokes, 158–77. Durham: Duke University Press, 2001.

Stoler, Ann Laura. *Race and the Education of Desire: Foucault's History of Sexuality and the Colonial Order of Things.* Durham: Duke University Press, 1995.

———. "Sexual Affronts and Racial Frontiers: European Identities and the Cultural Politics of Exclusion in Colonial Southeast Asia." In *Tensions of Empire: Colonial Cultures in a Bourgeois World,* ed. Cooper and Stoler, 198–237. Berkeley: University of California Press, 1997.

Stoler, Ann Laura, and Frederick Cooper. "Between Metropole and Colony: Rethinking a Research Agenda." In *Tensions of Empire: Colonial Cultures in a Bourgeois World,* ed. Cooper and Stoler, 1–56. Berkeley: University of California Press, 1997.

Sturdevant, Saundra Pollock, and Brenda Stoltzfus. *Let the Good Times Roll: Prostitution and the U.S. Military in Asia.* New York: New Press, 1992.

Sundquist, Eric J. *Faulkner: The House Divided.* Baltimore: Johns Hopkins University Press, 1983.

Suzuki, Bob H. "Education and the Socialization of Asian Americans: A Revisionist Analysis of the 'Model Minority' Thesis," *Amerasia* 4.2 (1977): 23–51.

Szyliowicz, Irene L. *Pierre Loti and the Oriental Woman*. New York: St. Martin's Press, 1988.

Tajima, Renee. "Lotus Blossoms Don't Bleed: Images of Asian Women." In *Making Waves: An Anthology of Writings by and about Asian American Women*, ed. Asian Women United of California, 308–17. Boston: Beacon, 1989.

Takagi, Dana Y. "Maiden Voyage: Excursion into Sexuality and Identity Politics in Asian America." In *Asian American Sexualities: Dimensions of the Gay and Lesbian Experience*, ed. Russell Leong, 21–35. New York: Routledge, 1996.

Takaki, Ronald T. *Iron Cages: Race and Culture in Nineteenth-Century America*. New York: Knopf, 1979.

——. *Strangers from a Different Shore: A History of Asian Americans*. 1989. Reprint, New York: Penguin, 1990.

Taylor, Charles. "The Re-birth of the Aesthetic in Cinema." *Wide Angle* 13.3–4 (1991): 12–30.

Tchen, John Kuo Wei. *New York before Chinatown: Orientalism and the Shaping of American Culture, 1776–1882*. Baltimore: Johns Hopkins University Press, 1999.

——. "Modernizing White Patriarchy: Re-Viewing D. W. Griffith's *Broken Blossoms*." In *Moving the Image: Independent Asian Pacific American Media Arts*, ed. Russell Leong, 133–43. Los Angeles: UCLA Asian American Studies Center and Visual Communications, Southern California Asian American Studies Central, Inc., 1991.

Thomson, James C., Jr., Peter W. Stanley, and John Curtis Perry. *Sentimental Imperialists: The American Experience in East Asia*. New York: Harper and Row, 1981.

Ting, Jennifer. "Bachelor Society: Deviant Heterosexuality and Asian American Historiography." In *Privileging Positions: The Sites of Asian American Studies*, ed., Gary Y. Okihiro et al., 271–80. Pullman, Wash.: Washington State University Press, 1995.

Tilton, Robert S. *Pocahontas: The Evolution of an American Narrative*. New York: Cambridge University Press, 1994.

Tompkins, Jane. *Sensational Designs: The Cultural Work of American Fiction, 1790–1860*. New York: Oxford University Press, 1985.

Truong, Than-Dam. *Sex, Money, and Morality: The Political Economy of Prostitution and Tourism in South East Asia*. London: Zed, 1990.

U.S. Congress Committee on Immigration and Naturalization. *Exclusion of Immigration from the Philippine Islands*. Washington, D.C.: Government Printing Office, 1930.

U.S. Department of Labor. *The Negro Family: The Case for National Action*. Washington D.C.: U.S. Government Printing Office, 1965.

Vaid, Urvashi. "Inclusion, Exclusion and Occlusion: The Queer Idea of Asian Pacific American-ness." *Amerasia Journal* 25.3 (1999–2000): 1–16.

Vergès, Françoise. *Monsters and Revolutionaries: Colonial Family Romance and Métissage.* Durham: Duke University Press, 1999.

Volpp, Leti. "American Mestizo: Filipinos and Antimiscegenation Laws in California." *University of California Davis Law Review* 33 (2000): 795–835.

Wallovitts, S. E. *The Filipinos in California.* San Francisco: R and E Associates, 1972.

Weisbrod, Carol. *Butterfly, the Bride: Essays on Law, Narrative, and the Family.* Ann Arbor, Mich.: University of Michigan Press, 1999.

Wichman, Siegfried. *Japonisme: The Japanese Influence in Western Art Since 1858.* London: Thames and Hudson, 1981.

Williams, Richard. *Hierarchical Structures and Social Value: The Creation of Black and Irish Identities in the United States.* Cambridge: Cambridge University Press, 1990.

Williams, William Appleman. "The Age of Corporate Capitalism." In *The Contours of American History,* 343–478. Chicago: Quadrangle, 1966.

Williamson, Joel. *New People: Miscegenation and Mulattoes in the United States.* New York: Free Press, 1980.

Wong, Eugene Franklin. *On Visual Media Racism: Asians in the American Motion Pictures.* New York: Arno Press, 1978.

Wong, Sau-ling Cynthia. *Reading Asian American Literature: From Necessity to Extravagance.* Princeton: Princeton University Press, 1993.

Wordell, Charles B. *Japan's Image in America: Popular Writing about Japan, 1800–1941.* Kyoto: Yamaguchi Publishing House, 1998.

Wu, William F. *The Yellow Peril: Chinese Americans in American Fiction, 1850–1940.* Hamden, Conn.: Archon Books, 1982.

Yoshihara, Mari. *Embracing the East: White Women and American Orientalism.* New York: Oxford University Press, 2003.

———. "Women's Asia: American Women and the Gendering of American Orientalism, 1870s–WWII." Ph.D. diss., Brown University, 1997.

Yu, Henry. "Mixing Bodies and Cultures: The Meaning of America's Fascination with Sex between 'Orientals' and 'Whites.'" In *Sex, Love, Race: Crossing Boundaries in North American History,* ed. Martha Hodes, 444–63. New York: New York University Press, 1999.

———. *Thinking Orientals: Migration, Contact, and Exoticism in Modern America.* New York: Oxford University Press, 2001.

Yuval-Davis, Nira. "Gender and Nation." *Ethnic and Racial Studies* 16.4 (1993): 620–32.

Index

ASIAN AMERICA

Caste and Outcast: Dhan Gopal Mukerji
EDITED AND PRESENTED BY GORDON H. CHANG, PURNIMA MANKEKAR, AND
AKHIL GUPTA, 2002.

*New Worlds, New Lives: Globalization and People of Japanese Descent in the
Americas and from Latin America in Japan*
EDITED BY LANE RYO HIRABAYASHI, AKEMI KIKUMURA-YANO, AND JAMES A.
HIRABAYASHI, 2002.

*Japanese Pride, American Prejudice: Modifying the Exclusion Clause of the
1924 Immigration Act*
BY IZUMI HIROBE, 2001.

Chinese San Francisco, 1850–1943: A Trans-Pacific Community
BY YONG CHEN, 2000.

*Dreaming of Gold, Dreaming of Home: Transnationalism and Migration
Between the United States and South China, 1882–1943*
BY MADELINE Y. HSU, 2000.

Imagining the Nation: Asian American Literature and Cultural Consent
BY DAVID LEIWEI LI, 1998.

*Morning Glory, Evening Shadow: Yamato Ichihashi and His Internment
Writings, 1942–1945.*
EDITED, ANNOTATED, AND WITH A BIOGRAPHICAL ESSAY BY GORDON H.
CHANG, 1997.

Dear Miye: Letters Home From Japan, 1939–1946
BY MARY KIMOTO TOMITA; EDITED, WITH AN INTRODUCTION AND NOTES,
BY ROBERT G. LEE, 1995.